The Economics of Professional Sports

FOURTH EDITION

Duane W. Rockerbie

University of Lethbridge

Table of Contents

Preface

Sports economics is a rapidly growing field in the economics literature. Academic journals and reference books are popping up across the economics landscape that are exclusively devoted to the field of sports economics. Two academic organizations have recently been founded to further research and discussions around the economics of sport: the North American Association of Sports Economists (NAASE) and the European Sports Economics Association (ESEA). A growing number of online web sites and blogs offer forums for people to exchange ideas. Why the recent interest in sports economics?

Sport can bring together individuals with otherwise very dissimilar interests in a way that no other industry can. Fans form a common bond when they cheer for their favorite professional team, cheer for their country in the Olympics or the World Cup, or just cheer for their kids when they play little league. The economic value of these forms of psychic consumption is worthy of study, particularly given the emerging field of the importance of happiness in economics.

Professional sports is also a cutthroat industry characterized by colorful owners who are keen to protect their profits. But like any other industry, there are many more business failures than successes (remember the USFL or the ABA?), so an astute business person needs to understand the nuts and bolts of how the industry works.

This book represents my lecture notes, materials from my published journal articles and chapters, as well as student contributions from my university course, The Economics of Professional Sports. It is not intended to be a highly theoretical course for fourth year students, instead, it is targeted to students with a first-year course in economics and some elementary calculus to try to demonstrate how economic tools can expand their way of thinking about the real world. However, the presentation is somewhat more rigorous than other textbooks in the discipline. Rather than try to cover a large number of topics, the book provides students with basic tools from a few examples that can be used to analyze many other topics in sports economics. There were no textbooks when I developed the course in 1998, so I wrote my own and here it is after many revisions.

I have shared many ideas with individuals about what topics to cover in this book, how they should be taught and what I needed to fix. There are too many helpful colleagues to thank in this space, but I would like to give particular thanks to a few: Jeremiah Allen, Jeffrey Davidson,

Stephen Easton, Danny LeRoy, Richard Mueller and all of my colleagues who attend the annual NAASE meetings. Special thanks to my students who always ask interesting questions and provide me with the most recent references to issues we discuss in class. As usual, any errors in this book are my sole responsibility.

Worked out answers to the Test Your Understanding questions are available by emailing me: rockerbie@uleth.ca except for my students until I provide them.

Duane W. Rockerbie

Chapter 1
An Introduction

The professional sports industry is an industry of growing interest in economics over the last twenty years or so. This chapter gives reasons why the professional sports industry deserves to be treated as a distinct field in economics. Why not write a book about the economics of the automobile industry, the shoe industry, or any other consumer product? Certainly there are texts devoted to those industries and others, but professional sports leagues possess unique characteristics, both in how they operate and how they are allowed to exist, that distinguish them from any other industry. These include:

1. *Antitrust protection*. In the United States and Canada, government legislation exists that protects consumers from unscrupulous businesses and promotes competition in industries. Businesses that violate these laws are subject to prosecution resulting in fines and potential jail time. Professional sports leagues are exempt from these laws and have been exempt for a long time. Owners argue that this special status is necessary in order to insure the survival of the professional sports leagues that fans so demand.

2. *League policies to control costs and share revenues*. The major professional sports leagues in North America utilize salary caps on both individual players and team payrolls to allow costs to increase in a controlled manner. They also

redistribute revenues from large market teams to small market teams in order to insure the financial stability of the league. Both of these practices could be considered illegal in any other industry.

3. *Restricting entry of new firms and new workers (athletes).* New teams that wish to enter an existing professional sports league must be approved by a majority of the existing owners. This also applies to existing teams that wish to relocate to new cities or sell their businesses to new owners. Athletes who wish to earn a living by playing for a team in a professional sports league must usually be drafted and be subject to league salary scales for rookie players. Player movement to new teams is usually tightly controlled.

Industries outside of the professional sports industry share none of these characteristics, hence they must be much more innovative and competitive in order to sell their products. Professional sports team owners and their players are often treated very differently from more ordinary citizens, much like movie stars and other celebrities.

Professional sports is also big business and most people consume the products produced directly or indirectly by the professional sports industry in some way. Many other industries rely on the professional sports industry to survive. From printed media, to national, local and specialty cable networks, to food services, marketing, construction, transportation and other industries that spin off of professional sports. While the economic size of the professional sports leagues themselves is not large, their importance to gross domestic product[1] (GDP) is significant. Plunkett Research estimated that the total revenue generated by the professional sports industry in the United States was $425 billion in 2012. The estimate of U.S. GDP for 2012 is $16.62 trillion, so the professional sports industry accounted for approximately 2.56% of annual GDP. That is twice the size of the U.S. auto industry and seven times the size of the movie industry.

Each chapter in this book will begin by listing the important concepts that will be covered. Students should review these concepts after reading the chapter to ensure that the important concepts are understood.

KEY CONCEPTS

- The continuing monopoly status granted to professional sports leagues allows them to violate laws that other industries cannot. Several landmark court rulings have allowed this status to continue.
- The labor market is more restricted in most professional sports leagues than is the case in other industries.
- Brief histories are provided of the four major North American sports leagues (NFL, NBA, NHL, MLB) are provided to provide some perspective on their evolution and importance.
- A brief summary of the economic issues that sports leagues face is given. These issues pertain mostly to labor markets, broadcasting rights and the level of competitiveness in the industry.

---

[1] Gross domestic product is a measure of the total sales of all final goods and services in an economy over a period of time, usually one quarter or one year.

1.1 Why Study Professional Sports?

Professional sports leagues possess three important characteristics that distinguish them from other industries. First, they are allowed to engage in business practices that, by law, are not allowed in other industries. Second, their labor markets are more restrictive, yet more lucrative for their employees, than other industries. Third, a single firm (team) in the professional sports industry cannot survive without the presence of other firms (teams). While we can think of a professional sports league as a single firm, we can also think of the teams that operate within the league as individual firms who agree on playing rules and business practices in order to insure survival of the league. We might think of the teams in a league as cooperating on a sort of joint venture.

A *monopoly* is an industry with only one firm hence it faces no competitors for the product it produces. As we shall see in Chapter 3, a lack of competition allows the monopoly to charge higher prices and engage in business practices that are detrimental to consumers than would otherwise be the case. There are actually not many examples of monopolies. Canada Post is the only provider of postal services in Canada and is protected from competition by the federal government. Of course, there are competitors when the product produced by Canada Post is interpreted more widely: courier companies, fax machines, e-mail, text messages and so on. As you can see, whether an industry is considered a monopoly depends upon how the product is defined.

While professional sports have many competing leagues in different sports, each team is a member of a league that acts as a monopoly when representing the interests of the owners of the member teams. If you want to establish a new professional hockey team in Vancouver, you will be competing against the Vancouver Canucks and the National Hockey

League (NHL) since you will not be invited to join the big league. To maintain its position of power and profit, the monopoly league must engage in practices to prevent the growth of competition from rivals in its sport. That means you and your new team. Rivalry and competition from other leagues can reduce profitability for all teams in all leagues (that play the same sport), new and existing. A professional sports league controls the establishment of new franchises in the league and where each franchise is allowed to operate. Usually a large majority of existing owners must support the establishment of a new franchise, and the owner of the new franchise must pay a large franchise fee to the existing owners for the right to join the league. Two teams are not allowed to operate within a certain geographic distance from each other according to league rules. So much for you being granted a new NHL team in Vancouver. If you wanted to establish a new dry-cleaning business in Vancouver, you would not have to obtain the permission of all the other dry-cleaning businesses that already operate there.

In a professional sports league, a common set of playing rules and a fixed playing schedule controls the quality and frequency of a team's games. The league also negotiates broadcasting contracts with national television broadcasters, like FOX Sports or NBC Sports, instead of each team negotiating separately for television rights to their games. This is done in order to maintain high royalties that are then distributed evenly to each team owner under the leagues revenue sharing system, although individual teams may negotiate their own contracts with local broadcasters for local games in many cases, but only with league permission. The professional sports league also negotiates national contracts for apparel and licensing of team logos with companies such as Adidas, Nike, Puma, Reebok, Russell Athletic and many others. These revenues are also distributed evenly among all teams in the league. You probably wouldn't want to share your revenue from your dry-cleaning business with every other dry-cleaning business in Vancouver and if you tried to, you could be caught and prosecuted for reducing competition.

The movement of players to different teams via free agency is restricted in order to maintain lower payrolls and to prevent teams from becoming too dominant. The use of a draft system also restricts which players can find employment in a professional sports league. In the NHL, only just over 200 players between the ages of 18 and 20 are selected every year to play in the NHL, although most of them do not play in the NHL, instead playing a few seasons in the minor leagues.[2] The league can also establish strategies on pricing, marketing and new franchises to deter entry by new rival leagues. All in all, a professional sports league places a lot of restrictions on the business practices of its owners, mostly in the interest of maintaining profits (although some owners will argue that profits are infrequent).

Most of these business practices are illegal. The Sherman Act in the United States and the Competition Act in Canada allow for the prosecution of firms who engage in illegal business activities, such as resale price maintenance (pricing low to prevent the entry of new firms) and colluding on prices. Major League Baseball (MLB) is informally exempt from the Sherman Act and the Competition Act based on a legal case decided in 1922. While the NBA, NFL and the NHL are not formally exempt, there is a common understanding that will should be treated the same as MLB should these leagues be challenged in court. Many attempts have been made to prosecute the four North American professional leagues with regards to free agency for players and the relocation of existing teams,

---

[2] The NHL success rate is about 19%. See
http://proicehockey.about.com/od/prospects/f/draft_success.htm

none of them successful. We will review some of the more notable cases later in the text. Consumers would surely be angered if local grocery stores banded together to form a "league", and then engaged in the same anti-competitive practices as professional sports leagues. Yet professional sports leagues are tolerated by consumers, and even complimented for dealing with rival competition and "greedy" players. This makes them unique and worthy of independent study.

1.2 The Size of the Professional Sports Industry

The economic size of an industry is hard to define, however if we think of the output of a professional sports team as putting fans in the seats, then attendance can be used as a measure of size. Attendance can seriously underestimate the economic size of the sports industry since teams earn revenue from many other sources besides ticket sales. Another measure of economic size is the total revenue for the industry, including revenues for industries that rely on the professional sports industry.

Attendance

Attendance in the professional sports industry in North America has been increasing rapidly since the early 1970's. Figure 1.1 plots total attendance for all Major League Baseball games since 1980 up to and including the 2016 season. Attendance increased by an annual average of 4.2% over the period. Excluding the work stoppage years of 1981 and 1994, the average annual attendance for MLB increased by a healthy 4.45%. This was largely due to new expansion franchises that increased the number of teams from 26 in 1980 to 30 in 2005 and to the construction of new stadiums that attracted more fans with greater amenities.

Figure 1.2 plots the total attendance for NBA games for the 1969-70 through 2015-16 seasons. Attendance increased by an annual average of 6.35%, excluding the 1998-99 work stoppage season. The NBA's attendance is notable for a flat period of attendance growth of only 0.2% from the 1977-78 to 1984-85 seasons. Part of this was due to new competition from the rival American Basketball Association (ABA) that operated teams in close proximity to NBA teams and played in the same months of the year. The ABA dissolved in 1979 with four teams[3] moving to the NBA. A new commissioner, new marketing efforts and franchise expansion resulted in a resurgence in NBA attendance in the late 1980's.

Figure 1.1
MLB attendance, 1980-2016.
Source: https://sites.google.com/site/rodswebpages/codes.

---

[3] These being the Denver Nuggets, New York Nets, Indiana Pacers and San Antonio Spurs.

NHL attendance is plotted in Figure 1.3 through the 2011-12 season. The average annual rate of attendance growth was 4.22% excluding the 1994 and 2004 work stoppage seasons. The 1967 to 1975 seasons experienced the fastest growth (16.2% annually) in the recent history of the NHL, largely due to expansion of the number of teams from the "original six". The drop in attendance from 1976 to 1980 can be attributed to efforts by the rival World Hockey Association (WHA) to capture some of the NHL's markets, although very few of the WHA teams in existence at that time operated in NHL cities (the WHA did play in the same months of the year as the NHL).

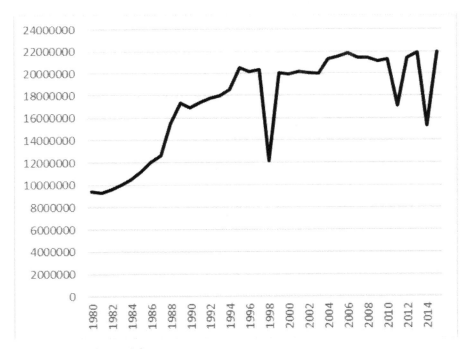

Figure 1.2
NBA attendance, 1968-69 to 2015-16 seasons.
Source: https://sites.google.com/site/rodswebpages/codes.

18

Figure 1.4 reveals that the historical pattern of attendance in the NFL is similar to the three other leagues, although attendance growth in the NFL has lagged behind them[4]. With the merger of the NFL and the AFL in 1970, and the collapse of the rival World Football League in 1974, attendance grew at an annual rate of 6.1% up to the 2005 season. Attendance fell dramatically in 1982, a work stoppage year notable for NFL teams hiring amateur players in place of the regular players, and did not recover to its 1981 level until almost ten years later.

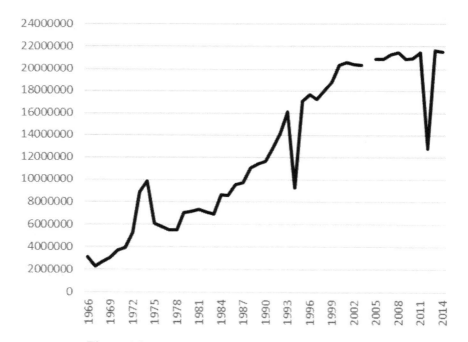

Figure 1.3
NHL attendance, 1960-61 to 2011-12 seasons.
Source: https://sites.google.com/site/rodswebpages/codes.

---

[4] NFL attendance data was provided by Nola Agha of SportsEconomics (www.sportseconomics.com).

Revenue and profit figures are difficult to find for professional sports teams since they are largely privately owned firms that are not required to make these figures public knowledge. Financial World and Forbes magazine estimate annual revenues and profits for the four professional sports leagues. They report annual revenues of $4.02 billion for the 1990 season, growing to $31.15 billion in the 2015 season. That translates to an impressive 27% average annual growth in revenues[5], although of course, some clubs fair better than others. Still these figures are small compared to many other industries. The status assigned to professional sports leagues by the media is far larger than their size in revenues would seem to warrant.

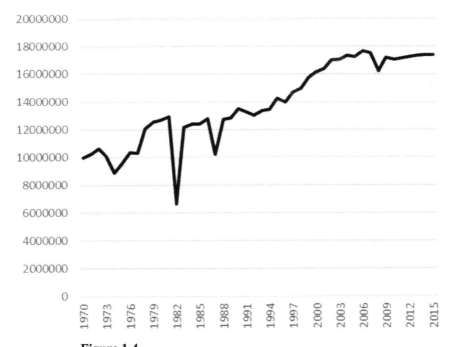

Figure 1.4
NFL attendance, 1966-2012.
Source: https://sites.google.com/site/rodswebpages/codes.

---

[5] This figure computed as $(31.15 - 4.02)/(1.35 \times 25) = 0.27$.

1.3 The Evolution of Professional Sports in the Early Years

Baseball

The first known game that had a playing field and a formal set of playing rules similar to today's rules was held at the Elysian Fields in Hoboken, New Jersey in June of 1846 (New York Knickerbockers versus the New York Base Ball Club). Twenty-one runs were required to win a game, which led to long games, some of which lasted a day and a half. This meant only men of nobility had the time to play and watch games. Amateur clubs dominated the game until the late 1860's.

Players, not owners, ran the rather disorganized leagues. In 1858 the National Association of Base Ball Players (NABBP) was formed, the first player union in sports. Rules were standardized across the country and a nine-inning limit to each game was adopted to allow for larger attendance and higher revenues. By 1860 there were players from sixty clubs in the NABBP and by 1867 there were players from three hundred clubs. Most were not paid. Fan attendance was limited. There were only 14 team cities with populations of over 100,000 (compared to 186 today) and none with a population of one million or more (compared to seven today).

The first team to pay its players and manager was the Cincinnati Red Stockings in 1869. They traveled extensively, even to Europe and Egypt, and won 56 consecutive games. The development of the railroad on the eastern seaboard and the Midwest led to many "professional" teams. Newspapers, anxious to increase circulation, covered game results and statistics, establishing a lasting relationship between sport and the media.

The presence of some paid players resulted in tensions between amateur and professional players on the same team. In 1871 the National

Association of Professional Base Ball Players was formed, which effectively eliminated amateur players. The Association was controlled by the players but only lasted five years. Until the later formation of the National League by club owners, the baseball market was very competitive. With low entry and operating costs, new clubs could be easily formed. Without entry barriers, there was no restriction on the number of clubs. The labor market was also competitive. All players were signed to single season contracts and were free to sign with any other team at the end of the season. Ticket prices were raised to ten cents to cover player salaries.

A profitable baseball operation was difficult during this short "free market" period. The lack of a fixed playing schedule, gambling, thrown games, player and fan rowdyism, and poor attendance led to financial pressure on the investors. Player turnover was high, teams were "raided" for the best players, and the league lacked competitive balance (the Boston Beaneaters won four of the first five pennants).

In 1876, the owner of the Chicago White Stockings, William Hubert, formed an association of professional clubs called the National League. Membership was restricted to only eight clubs and franchises were awarded only to well-financed investors in cities with a minimum population of 75,000. This greatly restricted the number of qualifying clubs. Only 24 cities would have qualified at the time. Each club had a monopoly right to its territory. The playing schedule was fixed to 60 games. To reduce rowdyism, players were subject to a disciplinary code, and liquor sales, gambling and Sunday games were banned.

Baseball became a serious business for its owners. The emphasis was on maximizing revenues through promotion and team success, and minimizing salary costs. Total revenue for the Boston Red Stockings from

1873 to 1882 was $272,339 and total profit was $17,423, for an average profit margin of 6.4 percent. The net worth[6] of the club was $767.93 in 1873 and $4,003.95 in 1882. The average growth rate of net worth was 20.1 percent and the total return to the owner was 26.5 percent per year. Over the period 1876 – 1900, 21 of 29 clubs were cancelled for a failure rate of 72 percent. But that is only one club per year or a failure rate of 3 percent, similar to current small business failure rates.

Players were paid several times a working man's wage, from $200 a year for a rookie, to $3,000 a year for a star player. Player salaries were typically two-thirds of a club's costs. League schedules were lengthened to increase revenues, from 84 games in 1879 to 140 games in 1889. Ticket prices were mandated at fifty cents across the league. Revenue sharing was instituted where visiting clubs received thirty percent of the gate, which hurt small market clubs.

Owners attempted to restrict salaries and the practice of free agent players to jump teams. In 1879, a reserve clause was introduced which stood until 1976. If a player did not agree on a contract by the end of the current season, the player was "reserved" through the next season at his current salary. This effectively eliminated free agents. Average player salaries fell by 20 percent between 1878 and 1880. Non-tampering agreements were reached with American Association clubs. Further collusion between owners resulted in a Limit Agreement in 1885, which limited player's salaries to a $2,000 maximum.

John Montgomery Ward, a player for the New York Giants, formed the Player's League in 1889, which lasted only one season. The league was a futile attempt to avoid the dreaded reserve clause. Players and owners shared in the profits and many National League stars jumped to the

---

[6] Net worth is the difference in value between the assets and liabilities of the club.

new league. The reserve clause created valuable property rights for the owner's, which could be exploited through cash sales of player's (formally banned in the late 1970's). Mike "King" Kelley, a star player at the time, was sold by Chicago to Boston for the huge sum of $10,000 in 1886 (about $2 million today)[7].

By 1889, with the National League, the American Association and the Player's League, there were 25 clubs competing for fans. In 1890, the National League absorbed four American Association clubs to form a 12-club league between 1892 and 1899. But by 1900, the National League had only 8 clubs, and the restricted entry prompted the formation of the American League by Ban Johnson (formerly the Western League) for the 1901 season. The American League quickly became more popular than the National League. Under the 1903 National Agreement, the National League and the American League agreed to function as separate and equal leagues.

The National Agreement began a lengthy period of financial stability in baseball. Between 1903 and 1920, baseball attendance grew about 50 percent, from 5,000 per game to 7,400 (today the average is about 27,000 per game). Because of the reserve clause, costs rose modestly compared to revenues. In 1920, the average club earned about $142,000 in profit. Profit margins averaged 11.2 percent and the average franchise value appreciation rate was about 15.8 percent per year, yielding a total annual return of 27 percent. Lofty profits led to the formation of the rival Federal League in 1917, which lasted only one season.

Basketball

---

[7] See the focus box in Chapter 2.

Basketball is attributed to Dr. James Naismith and first appeared in Massachusetts in 1891. Originally the game was played with nine players per team, peach baskets fixed to balconies of the gym, and a soccer ball. As it evolved between 1891 and 1900, the rules were very fluid. There was no limit to the number of players on the bench (Cornell University typically played with a 50-man squad) and play was defensive and rough. Games were typically low scoring.

By 1900, the rules of play included five-man teams, two-point field goals, and a one-point foul shot. Barnstorming clubs soon appeared and promoters would stage games packaged with dances and music to draw customers. Players were paid any residual after the gym rental and the promoter's fee was paid. Originally, players were hired by the promoter on a per-game basis. Star players did not exist as team rosters varied for every game. The first professional league, the National Basketball League, was formed in 1898 among clubs in Philadelphia. Very little financial information is available for the early period up to the 1920's, but franchise turnover was high.

Basketball leagues were regional until the formation of the American Basketball League (ABL) in 1925. The ABL lasted until 1931, when it became inactive, but was revived in 1933 as an eastern regional league. The National Basketball League (no relationship to the former) was formed in 1937 with 14 clubs. Five clubs folded in 1938, and by 1942 the league was down to four clubs. The NBL expanded to 12 clubs after World War II, but faced competition from the rival 11 club Basketball Association of America (BAA). The NBL established clubs in areas where amateur basketball was popular and where most of the players (who were white) originated. The BAA adopted a big-city strategy. Per game attendance in the BAA was in the 3,500 to 5,000 range in Boston, Philadelphia and New York.

The National Basketball Association (NBA) was formed in 1949 out of the remaining owners of the NBL and the BAA. Originally composed of 17 clubs, the league had shrunk to eight clubs by 1954. After the 1956-57 season, the NBA encouraged movement of teams to larger cities. The Milwaukee Hawks moved to St. Louis, Fort Wayne moved to Detroit, Rochester moved to Cincinnati. By the 1963-64 season, the league had nine clubs located in the country's largest cities. Average attendance was about 5,000 per game. Expansion of clubs and racial integration has increased attendance to about 15,000 per game today.

Football

The first organized football game was between Princeton and Rutgers in 1869. The game resembled rugby and Rutgers won the game six "goals" to four. Twenty-five players for each team were on the field and eleven-man teams did not appear until 1880. The rule of ten yards in four downs did not appear until 1912. Scoring seems unfamiliar by today's standards. A safety was one point, a touchdown was two points, an after-touchdown conversion was four points, and a field goal was five points. The current scoring system was not introduced until 1912. The game as played by colleges was very rough and injuries were frequent. In 1905 this led to the formation of the Intercollegiate Athletic Association, the precursor of the NCAA.

Professional football took much longer to appear than baseball or basketball. In 1920 the American Professional Football Association (APFA) was organized by George Halas, owner of the Chicago Bears. A franchise cost $25. The National Football League (NFL) that was established in 1922 grew out of the APFA. Few clubs were located in large cities. Attendance was low compared to current numbers: about 3,600 to 5,000 per game in the 1923-24 season.

College games typically outdrew professional games by a large factor and continued to do so for several decades. The few clubs located in large cities outdrew their small-city rivals by a factor of 2 or 3 to 1. During the period from 1920 to 1929, twenty-nine franchises folded. Gradually franchises were established in the big cities. By 1960 there were 13 clubs and attendance averaged about 23,000 per game. Still the lack of entry and competition resulted in the establishment of the rival American Football League (AFL) in 1960 by Al Davis. The AFL-NFL war resulted in reduced profits for both leagues and the two leagues merged in 1970.

Hockey

The National Hockey League was organized in 1917 in Montreal following the suspension of operations by the National Hockey Association of Canada Limited (NHA).[8] The Montreal Canadiens, Montreal Wanderers, Ottawa Senators and Quebec Bulldogs attended the founding meeting where the delegates decided to use NHA rules. The Toronto Arenas were later admitted as the fifth team as Quebec decided not to operate during the first season. Quebec players were allocated to the remaining four teams. An emergency meeting was held January 3 due to the destruction by fire of the Montreal Arena, which was home ice for both the Canadiens and the Wanderers. The Wanderers withdrew from the league, reducing the NHL to three teams. The Canadiens played their

---

[8] An excellent economic history of the early years of the NHL is J. Ross, Joining the Clubs: The Business of the National Hockey League to 1945, Syracuse University Press, 2015.

remaining home games at the 3,250-seat Jubilee rink. Quebec did not play in 1918-19.

Hamilton and Ottawa were awarded franchises in 1920. All teams played a split-schedule of 24 games up to the 1922 season. In 1923, the clubs agreed that players could not be sold or traded to clubs in any other league without first being offered to all other clubs in the NHL. Also in 1923, the first US franchise was awarded to Boston. In 1924, the Canadian Arena Company of Montreal was granted a franchise to operate the Montreal Maroons. The NHL was now a six-team league with two clubs in Montreal. The league schedule extended to 30 games.

Labor strife began early in the NHL. In 1925, Hamilton finished first in the standings, receiving a bye into the finals. But Hamilton players, demanding $200 each for additional games in the playoffs, went on strike. The NHL suspended Hamilton's players, fining them $200 each. The Stanley Cup finalist was to be the winner of NHL semi-final between Toronto and the Montreal Canadiens.

Franchises were granted to Pittsburgh and New York (Americans) in 1926. The Hamilton club folded. The season was extended to 36 games to raise ticket revenues. The Stanley Cup came under the control of the NHL. In previous seasons, the winners of the now-defunct Western or Pacific Coast leagues would play the NHL champion in the Stanley Cup finals. Toronto renamed its franchise the Maple Leafs. In 1931, the schedule was expanded again to 48 games and the NHL ranks had been reduced to 8 teams.

The Montreal Maroons withdrew from the NHL on June 22, 1938, leaving seven clubs in the League. Expenses for each club were league regulated at $5 per man per day for meals and $2.50 per man per day for accommodation. Shortly thereafter, the Brooklyn Americans withdrew from the NHL leaving six teams: Boston, Chicago, Detroit, Montreal New York and Toronto. The schedule was raised again to 50 games to raise revenues.

The NHL entered a period of remarkable stability with the "original six" franchises up to 1969. Further expansion has increased the NHL to 28 clubs today.

1.4 Professional Sports Outside North America

Soccer is truly the world's game and is more popular than the four professional sports leagues in North America combined. Professional soccer leagues exist in almost every developed country. England has the Premiership League, thought to be the richest soccer league in the world. Germany has the Bundesliga, Italy the Serie A (pronounced "Serie Ah"), Spain the Primera league, and so on. Major leagues also exist in South America, Africa, the Middle East, Russia and Southeast Asia. The structure of the leagues is roughly the same, regardless of the country. A premier league sits atop soccer in each country with clubs representing the largest cities, followed by first, second and third division leagues, which represent smaller cities. A relegation system works to ensure that each club play to its best ability. The bottom three teams in each league are relegated down to next lower league for the next season. The top three teams in the lower league are then promoted to the higher league. Being relegated could mean a large drop in profits for the next season.

In the top leagues, each club can play a tremendous amount of games in a season. Besides trying to win the premier league championship as the club with the best overall record, clubs also play for various regional championships. In Europe, clubs vie for the Europa Cup each year, which is a tournament of over 100 of the best-ranked teams in Europe (rankings computed by UEFA). This tournament takes an entire season (August through May) to complete with clubs traveling all over Europe. The UEFA Champions League is the most prestigious of the European cups with only a few of the best clubs in Europe competing. Each country also has a national cup given to the winning club of a round-robin tournament. The FA Cup in England is one of these. Of course, tournaments involving national teams are also very important. Europe has the European tournament once every four years and South America has the Copa America tournament once every two years, culminating with the prestigious World Cup held every four years. Television rights alone for the 2006 World Cup in Germany garnered over $1 billion for FIFA, $2.7 billion for the 2010 World Cup in South Africa and $2.4 billion for the 2014 World Cup in Brazil.

The purpose of all these games is to extract the highest profit from fans and television networks. Financial data for soccer is extremely secretive as most clubs are privately owned by consortiums. The largest clubs around the world earn huge profits. Some clubs have publicly owned shares listed on stock exchanges. This encourages them to maximize revenues and reduce uncertainty for their shareholders. An indication of the large amounts of money involved is provided by Rupert Murdoch's failed attempt to purchase the successful Manchester United club of the English Premiership. His offer of $1 billion was eventually rejected by the British government on the grounds that it would create excessive market power for Murdoch's businesses. Murdoch owns the BSkyB network, which holds exclusive broadcasting rights for Premiership games (as well as the FOX network in North America)[9].

---

[9] Murdoch's BSkyB network still owns 11.2% of the outstanding shares of Manchester United.

Broadcasting royalties to English Premier League (EPL) clubs reached approximately £560 million in broadcasting royalties for the 2007-08 season, increasing from only £200 million in the 1997-98 season. The English FA raised this amount to approximately £30 million for the 1998-99 season in response to a bid by foreign investors to create a new European super-league, composed of the best clubs in Europe[10]. The new league promised each member club over £100 million per season in broadcasting royalties. Television rights for UK and European soccer were estimated to be worth over $2 billion per season. The proposal fell apart due to a lack of financial commitment by investors. Royalties for the 2016-17 season reached $4.3 billion for the EPL.[11]

Forbes magazine computes an annual list of the world's richest professional sports teams based on revenues and the market value of their assets (stadiums and so on). For 2016, the Dallas Cowboys (NFL) topped the list at a valuation of $4 billion, followed by Real Madrid (La Liga) at $3.7 billion, FC Barcelona (La Liga) at $3.6 billion and the New York Yankees (MLB) at $3.4 billion.

One must assume that the huge potential profits from European soccer are still untapped. With satellite broadcasting around the world, professional rugby, Australian rules football and even cricket, are enjoying tremendous growth in popularity and profits.

League	Team	Valuation ($billions)
NFL	Dallas Cowboys	$4.0
La Liga (Spain)	Real Madrid	$3.7

[10] "Winners Take All", *The Economist*, August 22, 1998, p. 49-50.
[11] https://www.washingtonpost.com/news/early-lead/wp/2015/02/13/massive-new-english-premier-league-tv-deal-has-the-rest-of-european-soccer-worried/?utm_term=.732ed40665ca

La Liga (Spain)	FC Barcelona	$3.6
MLB	New York Yankees	$3.4
EPL	Manchester United	$3.3
NFL	New England Patriots	$3.2
NBA	New York Knicks	$3.0
NFL	Washington Redskins	$2.9
NFL	New York Giants	$2.8
NBA	Los Angeles Lakers	$2.7

Table 1.1
Top 10 richest professional sports teams
Source:https://www.forbes.com/pictures/mli45fgemg/1-dallas-cowboys/#1533569617b5

1.5 Economic Issues

Monopoly Behavior

A sports league is a collection of team owners who agree on a common set of operating procedures, which insure larger profits than if each owner acted on his or her own. These procedures include restricting entry of new teams, assigning exclusive franchise territory, and agreeing on a revenue-sharing formula, salary cap or luxury tax. Some of these practices are illegal in any other industry, however baseball (and the other leagues) is formally exempt from the laws banning these practices (called antitrust statutes) since a unanimous court decision in *Federal Baseball versus National League* in 1922. The ruling was that baseball did not operate interstate commerce and was therefore exempt. The legal standing of collusion in baseball has been reaffirmed by several court decisions since then. This allows owners to collude on prices, revenue splits, advertising and player salaries.

The other leagues do not enjoy formal exemption except in two areas. First, when a collective bargaining agreement exists or remains in force, despite a labor dispute, player-league contracts are exempt from antitrust statutes. Second, in 1961 Congress passed the Sports Broadcasting Act (amended in 1966), which extended the antitrust exemption to the negotiation and sale of broadcasting rights. This makes league packaging of rights for sale to the networks perfectly legal.

All leagues establish rules governing the awarding of franchises, conditions of entry and relocation, the market for players, and playing regulations. These agreements attempt to be joint-wealth maximizing and collusive for the owners. In order for new teams, or firms, to enter the industry, permission must be obtained from the existing firms. Famous exceptions are the Oakland Raiders (NFL) move to Los Angeles in 1982 and the San Diego Clippers (NBA) move to Los Angeles in 1984. Teams must collude somewhat just to establish uniform playing rules which establish agreement on a winner and a true champion. Also collusion on a league schedule is necessary to maintain an even number of quality games, particularly when teams differ greatly in quality. Chapter 4 discusses the business end of running a professional sports franchise.

Collusion in the form of entry restriction, revenue sharing and territorial rights generally does not affect the quality of play; rather it exists only to maintain profits. Owners argue these rules are necessary to protect franchise values, yet they do not exist for any other industry. Most of the franchise value is composed of player contracts and exclusivity in a geographical market, not meaningful physical assets. Some argument could be made that restricting entry insures an adequate supply of quality players. Some restrictions on entry and on rival leagues may be in the interests of sports fans

Gate receipts still account for the majority of a team's revenues, along with concessions and broadcast rights. The revenue sharing arrangements in professional leagues tend to discriminate against small market clubs In 1991, the top baseball club earned 2.5 times the revenue of the smallest club. By 2004, the gap increased to 3.3 times the revenue of the smallest club, but the gap had shrunk to 2.5 times in the 2016 season. In the NHL, the top club earned 2.6 times more revenue than the smallest club did in 1991, shrinking slightly to 2.2 times in 2015. Of course, in the long-run teams will maximize profits at an optimal winning percentage which varies by each team. It is no accident that large city teams have tended to dominate the pro leagues as they have a higher potential revenue source. Chapter 5 will discuss issues of league policies to promote parity, and whether they work.

League expansion is not limited by the market size of cities that do not have a team. However it is in the best interests of owners not to locate a franchise in every city that can support one for two reasons. First, demand for a new or existing franchise by a city currently without one maintains the potential of high capital gains for owners. Second, credible threats of movements to new cities that desire a franchise preempts entry of new rival leagues without actually incurring the cost of a new franchise. An example is the constant threat of moving the Oakland Raiders to a different city. Chapter 6 discusses economic models of entry of new teams and the existing league's response. Chapter 7 reviews the economics of new stadium and arena construction and the destructive behavior of cities to bid for professional sports franchises.

The Labor Market

Historically all of the leagues established collusive agreements that governed the selection (entry drafts), contractual arrangements (reserve clause), and distribution of players among clubs. Exploitation of players kept salaries far below the value of the player to a team up to 1976 in baseball, in basketball until the mid-1970s, and in football and hockey until just recently. The first league players to be deemed free agents through binding arbitration were Andy Messersmith (Dodgers) and Dave McNally (Orioles) in 1976. The owners subsequently fired the arbitrator on the cases, hired by the owners, after the ruling. The only other market with such a labor structure among owners was the motion picture industry in its early years.

There is still not an open and competitive market for player services. Rather, an elaborate set of rules determines which teams can negotiate with which players, designed to benefit the owners. For instance, drafted players can only negotiate with the team who drafted them.

At current salary levels, a superstar baseball or basketball player makes up to fifty times the salary of a rookie player. Certainly it is not true that a superstar player is fifty times more productive as a rookie. Salary differentials provide an economic incentive for all players to perform at their maximum level. Rather than monitor players, players signal their own quality. Essentially they are offered a two-part contract. One part is payment for expected performance. The other part is a prize determined by the probability that a player becomes a superstar player, which is endogenously determined. This shifts the cost of ensuring player performance to the players themselves.

The team that will pay the most salary is the one that expects the largest increment in revenue from that player's service. This is why the best players tend to end up on the big-city teams. Even if players do not have unrestricted movement around teams, differences in revenues generated by players will insure that players end up on the teams where they are paid the most, if player sales are allowed. Under free agency, the players receive more of the revenues they generate. Chapter 8 reviews these labor issues.

Sport	Athlete	Salary	Endorsements	Total
Soccer	Christiano Ronaldo	$56 m	$32 m	$88 m
Soccer	Lionel Messi	$53.4	$28	$81.4
Basketball	LeBron James	$23.2	$54	$77.2
Tennis	Roger Federer	$7.8	$60	$67.8
Basketball	Kevin Durant	$20.2	$36	$56.8
Tennis	Novak Djokovic	$21.8	$34	$55.8
Football	Cam Newton	$41.1	$12	$53.1
Golf	Phil Mickelson	$2.9	$50	$52.9
Golf	Jordan Spieth	$20.8	$32	$52.8
Basketball	Kobe Bryant	$25	$25	$50

Table 1.2
Top 10 highest paid athletes ($ millions)
Source: ttps://www.forbes.com/sites/forbespr/2016/06/08/forbes-releases-the-worlds-highest-paid-athletes-list-2016/#6fcec2765b96

Television Broadcasting

In the early years of television, broadcast rights were negotiated locally. Most clubs simply sold the broadcast rights to a certain station. Other teams purchased airtime and produced the broadcasts themselves. By reciprocal agreements among clubs, broadcasts to the home market were blacked out when the team was playing at home; only away games were broadcast. In 1946 the major leagues adopted a rule preventing the broadcast of other clubs' games into the home territory when games of the club were at home. This practice was clearly anti-competitive. Under pressure from the Justice Department, leagues modified these rules in 1950.

The first league-wide packaging of rights was between the NBA and NBC in 1954. Major league baseball quickly followed suit, also with NBC, and the NFL completed a deal with CBS. In 1960, the American Football League (AFL) pooled its broadcasting rights and sold them to ABC. By colluding, the leagues eliminated interclub competition to sell rights and increased their share of the profits relative to the networks' share.

The courts struck down the CBS-NFL contract and the status of pooled broadcast rights was in doubt across sports. However in 1961, Congress passed the Sports Broadcasting Act, which permitted leagues to operate as cartels in the negotiation and sale of broadcast rights. After the AFL-NFL merger in 1970, the new NFL allowed each of the big three networks to broadcast some games. This strategy effectively eliminated any potential TV contract for a rival league.

The rapid growth of cable broadcasting in the 1980's saw the emergence of all-sports broadcasting networks (ESPN, TNT, Sportschannel, etc.). Large contracts awarded to national networks have been gradually replaced by smaller contracts awarded to the cable networks. Rupert Murdoch's FOX network is an exception to this trend, acquiring broadcast rights for the NFL, MLB and the NHL. The FOX strategy is innovative. By providing a network of regional stations, broadcasting local content, FOX provides more specific events to its viewers, yet can still provide national coverage across all the stations.

Brief Review of Concepts

- A professional sports league is a collection of team owners who agree on a common set of operating procedures in order to maximize joint profits. These procedures include restricting entry of new leagues, assigning exclusive franchise territories, and agreeing on a method to distribute revenues and players. Baseball is formally excluded from anti-trust laws, while the other leagues benefit from more informal exclusion.
- Leagues usually earn larger profits than if each team operated independently. Restricting the supply of games is necessary to insure higher profits.
- Team revenues are composed mostly of gate receipts, concessions and marketing, and broadcast rights. Small market clubs generally do not do as well as large market clubs, however this is still profit maximizing for the league.
- Players were usually paid far below the value of their output to the club up to the late 1970's in all leagues. The establishment of binding arbitration and free agency allowed players to capture a larger share of their output.
- Player movement is still restricted in professional sports through the use of entry drafts and different categories of free agents. There is an economic incentive for players to perform at their maximum level, since the player's compensation is dependent upon his performance statistics. In this way, the cost of monitoring player performance shifts from the owner to the players.
- The highest paid players are the ones thought to contribute the most to revenues for the owner. Since large city teams tend to generate more revenues, the better players tend to end up playing for them.
- Broadcast rights were negotiated locally until the mid-1950's. Leagues then colluded to negotiate broadcast rights to maximize profits. The Sports Broadcasting Act of 1961 granted the leagues the right to collude on league-wide broadcasting contracts.

Focus box: Roone Arledge, sports broadcasting innovator.

In 1954, Roone Arledge was a 23 year-old corporal waiting for his discharge from the army. After his graduation from Columbia University in 1952, he worked briefly for the Dumont television network where he developed a keen interest in the rapidly growing television industry. At that time, television technology and programming were primitive. Talk shows, variety shows and family-oriented sitcoms ruled the airwaves (no cable) and all programming was live. After leaving the army, Roone Arledge rejoined with Dumont and won an Emmy award in 1955 for producing *Hi Mom*, a children's program featuring Shari Lewis and her collection of puppets. From such small beginnings, Arledge came to be the undisputed king of television sports broadcasting and the president of the ABC network.

Arledge had joined ABC by 1961 to produce sports programs. ABC's sports lineup was limited to college football games; CBS broadcast NFL games every Sunday. With no imminent professional sports league contract, Arledge developed the new program *Wide World of Sports*, which was a haphazard collection of whatever sporting events ABC could purchase rights to. The program was wildly successful and stayed on the air until the 1980's when specialty sports channels gobbled up programming rights. Arledge also produced *The American Sportsman*, which featured a weekly hunting or fishing expedition to some corner of the world. While these two programs were popular, they were not major league and could not propel ABC into the same position as CBS and NBC.

The pursuit of the television rights to the Olympic games was Arledge's master stroke. During the cold war, any competition pitting American against Soviet athletes garnered viewers. "In those days," says Arledge, "if you had an American against a Russian, it didn't matter what they were doing, they could have been kayaking and people would watch." Still, televising the Olympics was a risky investment for any television network due to the high production costs. ABC paid $50,000 for the rights to the 1960 Winter Olympics in Squaw Valley and then cancelled the deal.

Arledge convinced the network to purchase the rights for the 1964 Winter Olympics in Innsbruck for $250,000, then went on to produce nine more Olympic games. Increasing television ratings caused broadcast fees to skyrocket: $3 million for the 1968 Summer Olympics in Mexico City, $13.5 million for the 1972 Munich Summer Olympics, and $25 million for the 1976 Summer Olympics in Montreal. The Munich games were the first to receive full network coverage in primetime. Few who lived at that time can forget ABC's coverage of the tragic slaying of 11 Israeli athletes by Palestinian terrorists, all produced in slick 40-minute packages by Roone Arledge. ABC won 29 Emmy awards for its Munich coverage.

Arledge was the first television executive to back the new American Football League (AFL) in 1961. The rebel nature of the league reflected Arledge himself. Arledge and ABC introduced many technical advances in game coverage that are standard today: slow-motion instant replay, player and statistical graphics and color commentators. ABC lost its AFL contract to NBC after four years and was shut out again from major league sports. This began a pattern of football broadcasting that continued into the 1990's: CBS broadcasting NFL (or NFC after the 1969 merger of the NFL and AFL) games, NBC broadcasting AFL (AFC) games. Arledge approached the newly merged NFL in 1970 to consider broadcasting football games on Monday nights. The NFL considered the deal, and after offering the games to CBS and NBC unsuccessfully, inked a new deal with ABC. *Monday Night Football* became a wild success with its controversial color commentator Howard Cosell.

Any attempt to obtain rights to Sunday NFL games by ABC was thwarted by rapidly increasing broadcast fees. CBS paid only $14 million for the rights to NFL broadcasts in 1964 and 1965. By 1982, the three networks paid a combined $2.1 billion for rights for five years. Rupert

Murdoch's new FOX network paid a staggering $1.58 billion in 1993 to broadcast only NFC games for five years.

In 1986, Arledge moved on to become president of ABC News and quickly turned it into the leader in television news broadcasting (*Nightline* and *20-20*). Despite his leadership in bringing professional and amateur sports to television viewers, Arledge's opinion of sports has turned sour. "The basic ill in sports today has got to be money", he says, "and it's ultimately going to corrupt everything. You have owners who can't control themselves giving all this money to players. You have 25 year-old kids making several million dollars a year and thinking they're entitled to it....They may see sports only as a means to a sneaker deal."

Source: "The Titan of Television", *Sports Illustrated*, August 16, 1994, p. 36-42.

Test Your Understanding

1. In Europe it is an accepted business practice for teams to sell players to each other in the transfer market, rather than trade for players as is more common in North America. Prior to the 2017-18 season, Paris St. Germain (France) purchased Neymar from FC Barcelona (Spain) for a reported world record fee of $191 million. Neymar will earn a salary much less than this ($31.7 million).

a) What economic factors do you think determined the large size of this transfer fee?

b) Why are European club owners happy to operate a transfer system and why do you think players might be unhappy about it?

2. "I have a hard time believing that athletes are overpriced. If an owner is losing money, give it up. It's a business. I have trouble figuring out why they would stay in business if they were losing money." Reggie Jackson, retired MLB player.

Owners often claim that they are losing money, yet they continue to stay in the business. What do you think are some ways in which this could happen?

3. You probably played with a Frisbee as a kid and perhaps you still do now. A Frisbee is a plastic disc that is thrown to other players. You might be surprised to know that a professional sports league existed for Frisbee players. Major League Ultimate (MLU) operated teams across the United States that played Frisbee football in football stadiums to modest but enthusiastic crowds. Players are paid travel expenses and small stipends to keep costs down. For 2013, the league secured a television contract with ESPN. The league hoped to expand its revenues and the number of teams, but operations were suspended in December 2016.

a) What difficulties do you see for league expansion?

b) If you were the MLU Commissioner, what policies could you have used to help insure the survival of the league?

4. The English Football Association (soccer) was formally established in 1863 and is the oldest professional sports league still operating in the world. The league is composed of many divisions that are ranked in order of quality. In all, there are 737 teams but most of these are local sides that play in small facilities. That is a lot of teams when you consider that England is about the geographic size of the state of Louisiana. Any amateur team may apply to join the FA and be placed into one of the divisions. At the lower ranks, most players are amateur and must keep full or part-time jobs. The promotion and relegation system requires that the top 3 teams in each division move into the next highest division, while the bottom 3 teams move down into the next lowest division.

a) North American leagues have only 30 or so teams spread over a wide area. Why do you think it would be hard to keep amateur players on a team?

b) Many of the largest and well-known teams in the FA operate only a few miles from each other. In North American leagues, teams are not allowed to do this in order to protect local markets from competition. Why does the FA not adopt such a practice?

Chapter 2
Basic Principles I

This chapter is the first of two chapters that lay out the necessary economic principles to be used throughout the text. The student is assumed to already know some basic principles from a previous introductory economics course, however a brief review should put all students on the same "playing field". The main points the student should learn in this chapter are:

- The definition of a demand curve, the Law of Demand and its assumptions, and what gives rise to the slope and shift of a demand curve.

- Price elasticity of demand, income elasticity of demand and cross elasticity of demand. What they are and what are they used for?

- The definition of a supply curve and what gives rise to the slope and shift of a supply curve.

- The concept of equilibrium. The mechanics of how a market moves to an equilibrium of demand and supply. The definition of consumer surplus and what it represents.

- Dynamics, or shifts in the demand and supply curve and their effects on prices and quantities.

- The special case of the all-or-nothing demand curve and why it is relevant.

- How player salaries are determined.

2.1 The Demand Curve

The demand curve is a hypothetical schedule that provides quantities of a product that consumers will purchase at different prices for the product. We will assume that every good has its own demand curve that is determined by market forces and consumer preferences. Demand curves cannot be easily observed in markets, but can be estimated using statistical methods that we will not cover here. Even though consumers cannot see a demand curve for a product they are considering purchasing, we will assume they act as if they can. A more suitable definition of a demand curve is a schedule showing the *maximum* price consumers are willing to pay for a given quantity of a good or service. Obviously consumers would like to pay something less than the maximum they are willing to pay, and some will, however the demand curve represents an upper bound on consumers' willingness to pay.

In order to draw a demand curve, the good or service must be carefully defined. For instance, the good provided by a Major League Baseball (MLB) team might be defined as a seat in the stadium for fans who buy tickets or a chance to cheer with other fans for the home team who watch the game at home or in a bar, or even an entertainment experience that competes with other sports, movies and cultural events. The definition of the good produced by the club partly determines the degree of competition faced by the club owner. If the good is defined as a seat in the stadium, the team might be defined as a monopoly (the sole producer in the industry) if there is no competing baseball team in the same city. New York and Chicago each have two baseball teams, while San Francisco and Oakland, and Los Angeles and Anaheim, have teams in close proximity. Generally these teams are still considered monopolies by sports economists, if only because they operate in different leagues (American League and National League). Teams that are monopolies have a great degree of market power and have the ability to set their own prices regardless of the prices other teams are charging. In general, a monopolist ream owner will charge a price on the ticket demand curve that is above what the price would be in a more competitive market. We will demonstrate this using economic theory in Chapter 3.

On the other hand, if the good is defined more broadly as entertainment, the team might be operating in a much more competitive environment, as there are many alternative forms of entertainment in a major city, including movies, concerts, theater, competing sports and other types of going-out entertainment. The team owner then cannot pick any price along the ticket demand curve since a price that is too high could result in financial losses. The competitive ticket price is below the monopoly ticket price, as we will show in Chapter 3. Organizations that face antitrust lawsuits, such as utility companies, often use very broad definitions of their products to argue why they do not charge a monopoly price. Cellular phone companies, like Telus or Rogers in Canada, argue that they are providing a communications product and there are many different competing forms of ways to communicate. For our purposes, we will define the product of a professional sports team as tickets to games since the price is easily observable. However, teams also receive revenues from other sources than ticket sales, such as concessions, parking and broadcast rights, but we will ignore those revenue sources until Chapter 4.

Sports leagues, like other entertainment industries, are differentiated from industries that produce physical goods in that there is not a direct association between the team's revenues and the team's output. For a dry cleaner, total revenues (price (P) x quantity (Q)) are directly related to how many items are dry-cleaned (Q). There may be different services provided by a dry cleaner (shirts, jackets, dresses, etc.), however each service has a clearly identified money price that makes calculating total revenue straightforward. For a professional sports team, total revenue is derived from ticket sales, but the team does not produce seats as a physical output. Rather the team produces games of some given level of acceptable quality, usually measured by wins or winning percentage, which may encourage fans to purchase tickets (seats). The degree to which the team's performance translates to the team's revenues is not a precise one, although it is positive (see Chapter 4). What the baseball team does produce is hits, home runs, stolen bases, strikeouts and so on. These performance outputs then contribute to the game played between two teams. The quality of these games then determines how many fans will buy the output that is important to the team owner – tickets. So tickets (bums in the seats) are a final output produced by intermediate outputs generated by the players on both teams. This involves two stages to producing the final output, unlike the dry cleaner. Movies, theater and other entertainment products produce their final output (tickets) in the same way, but with different inputs.

Back to demand curves. All demand curves are assumed to obey the *Law of Demand*: as the price of the good falls, the quantity purchased of the good increases. If the ticket price for a hockey team is plotted on a vertical axis, with higher prices as we move up the axis, and the number of tickets sold (Q) is plotted on a horizontal axis, with more tickets sold as we move to the right along the axis, according to the *Law of Demand*, the demand curve for tickets slopes downward. A hypothetical demand curve for a hockey team is drawn in Figure 2.1[12]. Its position and degree of negative slope in Figure 2.1 is not important for now – we will just assume we can see this demand curve. The team owner faces this demand curve

---

[12] The demand curve is drawn as a straight line in Figure 2.1 for convenience. Demand curves are not really observable, but they can be measured using statistical methods.

and can choose any price along it, but not above it at a given quantity. It is an upper bound. The owner could charge a price below the demand curve at a given quantity, but this would not earn as much revenue as could be earned by charging the price at the demand curve. We will assume that team owners must pick a price that is a point on the demand curve at a given quantity, not above or below it.

One might think of exceptions to the *Law of Demand*, for instance, expensive luxury seats or boxes that sell out despite their rising prices. This would make the demand curve for these tickets appear to be upward sloping[13]. In this case, the fan is not just buying a seat, rather he or she is buying a combination of goods. Table food and beverage service, a better view, telephones, privacy and status are also included in the price. Each of these goods has a demand curve, which we can assume is downward sloping, so how can the outcome of all these demand curves be upward sloping? As we shall see later in this chapter, changes in incomes, prices of other goods, and tastes can shift a downward sloping demand curve in Figure 2.1 so that certain price-quantity combinations that consumers choose can appear to be an upper sloping line.

---

[13] Demand curves that appear to be upward sloping used to be referred to as Giffen goods, named after a Scottish economist Robert Giffen. He observed that as poor families experienced increases in their incomes during Victorian times, they purchased higher priced goods. As we shall show, this is not a violation of the Law of Demand if incomes are increasing. There is not much evidence that true Giffen goods exist.

48

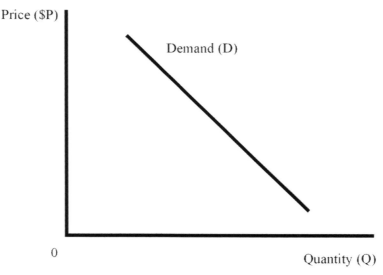

Price ($P)

Demand (D)

0

Quantity (Q)

Figure 2.1

The Law of Demand: A decrease in the average ticket price increases the quantity demanded for tickets. This is reflected in a downward movement along the demand curve. All demand curves are assumed to slope downward.

Analytical example: Picking points from a demand curve.

Question: The demand curve for tickets for the new Los Angeles Surfers NFL team is given by P = 100 − 0.001Q where P is the ticket price and Q is the number of tickets sold. How many tickets will be purchased when the ticket price is: $100, $50, $25, $10?

Answer: The equation for the demand curve is a straight line with a vertical intercept of $100 and a slope of -0.001. Solve the demand curve equation for Q on the left-hand side. Q = 100,000 − 1000P. Now insert the ticket prices.

Q = 100,000 − 1000(100) = 0
Q = 100,000 − 1000(50) = 50,000
Q = 100,000 − 1000(25) = 75,000
Q = 100,000 − 1000(10) = 90,000

2.2 The Slope of the Demand Curve

A demand curve for a good can be relatively steep or flat depending on what the good is. For the team owner, it is important to have some idea what the slope of the ticket demand curve is when making pricing decisions. The slope of the demand curve for tickets is determined by the availability of *substitute goods*. If baseball tickets have many substitute goods available, the demand curve for tickets will be relatively flat reflecting the fact that an increase in the average ticket price will cause many fans to switch their purchases to other forms of entertainment and reduce their purchases of baseball tickets. In Figure 2.2, the demand curve labeled D_1 has many substitutes. An increase in the average ticket price from \$25 to \$30 results in a drop in ticket sales from 25,000 per game to only 15,000 per game due to the flat slope of D_1. You can already see that a team owner might not want to contemplate this price increase.

A baseball team that faces very few substitutes available will have a relatively steep demand curve and fans will be more insensitive to increases in ticket prices. If Figure 2.2, the demand curve labeled D_2 has few substitutes in the eyes of fans. A team owner who increases the average ticket price from \$25 to \$30 experiences a loss in ticket sales of only 2,000 tickets per game. You can see already that a higher ticket price could increase revenue for a team facing a steep demand curve for tickets, even if there are a few empty seats.

Most National Football League (NFL) sell-out every game despite having very high average ticket prices. This does not mean that fans believe there are *no* substitutes for the club's games, rather that the team has reached a stadium capacity constraint and cannot sell any additional tickets. There are always *some* substitutes available for any good, so if ticket prices are raised too high, even in the NFL, drops in attendance will result. Economists do not believe that a good with no substitutes exists, but it is a curious case. The demand curve would be completely vertical since the price could be raised without limit and not reduce sales. Can you think of such a good?

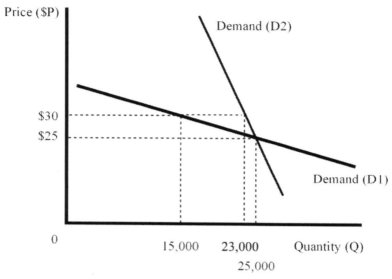

Figure 2.2
Goods with many substitutes have relatively flat demand curves as consumers will be sensitive to prices changes. The opposite is true for goods with few substitutes. There is no such thing as a good with *no* substitutes.

2.3 Shifts in Demand Curves

In order to draw a demand curve in a fixed position, we must assume that the state of the world never changes. More specifically we must assume that real incomes, prices of substitute goods and tastes are do not change. *Real income* is the purchasing power of one's dollar income. Increases in prices with no increase in one's dollar income will lower real income since the same dollar income cannot purchase as many goods and services. An increase in real income for consumers will shift the demand curves for many products (but necessarily all products) to the right. We call this an *increase in demand*. An increase in the quantity of tickets sold due to a drop in the ticket price is a movement along a fixed demand curve. We distinguish this case from a shift in the demand curve by calling it an *increase in quantity demanded*. For the baseball team owner, an increase in real income (imagine a helicopter dropping money with no change in prices) raises the quantity demanded for tickets at the original average ticket price of $25 in Figure 2.3 from 25,000 to 30,000 tickets per game. The demand curve for tickets has shifted to the right since the quantity demanded of tickets will be higher at any price. A fall in real income will have the opposite effect.

We will assume that sports tickets are a *normal good*. Increases in real income shift the demand curve to the right for normal goods so that expenditures on the good increase. Expenditures on *inferior goods* fall as real income increases (the demand curve shifts to the left). These are generally very staple goods of low quality. When your real income increases by enough, you might prefer to buy the better-quality lawn fertilizer than the cheap stuff. The better-quality fertilizer is a normal good and the cheap fertilizer is an inferior good. Economics studies have found that tickets for professional sports teams are normal goods.

An increase in the price of a substitute good for baseball tickets has the same effect in Figure 2.3. At the average ticket price of $25, some of those who formally purchased the now higher-priced substitute good, say a movie ticket, will now purchase a baseball ticket, shifting the ticket demand curve to the right by some amount. An increase in tastes for baseball tickets will also shift the demand curve to the right in Figure 2.3, however changes in tastes can have unpredictable effects. Towards the end of the 1994 MLB season, team owners locked out the players in a labor dispute. All September regular season games, playoff games and the World Series were cancelled. Fans were so discouraged from buying baseball tickets that ticket sales did not recover to the 1993 regular season level until five years after the lockout. A change in fan tastes shifted the demand curve for MLB tickets to the left for some time.

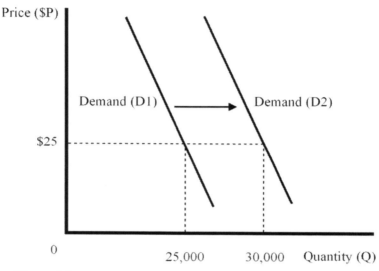

Figure 2.3
An increase in real income, an increase in the price of a substitute good, or a change in tastes towards sports tickets, will shift the demand curve for tickets to the right. At the same price of $25, the demand for tickets is higher.

Professional sports clubs do have some ability to influence the local ticket demand curve they face. A rather unique feature of the professional sports business is that improvements in the quality of teams can shift the demand curve for tickets to the right. This could be the case when a club acquires more talented players through trades and free agency and enjoys greater team success on the field. Casual evidence suggests that fans do appear to support clubs that are more successful on the field.

Figure 2.4 plots club revenues against win-loss percentage for MLB clubs for the 2008 season (other recent seasons are very similar). Each point in the scatter plot represents one MLB team. A rough line drawn through the middle of the cloud of points is upward sloping, suggesting that revenue increase as winning percentage increases. Can you guess which team is the point at the extreme right in the plot? In other industries, firms can shift the demand curve they face to the right through the use of advertising or improving the quality of their product, an output. In professional sports, improving the quality of an input (labor or talent) can have the same effect. Some clubs choose not to do so and spend season after season in the basement. Perhaps this is because the shift in their demand curve would not be large enough to warrant the higher costs of player talent. As we shall see in Chapter 4, revenue sharing in MLB provides an incentive for some teams to keep the payroll small and suffer losing seasons.

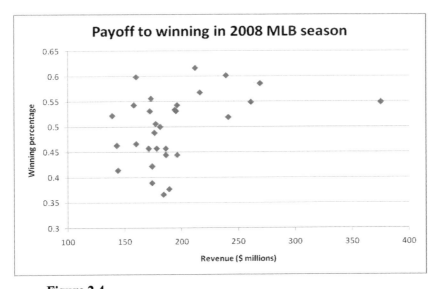

Figure 2.4
Increasing the level of player talent can result in greater team success and revenues. In this case a club has shifted its demand

curve for tickets to the right (holding real incomes and the prices of substitute forms of entertainment constant).

Brief Review of Concepts

- The demand curve for a particular good or service is a schedule representing the maximum amount consumers are willing to pay for a given quantity of the good or service. According to the Law of Demand, price and quantity demanded are inversely related.
- A change in the quantity demanded is a movement along a fixed demand curve, caused by a change in the product's price.
- The slope of a demand curve is flatter the more substitute goods are available. Consumers will be more price-sensitive when many similar goods are available.
- An increase in the price of a substitute good or an increase in real income will shift the demand curve to the right.
- The definition of the product is critical to determining the demand curve.

2.4 Elasticities

Knowing whether the ticket demand curve is relatively flat or steep is not enough for team owners to make accurate pricing decisions. The *price elasticity of demand* is a numerical value, which describes the sensitivity of quantity demanded to changes in the price of a good. It is computed as the percentage change in quantity demanded divided by the percentage change in price along a fixed demand curve.

$$\eta_D = \frac{\% \Delta Q}{\% \Delta P} = \frac{(Q_1 - Q_0)/((Q_1 + Q_0)/2)}{(P_1 - P_0)/((P_1 + P_0)/2)} \qquad (2.1)$$

where P_0 and Q_0 are the original price and quantity demanded, and P_1 and Q_1 are the new price and quantity demanded. Consider the demand curve for baseball tickets that a hypothetical owner faces in Figure 2.5. At an initial average ticket price of $50, the quantity demanded of tickets per game is 15,000. If the club owner drops the average ticket price[14] to $40, quantity demanded rises to 18,000 seats in our example.

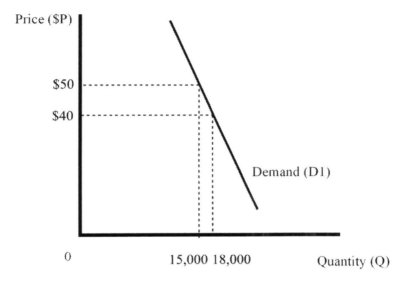

Figure 2.5
The price elasticity of demand measures the responsive of quantity demanded to price changes. In this example, when the average ticket rose from $40 to $50, the quantity demanded of tickets fell from 18,000 per game to 15,000 per game. The computed elasticity is –0.82 meaning that for every 10% increase in ticket prices, ticket sales fall by 8.2%. Since the price increase is greater than the fall in ticket sales, ticket revenue will rise as a result of the price increase.

The price elasticity of demand is computed as

$$\eta_D = \frac{(18,000 - 15,000)/((18,000 + 15,000)/2)}{(\$40 - \$50)/((\$40 + \$50)/2)} = -0.82$$

---

[14] Reductions in ticket prices are very uncommon in professional sports. One exception is the Montreal Expos who dropped ticket prices by over 30% between the 1997 season and their last season 2004. The club was sold and relocated to Washington, D.C. for the 2005 season.

meaning that ticket sales rise by 0.82% for every 1% fall in ticket prices. If the absolute value (drop the negative sign) of the price elasticity of demand is greater than one, the demand curve is said to be *elastic*, implying that quantity demanded is very sensitive to price changes. A price elasticity less than one in absolute value is said to be *inelastic*, implying that quantity demanded is not very sensitive to price changes. The demand curve for tickets in Figure 2.5 is inelastic over the range of ticket prices and quantities demanded observed.

Elasticity value	Demand sensitivity to price changes	Revenue effect for a price decrease
$|\eta_D| > 1$	Elastic	Revenue increases
$|\eta_D| < 1$	Inelastic	Revenue decreases
$|\eta_D| = 1$	Unit-elastic	Revenue unchanged

Club owners are very interested in knowing the price elasticity of demand for their games since elasticity determines what happens to total revenue when the ticket price changes. In Figure 2.5, total revenue before the drop in ticket prices is $50(15,000) = $750,000 while it is only $40(18,000) = $720,000 after the price reduction. The increase in ticket sales is not enough to make up for the drop in ticket prices and total revenue has fallen. This is always true with an inelastic demand curve. On the other hand, an increase in ticket prices from $40 to $50 will raise total revenue with an inelastic demand curve[15].

If the demand curve for tickets is elastic ($|\eta_D| > 1$), total revenue will rise with reductions in ticket prices and will fall with increases in ticket prices. Estimating price elasticities is difficult for team owners since

---

[15] The Montreal Expos found this out the hard way. Total revenues from ticket sales fell drastically in the 1997-98 season despite some increase in attendance. Despite this, ticket prices fell again for the 1998-99 season.

income, substitute goods prices and tastes must be held constant so the demand curve does not shift. Surprisingly there is very little in the academic literature concerning estimates of price elasticities for professional teams or leagues. This is probably due to the difficulty in obtaining reliable ticket price data going back in time. Lee, Park and Miller (2006) estimated price elasticities for a sample of MLB clubs that appear in Table 2.1 below. Which clubs would appear to benefit the most from raising their ticket prices?

Anaheim	-0.88	New York (Yankees)	0.73
Atlanta	-0.57	Oakland	-2.20
Baltimore	-0.72	Philadelphia	-0.42
Boston	0.57	Pittsburgh	-0.64
Chicago (Cubs)	-0.56	San Diego	-1.32
Houston	-2.31	San Francisco	-0.62
Kansas City	-1.46	St. Louis	-0.59
Milwaukee	-1.14	Texas	-0.21
Minnesota	-0.46		

Table 2.1
Price elasticity estimates for MLB clubs (1970–2003)

It is important to note that the price elasticity of demand takes on different values along a fixed demand curve. A formal discussion is left for Chapter 3, however the further down the demand curve the price falls, the smaller the price elasticity of demand (more inelastic).

The price elasticity of demand can be found algebraically from a demand equation. A typical specification is $Q = AP^{-\varepsilon}$ where A is the vertical intercept of the demand curve. Taking the natural logarithm of both sides gives $lnQ = lnA - \varepsilon lnP$. It is easy to show that ε is the absolute value of the price elasticity of demand. We know that $\partial lnQ/\partial lnP = \frac{1}{Q}dQ/\frac{1}{P}dP$ using rules of differentiation. But this division is just $\%\Delta Q / \%\Delta P$ which is the price elasticity of demand defined in (2.1). Often when economists wish to estimate the price elasticity of demand for a product, they estimate a least squares regression of the natural log of the quantities purchased against the natural log of the prices observed. The slope coefficient is an estimate of the price elasticity of demand.

The *income elasticity of demand* gives an indication of the sensitivity of ticket sales to changes in real incomes. Real income is the purchasing power of income. Typically real income is computed by dividing dollar income by a consumer price index, but we shall ignore these difficulties here. We have already seen that an increase in real income will shift the demand curve to the right for a normal good. The income elasticity of demand provides an estimate of how far the demand curve will shift along the horizontal quantity axis in Figure 2.3. The income elasticity of demand is computed as the percentage change in demand (not quantity demanded) for a given percentage change in real income.

$$\eta_I = \frac{\%\Delta Q}{\%\Delta I} = \frac{(Q_1 - Q_0)/((Q_1 + Q_0)/2)}{(I_1 - I_0)/((I_1 + I_0)/2)} \tag{2.2}$$

where Q_0 and I_0 are the original quantity demanded and real income, and Q_1 and I_1 are the new quantity demanded and real income. If the income elasticity of demand is positive, we are dealing with a normal good; if it is negative, we are dealing with an inferior good.

Suppose that real incomes rise by 5% on the average in the baseball Mudhens home market during the off-season (this would be a healthy increase). As a result, suppose that fans purchase 18,000 tickets per game for the upcoming season instead of the 15,000 tickets per game purchased last season. This means the demand curve for tickets for the Mudhens has shifted to the right with the increase in real income as in Figure 2.3. The income elasticity of demand is computed as

$$\eta_I = \frac{(18,000 - 15,000)/((18,000 + 15,000)/2)}{0.05} = 3.64$$

meaning that ticket sales rise by 3.64% for every 1% increase in real income. In this example, Mudhens tickets are a normal good since sales increase as income rises.

Goods whose income elasticity of demand is greater than zero are normal goods, while those whose income elasticity of demand is less than zero are inferior goods. Table 2.2 below provides income elasticities for the National Hockey League (NHL) from a number of studies. The numbers suggest that NHL tickets are either a weakly normal good or a weakly inferior good, depending on the study.

Income elasticities are tricky to estimate since real income does not change very quickly over time in metropolitan cities. Typically one specifies a demand equation like $Q = AI^\beta P^{-\varepsilon}$ then takes the natural log of both sides to find $lnQ = lnA + \beta lnI - \varepsilon lnP$. The slope coefficient β from a least squares regression is the income elasticity of demand.

Study	League	Time period	Income elasticity
Jones (1983)	NHL	1946-67	-0.002
Paul (2003)	NHL	1999-2000	-0.0002
Jones et al (1996)	NHL	1983-84	-0.167
Jones (1993)	NHL	1983-84	0.100
Jones (1992)	NHL	1981-84	0.88

Table 2.2
Estimates of income elasticities

Brief Review of Concepts

- The price elasticity of demand measures the percentage change in the quantity demanded for a given percentage change in the price of the good. The demand curve is said to be elastic (inelastic) if the price elasticity of demand is greater than (less than) one.
- Lowering the price raises (lowers) total revenue if the demand curve is elastic (inelastic).
- The income elasticity of demand measures the percentage change in demand for a given percentage change in real income. Goods with an income elasticity of demand greater (less) than zero are said to be normal (inferior) goods.

2.5 The Supply Curve

Since we have decided that tickets are the final output of a professional sports team, since that is what revenue is obtained from, we need to consider what the ability of team owners to "produce" tickets. In the more standard case of businesses that produce a physical good, like a cellular phone or a loaf of bread, the output is produced using a range of *inputs* or *factors of production*. These can include labor, raw materials, capital (machines), energy, land, knowledge, organizational skills and so on. The ability of the business to hire these factors in large enough quantities will determine the amount of output that can be produced. Professional sports organizations also hire factors, the most important of which is the stock of talent that is carried by the players on the roster. Other factors can include coaching, equipment, a stadium or arena, transportation, medical care and so on.

We introduced the demand curve for tickets already in this chapter but we have not explained what ticket price a team owner will choose on the demand curve. To do this, we require a second curve in Figure 2.1. The supply curve represents the *minimum price* a producer must receive to produce a given quantity of goods or services. Thus the supply curve is a lower bound on the producer price for a given quantity of goods, but he may be able to extract a higher price. Stated another way, the supply curve gives the quantity of output the producer will make available at each price. There is no Law of Supply that is like the Law of Demand. The supply curve can slope upward or downward depending on the cost conditions facing the firm. Conventionally it is drawn upward-sloping since, in most industries, to produce more output firms must hire more factors of production (labor, capital, land, etc.) which raises the minimum price the firm needs to produce more output. However if firms are able to purchase factors of production in bulk and receive a lower unit price per unit of factor, the minimum price the firm needs could fall as more factors are purchased.

We will assume that "producing" more tickets requires acquiring more expensive talent for the team so the supply curve is upward-sloping, even though the amount of other factors needed may not increase by much. Figure 2.6 provides an example of a supply curve for tickets. The interpretation is that the team must receive an average ticket price of at least $25 to provide 20,000 tickets per game in order to avoid losses. The team would like to charge a higher price than $25, but as we shall see later, its ability to do so is constrained by what fans are willing to pay for tickets.

2.6 The Slope of the Supply Curve

The slope of the supply curve is determined by the availability of factors of production. If factors are scarce, and producing more output requires the bidding away of factors from other businesses, costs can rise quickly and the supply curve will be relatively steep. This is often true for high technology industries where factors of production are scarce and expensive. Other industries, such as fast food, employ mostly unskilled labor and inexpensive factors resulting in a relatively flat supply curve. The minimum price needed to produce output will increase very gradually. If factors of production are abundant and cheap, the supply curve will be relatively flat.

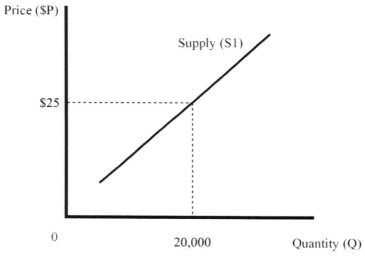

Figure 2.6
The supply curve of tickets gives the minimum ticket price the team owner must receive to supply a given amount of tickets. In this case, at least $25 per ticket is needed to produce 20,000 tickets per game.

Business owners can judge how quickly costs will increase with more output if they know the value of the price elasticity of supply. The *price elasticity of supply* measures the percentage change in the quantity supplied for a given percentage change in the product price.

$$\eta_S = \frac{\%\Delta Q}{\%\Delta P} = \frac{(Q_1 - Q_0)/((Q_1 + Q_0)/2)}{(P_1 - P_0)/((P_1 + P_0)/2)} \qquad (2.3)$$

The terms P_0 and Q_0 are the original price and quantity supplied, and P_1 and Q_1 are the new price and quantity supplied. Suppose that the quantity of tickets supplied in Figure 2.6 increases from 20,000 to 25,000, requiring an increase in the minimum average ticket price from \$25 to \$30. The price elasticity of supply is computed below.

$$\eta_S = \frac{\%\Delta Q}{\%\Delta P} = \frac{(25{,}000 - 20{,}000)/((25{,}000 + 20{,}000)/2)}{(30 - 25)/((30 + 25)/2)} = 1.22$$

The calculated price elasticity of supply indicates that a 1% increase in the minimum ticket price will allow an increase of 1.22% in ticket output. The supply curve is said to be elastic if the price elasticity of supply is greater than one; inelastic if the price elasticity of supply is less than one. Unlike the price elasticity of demand, there is no direct connection between the value of the price elasticity of supply and team revenue since fans might not purchase all of the tickets that the team owner makes available (that is determined by the demand curve).

In Figure 2.7, the supply curve can shift to the right due to:

1. an increase in the number of firms in the industry
2. natural occurrences like good weather for farmers
3. a decrease in taxes that businesses pay
4. new technologies which allow for higher output with the same amount of factors
5. an increase in the amount of factors available that does not affect factor prices.

For professional sports teams, another important reason the supply curve of tickets can shift to the right is a publicly funded increase in the seating capacity of the stadium or arena that does not increase costs for the team. This is particularly true if the team is selling out every game. We explore this possibility more fully in Chapter 3. In Figure 2.7, at the same price of $25, the club can produce more output (from 25,000 to 30,000), hence the supply curve has shifted to the right. We shall focus on industry or league supply curves, not supply curves for individual teams.

Analytical example: Picking points from a supply curve.

Question: The supply curve for tickets for the new Los Angeles Surfers NFL team is given by $P = -5 + 0.001Q$ where P is the ticket price and Q is the number of tickets that can be made available for sale. How many tickets can be made available when the ticket price is: $100, $50, $25, $10?

Answer: The equation for the supply curve is a straight line with a vertical intercept of $5 and a slope of 0.001. Solve the supply curve equation for Q on the left-hand side. $Q = -5,000 + 1000P$. Now insert the ticket prices.

$Q = -5,000 + 1000(100) = 95,000$
$Q = -5,000 + 1000 (50) = 45,000$
$Q = -5,000 + 1000(25) = 20,000$
$Q = -5,000 + 1000 (10) = 5,000$

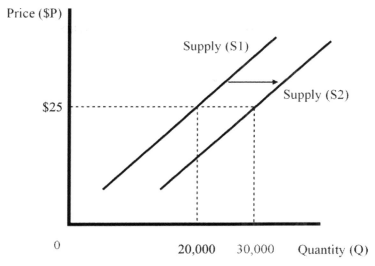

Figure 2.7
The supply curve provides the *minimum* price the producer needs
to produce a given amount of output. It is assumed to be upward
sloping due to the higher costs incurred by the producer to produce
more output. The supply curve will shift to the right as greater
technology lowers costs, more factors of production become
available, or as new firms enter the industry.

Brief Review of Concepts

- The supply curve is a schedule giving the minimum price a
  producer needs to produce a given amount of output. The supply
  curve can slope in any direction depending upon the cost
  conditions facing the firm. Generally it is drawn as upward
  sloping.
- The supply curve will be relatively flat if factors of production are
  abundant and cheap. The price elasticity of supply measures the
  percentage change in the quantity supplied for a given percentage
  change in the product price.
- The supply curve will shift to the right when the number of
  producers increases, factor prices fall, productivity increases, taxes
  decrease, or as the result of a natural occurrence.

66

2.7 Equilibrium

The demand curve and the supply curve for a product produced by a business can be drawn in the same picture as in Figure 2.8. The market price of the good is found where the two curves intersect. In Figure 2.8, the demand and supply curves for the Mudhens intersect at an average ticket price of $25, resulting in 20,000 tickets per game being sold. At this price, the maximum amount the last consumer willing to pay for the 20,000[th] ticket is just equal to the minimum amount the producer must receive to produce that ticket. Every consumer who wants to buy a ticket at the $25 price can do so. There will be no shortage or surplus of tickets.[16] In economics, we often say that prices are determined at the margin, meaning that the market price is determined by what the last consumer is willing to pay for the last ticket. Since the demand curve is the maximum price consumers are willing to pay, each consumer before the last consumer is willing to pay more than $25 per ticket since the demand curve is above $25 at ticket quantities less than 20,000, however they do not have to.

The price at the intersection of the demand curve and the supply curve is called the *equilibrium* price. The concept of equilibrium has different meanings in different disciplines. In economics, we use the term equilibrium to describe a position where any movement away from it results in a movement back to the same position over a period of time. In the sciences, the movement back to the equilibrium is the result of physical forces of nature; in economics, it is due to market forces that are the sum of choices made by individual consumers based on their own preferences. To see how this process works, suppose the average ticket price is higher than

---

[16] Why then do we often observe empty seats in stadiums and arenas? As we shall see in the next chapter, charging a ticket price that equates demand and supply is not the same as filling the stands. In some cases, it is profitable for the team owner to leave some seats empty.

the equilibrium ticket price. At an average ticket price of $30, the team owner can afford to put 30,000 bums in the seats by hiring more factors of production, in this case, increasing the stock of talent on the team. So it is the higher ticket price that allows the owner to "increase production" – without the higher ticket price, the owner could not afford the greater stock of talent. Unfortunately for the team owner, the demand curve he or she is facing in the local market indicates that fans will purchase only 10,000 tickets per game at the $30 ticket price. The difference of 20,000 tickets per game is a *surplus* of tickets produced over and above the amount that will be purchased by fans. Inventories of unsold tickets will accumulate. This sends a signal to the team owner to lower "production" by lowering the stock of talent on the team and to subsequently lower the ticket price. As output falls and ticket inventories are sold off, production moves down the supply curve towards 20,000 tickets per game. As the ticket price falls, the quantity demanded of tickets increases as more marginal consumers are willing to pay the lower ticket price. Consumers move down their demand curve towards 20,000 tickets per game. As long as the quantity supplied of tickets is greater than the quantity demanded, output and price will fall until the equilibrium price of $25 and quantity of 20,000 tickets per game are restored. At this point, all the tickets that are made available for sale are purchased by fans.

We could have just as easily started at a price below the equilibrium price to demonstrate the movement back to the equilibrium price. Consider the price of just $20 in Figure 2.8. At this low price, fans would like to purchase 30,000 tickets per game as indicated by where the price intersects the demand curve. However the price of $20 is too low for producers to take on much in the way of costs, so they cut their team talent stock and offer only a small number of tickets, 10,000, as given by where the $20 price intersects the supply curve. The resulting difference of 20,000 tickets per game is a *shortage*. Since only 10,000 tickets per game are actually produced at a price of just $20, consumers bid up the price in order to ration the available quantity. As the ticket price rises, some consumers no longer wish to purchase them (we move up the demand curve), while the higher price allows the team owner to incur higher costs and increase production. The fact that consumers are lining up to buy tickets, and are willing to pay a higher price, sends a signal to the team owner to increase output and incur higher talent costs (move up the supply curve). This process continues until the shortage is eliminated at the equilibrium ticket price of $25. At that price, all the consumers willing to pay $25 per ticket can purchase them and the market is cleared.

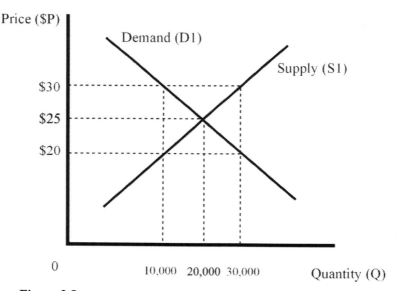

Figure 2.8
The price of $25, where the demand and supply curve intersect, is called the equilibrium price. At this price, every consumer who wishes to buy a ticket at an average price of $25 can do so. There is no shortage or surplus. At a price of $30, a surplus of 10,000 tickets will result since the price is too high. At price of only $20, a shortage

of tickets will result since the price is too low. Market forces move the price and quantity sold back to the equilibrium price.

2.8 Consumer and Producer surplus

Consumer surplus is an important concept used to show the value to society from a good or service. As we shall see, free markets work to maximize consumer surplus, which is one reason why free markets are espoused by economists. In a free market, prices are always equilibrium prices determined by demand and supply curves for each good and service, whereas in a market with some sort of government interference in the determination of prices, consumer surplus is not maximized. To understand consumer surplus, we need to think a little more deeply about what the demand curve for tickets represents. Consider Figure 2.9 where a demand curve for tickets is drawn without any need for a supply curve. Think of each point on the demand curve as the maximum price each person will pay to purchase a game ticket when sorted from highest to lowest. Near the top of the demand curve, the first few individuals are willing to pay a very high price for a ticket since they value them so much. As we move down the demand curve, ticket prices fall since each successive person is not willing to pay as much for a ticket as the previous person. Each point on the demand curve represents the *marginal valuation* of a ticket for each individual.

The *consumer surplus* is the difference between the maximum price an individual is willing to pay (the marginal valuation) for a ticket and the price that he or she actually pays, summed over all consumers on the demand curve. In Figure 2.9, all those consumers who are willing to pay a ticket price higher than $25 receive a "surplus" since the ticket price they actually pay is only $25. This is the economic concept of value. All those individuals above the equilibrium price of $25 on the demand curve believe that stadium tickets are worth more than $25 up to the last person at ticket sales of 20,000 per game. The last person receives no surplus since the maximum amount he or she is willing to pay for a ticket is just equal to the price he or she actually pays ($25). All those consumers on the demand curve below the equilibrium price choose not to buy a ticket since their marginal valuation of a ticket is below the market price. Hence the consumer surplus is measured as the area inside the shaded triangle above the equilibrium price and below the demand curve.

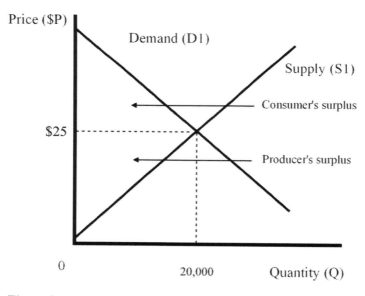

Figure 2.9
Consumer surplus is defined as the sum of the difference between the maximum amount each consumer is willing to pay for a given quantity of tickets, and the price actually paid (P_o, the equilibrium price) for all consumers. Consumer surplus is a measure of the value of a given amount of output to society. The value of a good is not its price, which is its marginal valuation.

The *producer surplus* is the difference between the equilibrium ticket price and the minimum ticket price necessary that allows the producer to supply a given amount of tickets, summed over all tickets on the supply curve. This is the area above the supply curve and below the equilibrium price in Figure 2.9. The producer gains a surplus since the marginal cost to produce each ticket, the point on the supply curve, is less than the ticket price, except for the last ticket sold. This is not the producer profit however, which is defined in the next chapter, instead it is more of an incentive to operate the business.

Analytical example: Calculating consumer surplus.

Question: The demand curve for tickets for the new Los Angeles Surfers NFL team is given by P = 100 - 0.001Q where P is the ticket price and Q is the number of tickets that can be made available for sale. What is the consumer' surplus at a ticket price of $40?

Answer: The equation for the demand curve is a straight line with a vertical intercept of $5 and a slope of 0.001. First find the quantity of tickets that will be sold each game at the $40 average ticket price. We already solved the demand curve for Q earlier in the chapter.

$$Q = 100,000 - 1,000(40) = 60,000$$

The consumer surplus is the area of the triangle below the demand curve and above the $40 price. The area of a triangle is always half the area of a rectangle.

Surplus = (1/2)[$100-

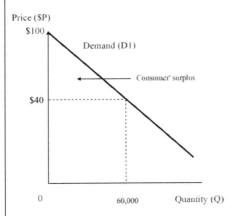

$$[\$40][60,000] = \$1,800,000$$

The consumer surplus in Figure 2.9 is the area between the demand curve and the equilibrium ticket price of $25. This is the total "value" to consumers and society of tickets to the professional sports game. The total "value" to the producer of the tickets is the producer surplus. If the market for tickets is free of government interference, the sum of the consumer surplus and the producer surplus will be maximized when the ticket price is $25. Consider a ticket price of $30 that is above the free market equilibrium price in Figure 2.10. Fans will purchase only 10,000 tickets at a ticket price of $30 according to the demand curve, even though the team owner will offer 30,000 tickets for sale. With only 10,000 tickets sold, the loss in consumer and producer surplus is equal to the sum of areas A and B. If the ticket price is only $20, ticket demand will increase to 30,000 per game, but the team will only be able to offer 10,000 tickets per game according to the supply curve. A shortage of 20,000 tickets will result. Again the actual quantity of tickets sold will only be 10,000 tickets since that amount is what the team will make available. The loss in consumer and producer surplus is again the sum of areas A and B in dollars.

The price of a good does not indicate its value: that is its consumer surplus. Goods deemed valuable by society, like clean water and air, typically have low prices in developed economies. They provide a great amount of consumer surplus and are thus provide great value, but that is because their prices are low.

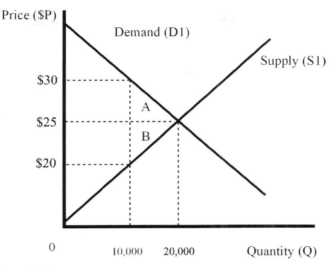

Figure 2.10
The equilibrium price always maximizes the consumer surplus to society. Consider the price $30 that is above the equilibrium price. The consumer surplus is much smaller and the producer surplus is the area below $30 and above the supply curve at 10,000 tickets. The area A+B is lost.

Brief Review of Concepts

- The equilibrium price and quantity purchased are determined by the intersection of the demand and supply curve. At this point, all those consumers willing to buy the good at the equilibrium price can do so. There is no shortage or surplus at the equilibrium.
- In the absence of government interference or other barriers, prices and quantities should always occur at their equilibrium points. Any movement away from the equilibrium will bring about a change in the product price, which causes a movement back to the equilibrium point.
- The consumer surplus measures the gain in wealth to society from the market for the product. It is the sum of the differences between the maximum price consumers are willing to pay for a product, and the equilibrium price they actually pay. The area under the demand curve and above the equilibrium price is the consumer surplus.
- The price of a good represents the marginal consumer valuation of the product, not the value of the product. Free markets maximize the consumer surplus.

Focus Box: Who Can Afford These Prices?

For the 2012 season, MLB ticket prices averaged $26.98, making baseball the most affordable professional sport for the fan. Tickets for premium seats average $89.47 in MLB. These are seats in special seating areas that are closer to the field and might have other amenities. The NFL average ticket price came in at a relatively hefty $78.38 with an average of $243.61 for premium seats. The NBA averaged $50.99 (premium seat prices not available) and the NHL averaged $57.49 ($134.14 for premium seats). A more telling statistic is the cost for a family of four to attend a game, which includes four tickets, four hot dogs, four small sodas, parking, two programs and two caps. The highest and lowest family costs for each league are given in the table below.

Highest and Lowest Game Prices (Family of four, US$), most current season		
	Highest	Lowest
MLB	Fenway Park (Boston): $337	Chase Field (Phoenix): $146
NFL	Cowboys Stadium (Dallas): $635	Everbank Field (Jacksonville): $343
NBA	Madison Square Garden (New York): $608	Time Warner Cable Arena (Charlotte): $198
NHL	Air Canada Center (Toronto): $626	Jobing.com Arena (Phoenix): $228

Source: http://sites.google.com/site/rodswebpages/codes

These costs are certainly high. What type of person can afford to attend major league sporting events? In 2012, the median household real income in the United States was $51,017 while the median income for

NFL season ticket holders was $104,100.[17] NFL season ticket holders averaged 104% higher incomes than the general population. In 1972, the same season ticket holder had an average income only 58% higher than the average household income. It would appear that attending sporting events is getting expensive and those in the upper end of the income distribution are those who can afford it.

2.9 Dynamics

Prices and quantities for some good change due to shifts in the demand and supply curves. In this section we analyze the effects of these shifts and dispel some common misperceptions of why prices and quantities change.

Increases in major league ticket prices can be the result of an increase in consumer demand for tickets. This can happen due to an increase in real incomes, an increase in the price of a substitute entertainment good, or just an increased preference on the part of consumers for major league sports tickets. The latter is particularly true if the team is winning and has the potential for a championship. The dynamics of the shift in the demand curve is shown in Figure 2.11. The demand curve for tickets has shifted to the right due to any or all of the previously mentioned factors. Initially, ticket prices might be slow to respond to the higher demand for tickets, particularly since most sports organizations maintain constant ticket prices throughout a regular season.[18] Playoff tickets can be substantially higher than regular season ticket prices.

---

[17] Source: http://www.sbrnet.com/newsletter/may20-2013.html

[18] This is not necessarily true. Many NHL teams now charge higher ticket prices for so-called premium games. Several examples are given in
http://ca.sports.yahoo.com/nhl/blog/puck_daddy/post/Why-NHL-teams-price-gouge-fans-for-premium-home-?urn=nhl,97847

In Figure 2.11, at the Mudhens initial average ticket price of $25, an increase in real incomes or an increase in the price of a substitute good, like professional football tickets, has shifted the Mudhens ticket demand curve to the right. At the current price, fans can afford to purchase 30,000 tickets per game but only 20,000 tickets will be made available (according to the ticket supply curve).A shortage of 10,000 tickets per game results and fans will be lining up to buy tickets. To alleviate the shortage, the club will have to ration tickets in some way other than raising their price, perhaps by a lottery or simply bearing with longer line-ups for tickets. The next season, the club can raise its ticket prices to alleviate the shortage. As the average ticket price is increased, some consumers will decide not to purchase tickets (those along the demand curve between the prices $30 and $25). At the new equilibrium price of $30 and ticket sales of 25,000 per game, ticket demand and ticket supply are equal and all those consumers willing to buy tickets at the higher equilibrium price of $30 can do so with no shortage.

Ticket prices can also change due to shifts in the ticket supply curve. Suppose that the Mudhens have decided to close a portion of the seating sections in their stadium and have covered these sections with tarps with advertising printed on them. In Figure 2.12, the supply curve of tickets has shifted to the left since at the original equilibrium ticket price of $25, fewer tickets are now made available. A shortage of 10,000 tickets per game results and fans line up to buy tickets. This sends a signal to the team owner to produce more tickets, but he or she can do so only by incurring higher costs. We move up the supply curve as the minimum price to offer tickets increases – this in turn lowers the quantity demanded of tickets as some fans now choose not to buy them at the higher price. At the new equilibrium ticket price of $30, 15,000 tickets per game are sold and there is no shortage of tickets.

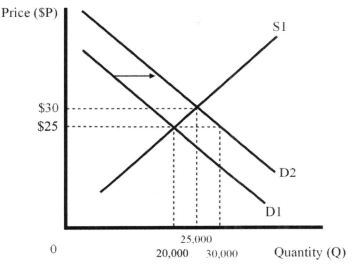

Figure 2.11
With slow price adjustment, the shift of the demand curve from D_1 to D_2 creates an initial shortage of tickets equal 10,000 tickets. Lineups send a signal to the team owner to raise the ticket price, and, as the price rises, quantity demanded falls and quantity supplied increases until 25,000 tickets per game is reached.

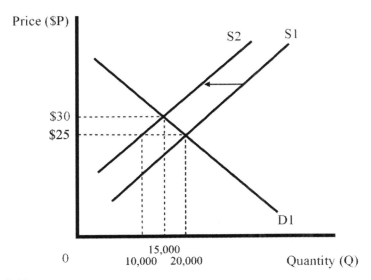

Figure 2.12

With slow price adjustment, the shift of the supply curve from S_1 to S_2 creates an initial shortage of tickets equal 10,000 tickets. Line ups send a signal to the team owner to raise the ticket price, and, as the price rises, quantity demanded falls and quantity supplied increases until 15,000 tickets per game is reached.

2.10 The All-or-Nothing Demand Curve

A smart team owner might be able to think of a way to extract the consumer surplus from sales of tickets since this is additional revenue for the owner. By selling tickets at a fixed price determined at the start of the season, the owner observe that scalpers are selling game tickets outside the stadium at prices much greater than the equilibrium ticket price. This is ticket revenue that is being collected by scalpers and not the owner, even though it is the owner that is "producing" the output. One way that the owner can capture this extra profit is to auction each ticket to the highest bidding fan. How much would each fan be willing to pay? Economics suggests that each fan will be willing to pay up to their maximum amount, but no more. Again, think of the ticket demand curve as the maximum amount each consumer is willing to pay for a single ticket, sorted from highest willingness to pay to the lowest. The first ticket goes up for auction and the highest bid will be very close to the first point on the ticket demand curve. The second ticket could then be auctioned to the next highest bidder and so on. The revenue from all tickets that are sold would be the total area under the demand curve up to the last ticket sold. In this way, the team owner captures the revenue he or she would have earned by charging the equilibrium price plus all of the consumer surplus. Fans would receive no consumer surplus since they have transferred it to the team owner by paying auction prices.

The auction method is useful if there are only a few tickets to sell, but when there are 75,000 tickets to sell for a football game, it is cumbersome and slow. There is another way the team owner can prevent scalping of tickets. Suppose that instead of selling tickets on a per game walkup basis, *all* tickets are sold as season ticket packages that includes one ticket for each home game for the entire season. Thus the fan faces an "all or nothing" choice in deciding whether to buy tickets. We define the all or nothing demand curve as the season ticket package price that transfers all the consumer surplus to the team owner. This is drawn in Figure 2.13. The all-or-nothing demand curve lies above the normal demand curve for single tickets since the owner charges a higher price than the walkup price (per game) in order to extract all of the consumer surplus.

The Mudhens walkup single game ticket price is $25, however the team owner could package all the single game tickets as a season tickets package and charge the all or nothing price of $30 per game (multiplied by the number of game tickets in a season). How do we know the price should be $30? The team owner charges the all-or-nothing price that increases ticket revenue by the amount of the consumer surplus. So the rectangle area between $35 and $25 at 20,000 tickets per game just equals the triangle area below the normal ticket demand curve and above the price of $25. A good rule of thumb is when area A just equals area B, the all-or-nothing price has been reached. Knowing what the all-or-nothing demand curve looks like allows the team owner to choose the season ticket price for any quantity of ticket sales.

Two conditions must be met for team owners to charge all-or-nothing prices. First, the team must be a local monopoly or else competition from other teams will prevent all-or-nothing pricing. Second, season ticket purchasers must be prevented from re-selling their tickets on their own (becoming scalpers) to those fans that are willing to pay a higher price on a walk-up basis. The walk-up market is a different fan from the season ticket market with a different demand curve. It seems unlikely that these two conditions are met in any professional sports market, however season ticket packages may be a way of capturing at least a portion of the consumer surplus instead of all of it, leaving less room for scalpers to make a profit.

Usually a significant portion of tickets are deemed season ticket seats and will not be sold on a per game basis. Most seats for NFL teams are sold on a season ticket basis – walkup tickets are unheard of for most teams. Season tickets might also be valuable to the team owner as a way to reduce the degree of uncertainty in ticket revenues since these tickets are essentially pre-sold at the start of the season. As we shall see in Chapter 7, personal seat license revenues can be a useful way to finance new stadium construction since the revenues are received quickly and they are not subject to variations in ticket demand.

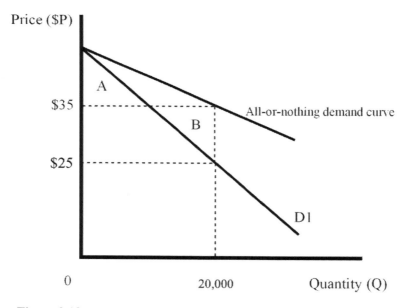

Figure 2.13
The All-or-Nothing demand curve lies everywhere above the normal demand curve since the team owner is able to extract a higher price from the consumer by charging for an "all-or-nothing" package of

season tickets. The all-or-nothing price P_1 transfers all of the consumer surplus to the team owner.

Analytical example: Calculating the all-or-nothing ticket price.

Question: The demand curve for tickets for the new Los Angeles Surfers NFL team is given by $P = 100 - 0.001Q$ where P is the ticket price and Q is the number of tickets that can be made available for sale. What is the season ticket price that will capture all of the consumer surplus for the team owner?

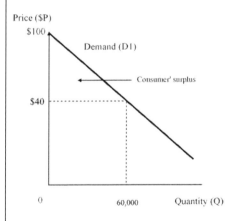

Price ($P)

$100

Demand (D1)

Consumer' surplus

$40

0   60,000   Quantity (Q)

Answer: We already calculated the consumer surplus to be $1,800,000 per game. Over 60,000 tickets per game, the ticket price could be raised by $1,800,000 / 60,000 = $30 to extract all of the consumer surplus. The season ticket price would be $40 + $30 = $70 per game multiplied by the number of home games. With 8 regular season home games in the NFL, the total season ticket package would be $70(8) = $560 instead of the $40(8) = $320 price for single game tickets to all home games. Alternatively the owner could charge $240 for a personal seat license (PSL) that gives the holder the right to buy a season ticket.

Brief Review of Concepts

- When the demand curve shifts to the right, the quantity demanded is initially greater than the quantity supplied, creating a shortage. The shortage sends a signal to the producer to raise output. To do so, the producer must incur higher costs and thus the price rises. The rising price prevents some consumers from purchasing the product. At the new equilibrium, the higher quantity demanded equals the higher quantity supplied.
- When the supply curve shifts to the right, the quantity supplied is initially greater than the quantity demanded, creating a surplus. This sends a signal to the producer to reduce output. Using fewer factors of production allows the producer to lower the price, encouraging more consumers to buy. At the new equilibrium, the product price will be lower and the quantity demanded will be greater.
- The all-or-nothing demand curve represents the maximum amount consumers will pay for an all-or-nothing quantity of the product (season tickets). Due to high market power, the producer can extract all of the consumer surplus by charging a price higher than the normal equilibrium price. Buyers must be prevented from re-selling the product to others.

2.11 Factor Pricing

Player salaries account for the majority of the costs of running a professional sports team. Why do some players earn far more than others? Are the rapidly rising salaries in all sports justified by the player's performance? Before answering these questions, we must develop the basic model of factor pricing used in economics. Factors are inputs used to produce outputs. In economics we usually group factors into capital and labor. Capital is composed of goods that are used to produce other goods, but are not final consumption goods themselves. Machines, buildings, education and training are all forms of capital. Professional sports teams do not use a lot of capital if we measure the output of the team as sales of tickets. In the short-run, we can safely assume that the capital stock is fixed for the team owner. The fixed capital the team uses is the arena or stadium, team buses and planes, and office equipment. These capital items do not change with the level of output of the team (tickets), except in the long-run if a new arena, or some other capital equipment is required.

Team owners hire players who bring a stock of their own talent to the team. Since team roster sizes are usually fixed (12 in the NBA, 23 in the NHL, 25 in MLB and 53 in the NFL), it does not make sense to think of a team owner hiring more or fewer players. Instead we think of each player having an individual stock of talent (t_i) that contributes to the total stock of talent on the team (T). The only way a team owner can increase the team's stock of talent is to hire players that are more talented and let lesser talented players go. It is total team talent that will, at least partly, determine the success of the team and the resulting revenue for the owner. We will assume throughout the rest of the book that greater team success brings more revenue to the owner and that is the incentive to acquire more talent.

$$T = t_1 + t_2 + t_3 + \cdots t_N = \sum_{i=1}^{N} t_i$$ where N is the number of players on the team roster.

We will assume that total team talent is subject to the *Law of Diminishing Marginal Productivity*. This means that as an increasing amount of a variable factor, like talent, is added to a fixed factor, like capital, to produce an output, output increases at a diminishing rate. For a professional sports team, the fixed factors might include coaching, practice facilities, equipment and transportation. We measure the output of players as winning percentage. As a team acquires more talented players in place of others, winning percentage should increase (holding constant the talent of other teams) and ticket sales will increase, but more slowly as the team stock of talent is higher. So ticket sales increase as team talent (and success) increases, but at a diminishing rate. The top figure in Figure 2.14 demonstrates this assumption. We often observe the law of diminishing marginal product in professional sports. Adding a superstar (very talented) player to a relatively poorly performing team can result in a large increase in team performance and ticket sales. Think of LeBron James when playing for the lowly Cleveland Cavaliers (NBA) early in his career. Adding a superstar player to a team already filled with superstars will probably do little to improve the team's performance and ticket sales, since performance and ticket sales are already high.

The *marginal product of talent* (MP_T) is the change in the total output (Q = winning percentage) when the team stock of talent (T) increases by one "unit".

$$MP_T = \frac{\Delta Q}{\Delta T} \tag{2.3}$$

When the team stock of talent is increased by a measurable amount, the MP_T can be found by measuring the resulting change in winning percentage and then using the equation for the MP_T. In economics, it is often the case that any change in the denominator of the equation is assumed to be very small, so small that it cannot be observed easily. This is because it allows the use of calculus to solve for the MP_T. We will not resort to calculus here. Graphically, the MP_T can be found by taking the slope of a line drawn tangent to any point on the total product curve in the top portion of Figure 2.14. A *tangent line* has the property that it just touches a single point on the curve and no other point. The slope of the tangent line decreases (becomes flatter) as output increases and we move up the total product curve, hence the marginal product of talent diminishes as total product rises. This is an assumption about how output behaves when a single factor (in this case talent) is increased and all other factors do not change. We call this the *Law of Diminishing Marginal Product*. This result comes from the assumption about the shape of the production curve. Note that total output is still increasing as the marginal product of talent diminishes. We will have more to say about these technicalities in Chapter 8.

A popular production function for winning percentage used in the sports economics literature is the logistic contest success function where there are N teams in a sports league.

$$w_i = \frac{N}{2} \frac{t_i}{t_1+t_2+\cdots+t_N} \qquad (2.4)$$

Most commonly we set $N = 2$ to simplify the analysis since adding more teams does not change any qualitative results.[19] With only two teams, the production function is $w_1 = \frac{t_1}{t_1+t_2}$ for team 1. The marginal product for team 1 is (using the quotient rule of differentiation)

$$\frac{\partial w_1}{\partial t_1} = \frac{(t_1+t_2)1-t_1}{(t_1+t_2)^2} = \frac{t_2}{(t_1+t_2)^2} = \frac{w_2}{t_1+t_2} > 0$$

You should be able to show that the marginal product of talent is diminishing in higher stocks of talent.[20] The greater is the stock of talent owned by team 2, the higher the marginal product of talent for team 1. This

[19] The production function for winning percentage must satisfy two criteria. First, the sum of all team winning percentages must equal $N/2$. Second, if all talent stocks are equal, each team should have a 0.500 winning percentage. You should be able to verify that (2.4) satisfies these criteria.
[20] This requires taking the second derivative of the production function and showing that it is negative.

is because when w_2 is high, w_1 is small since in a two-team league $w_1 + w_2 = 1$ (excluding tie games). Team 1 then has a low stock of talent and its marginal product is large (check the slope in Figure 2.14 when the stock of talent is small).

The team owner considers the *marginal revenue product* of talent to be the change in team revenue when one more unit of talent is added to the total talent stock of the team since it is revenue that the owner cares about. Adding one more unit of talent to the team increases the team winning percentage by the marginal product of talent. A higher winning percentage will shift the demand curve for tickets upward by some amount and result in more ticket sales and more revenue for the team owner. We leave exactly how much the demand curve shifts to the next chapter.

The MP_T can be easily converted from units of tickets to dollars by multiplying the MP_T by the average ticket price. We call this the *value of the marginal product* of talent (VMP_T). Economics suggests that the team owner will acquire costly talent until the *wage rate per unit of talent (W_T)* for each team will just equal the VMP_T.

$VMP_T = P \bullet MP_T$

Rule: Hire talent until $W_T = VMP_t$

Of course, the VMP_T can differ among teams due to the size of the local market. Teams that operate in large cities with high average incomes are much more likely to attract fans willing to pay a high ticket price, resulting in a higher VMP_T and resulting W_T. The minimum salary paid to a player is his or her own stock of talent (t_i) multiplied by the marginal product of talent, in the absence of a reserve clause.

Rule: Player salary $= W_T \bullet t_i = VMP_T \bullet t_i$

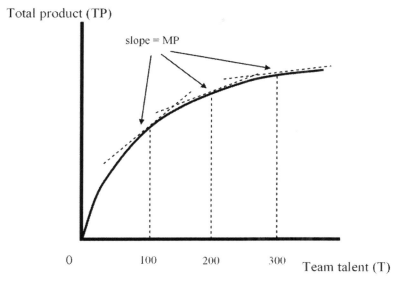

Figure 2.14
The total product (*TP*) schedule is assumed to be upward sloping since as more team talent (*T*) is acquired, however the function increases at a diminishing rate. The marginal product (*MP_T*) of talent is the change in total product when the owner purchases one more unit of talent The MP_T is the slope of the *TP* schedule at any level of talent measured by the slope of a tangent line.

More talented players will be paid more as they have higher t_i's, but the wage rate per unit of talent is the same for each player in the calculation of salaries. This is demonstrated in Figure 2.15 for a player who is a member of a team with a team stock of talent of 200 units. The marginal product of talent is assumed to be 100 tickets per game at this point on the marginal product curve. At an average ticket price of $25, the VMP_T is $2,500. The interpretation of this is that adding one more unit of talent to the team will add an additional $2,500 in ticket revenue to the team owner. Note that the VMP_T is determined for all players on the team by the last unit of talent that is acquired by the owner. On all previous units of talent, the team owner receives a surplus equal to the area under the marginal product curve and above the MP_T of 100 tickets per game. The owner will continue to acquire costly talent until the surplus is maximized at 200 units of talent. This will maximize ticket revenue from hiring talent and bringing fans in to the stadium. The total payroll for the team is just $VMP_T \bullet T$ which is $2,500(200) = \$500,000$ and is the rectangular area in Figure 2.15. If the salary paid to the player is less this, the player can negotiate with other teams or ask the owner for a raise.

Salary negotiation is always about who receives the surplus value from talent – the player or the owner. In a free agent market, the player can attempt to extract the surplus value from the owner by asking for a high salary, on the threat of signing with another team. Under the old reserve clause, players were typically paid less than their marginal product so the owner extracted a large surplus value from the player. Skilled player agents have created a very successful industry in extracting a player's full surplus value. In this case, the player may receive his or her salary according to the talent rule, plus all of the surplus value. The owner will not pay a salary beyond this amount since no profit will be earned on talent.

The difference between the salary a player earns and the salary that the player could earn by finding alternative employment in another industry is called the player's *economic rent*. This is a result of the unique skills that a player possesses that would have no use in any other industry. It is likely that most professional athletes earn very large economic rents since their salaries in their alternative occupations are low, unless they have obtained useful degrees while training in college and university.

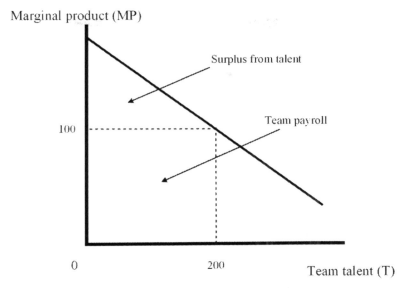

Figure 2.15
The player's salary is determined by his or her MP. The difference between the value of the player's output (the area under the MP schedule up to 200 talent units) and the team payroll ($25(100)(200) = $500,000) is the surplus value that the team owner receives.

2.12 Rookie Salaries: An Application of Expected Value

All professional sports leagues establish minimum starting salaries for first-year (rookie) players that are far above the income the player would earn if not playing professional sports. The minimum salary for NHL players is $550,000 for the 2013-14 season, $405,000 in the NFL, $490,000 in the NBA and MLB. The opportunity cost (C) is the income that the rookie player would earn if he or she did not make it to the professional league. Starting salaries must be high in order to give an incentive for good players to take the risk of working through college or university, grinding through the minor leagues, and entering the rookie draft. Each player has a probability (p) of making it to the major leagues that is quite low, even for very talented players. The player does have an ability to affect his or her own probability through demonstrating ability, lobbying efforts, etc., but often this is costly.

Analytical example: Calculating a player's salary, the team payroll and the surplus to the owner.

Question: The total product for the owner of the Los Angeles Surfers NFL franchise from acquiring costly talent is given by the equation $Q = 1000T - T^2$. This results in a MP_T schedule given by the equation $MP_T = 1000 - 2T$ (don't worry how). The owner would like a good team and decided to hire 400 units of talent. If the average ticket price is $40, what will a player be paid with 20 units of talent, what will the team payroll be and what will be the surplus from talent to the owner?

Answer: The MP_T with 400 units of talent is $1000 - 2(400) = 200$ tickets. The VMP_T is then $40(200) = $8,000. A player with 20 units of talent will be paid $8,000(20) = $16,000 per game and the team payroll will be $8,000(400) = $3,200,000 per game. An NFL team plays 8 regular season home games, so the payroll for the season is $8(3,200,000) = $25.6 million. The surplus to the owner is the area of a triangle: $0.5(1000-400)(400)($40) = $4.8 million per game or $38.4 million for the season. Essentially players and owners receive nothing for road games since the ticket revenue accrues to the other team.

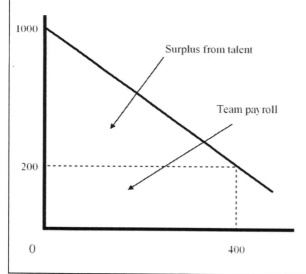

We can treat the decision to invest in training and foregoing other forms of income as a gamble. Let's assume that if a player gambles but does not make it to a professional team; he or she will earn no income since the opportunity to earn C has been given up[21]. A player who is *risk-neutral* will demand a starting salary S up to the point where $pS + (1-p)0 = C$. We call the left-hand side of the equation the *expected value* of the gamble. A risk-neutral person does not consider the riskiness of the gamble in making the decision to train. Instead, a risk-neutral person only cares which side of the equation is larger and will choose thusly. Suppose the athlete can earn $40,000 instead of playing basketball in the NBA and the player's probability of making it onto an NBA team is 0.01. The minimum salary the athlete will demand is found by solving the equation for the salary: $S = C/p = \$40,000/0.01 = \$4,000,000$. If an athlete is *risk-averse*, he or she will demand a starting salary higher than $4,000,000 to compensate for the risk in the gamble. If an athlete is *risk-loving*, he or she will accept a starting salary lower than $4,000,000 since he or she prefers the gamble to the certain outcome of $40,000. Whether a player is risk-averse, risk-neutral or risk-loving depends on the athlete's preferences. Since the probability of making it to a major professional sports league is very small, the fact that many athletes still try might indicate they are risk-loving. However economics usually asserts that individuals are risk-averse.

Brief Review of Concepts

- The definition of output is difficult for the major league sports organization. Players produce measurable performance statistics and wins. Owners care only how wins translate into ticket sales. We will define the output as ticket sales.
- A player's marginal product is the change in the total output of the team when he or she plays an additional minute or game.
- The team owner will pay a player the marginal product of talent multiplied by the player's own stock of talent units.

---

[21] It would be simple to allow the player to earn some salary different from C if they fail to make a professional team.

- The difference between the total revenue generated by a player and the player's salary is the surplus to talent. The surplus is a return to the team owner. Salary negotiations always involve a battle between the player and the owner over the surplus.
- Players who are risk-averse will demand a starting salary greater than their opportunity cost of employment in order to be compensated for taking the risk of reaching the majors. Players who are risk-loving will play for less than their opportunity cost. Starting salaries are typically much higher than salaries in other occupations due to the low probability of making a major-league team.

Test Your Understanding

1. The current trend in major league baseball is to build smaller stadiums that reflect the way older stadiums looked 60 years ago. This usually means a decrease in the number of seats in the stadium. Assuming that clubs care about revenues and profits, and they know what the demand curve they face looks like, why would they move towards smaller stadiums? Is there an elasticity condition for this?

2. Explain how each of the following will affect the demand and supply curves for tickets and the resulting effect on the equilibrium ticket price.

   a) An increase in the prices of hot dogs, beer and other concession items at the stadium.
   b) An increase in the price of a PSL to buy seasons tickets.
   c) A rival league establishes a team in the same city.
   d) An improvement in the quality of team.
   e) A large increase in medical insurance costs for the team owner.

3. Ted Texas is the owner of a football team. After hiring an economist to do some market survey work, Ted has learned that the price elasticity of demand for tickets in his local market is equal to -1.15. The average ticket price for football games is $75. Ted would like to see attendance increase by 10%. By how much

will Ted have to change the average ticket price to do this? What will be the percentage change in Ted's ticket revenue (tricky)?

4. Suppose an NFL club has just finished construction of a new stadium that it financed itself. It is deciding on how to price its season ticket package for a particular seating section of the stadium that has drink service and other amenities. The team plays a total of eight home games.

a) Suppose the demand curve for tickets that the club faces in this seating section is given by $P = 600 - 0.1Q$ where P is the average ticket price and Q is the number of tickets sold per game. If the club is averaging 5,000 spectators per game in this seating section, what will be the average price of a single game ticket? If a seasons ticket package is simply composed of single game tickets which can be purchased individually, what is the price of the season ticket package?

b) The club is considering selling season's tickets as an all-or-nothing package and have hired you to figure out what the price of the package (for all home games) should be. What is the maximum amount of consumer surplus that you can extract from fans? What will be the maximum all-or-nothing season ticket price for this seating section? If the difference is to be made up with a PSL, what is the price of the PSL?

5. Suppose that a major-league baseball club can hire talent units in order to improve the performance of the team. Better performance translates into higher ticket sales. Also suppose that the players the club hires can be broken down into talent units. The table below gives the number of tickets that are sold per game for each level of talent units.

Talent units	Tickets sold	Talent units	Tickets sold
10	2,000	60	18,000
20	4,000	70	25,000
30	7,000	80	31,000
40	11,000	90	35,000
50	14,000	100	38,000

a) Define the law of diminishing returns as it applies here. Does this output schedule satisfy the law of diminishing returns? Why?

b) Compute the marginal product of talent at each level of talent units starting from 20.

c) If the average ticket price is $15 and the club decides to hire 90 talent units (maybe this is a better than average team), what should be the total payroll per game?

d) Compute an estimate of the surplus value received by the club owner when he hires 70 talent units.

6. Steve Stunning is a promising high school basketball player that has just received a scholarship to attend a university and play for the basketball team. Alternatively, he could work in his family business and earn a good income of $100,000 per year, but if he accepts the scholarship, he must give up this opportunity. Steve knows that the probability of being drafted by an NBA team is small, only 0.09, but better than most university players.

a) What salary will Steve demand if he is drafted by an NBA team if he is risk-neutral? What if he is risk-averse?

b) Suppose that if Steve is not drafted to an NBA team, he can earn an income in the family business, but only $50,000. How does this change the answer in part a?

7. Another popular contest success function is given by

$$w_1 = \frac{1}{N-1}\left(\frac{t_1}{t_1 + t_2} + \frac{t_1}{t_1 + t_3} + \frac{t_1}{t_1 + t_4} + \cdots + \frac{t_1}{t_1 + t_N}\right)$$

Here we have assumed that team 1 plays every other team only once so that each term in the bracket is essentially the probability of winning each game.

Show that this contest success function satisfies the two criteria in footnote 19 by restricting the league to just 3 teams. Hint: each team will have a winning percentage defined as above, just with different subscripts

Focus Box: The First Superstars in Professional Sports.

Major league baseball produced the first legitimate superstars in professional sports. Superstars can be deemed as players who perform at a level far above their peers and are paid accordingly. Mike "King" Kelly was a scrappy, dirty player for the Chicago White Sox in 1886, who was sold to the Boston Beaneaters for the unheard of sum of $10,000. He had just finished leading the White Sox to a World Series victory. Kelly was probably the best player of his time and fans in Boston went wild after his acquisition. During the "dead ball" era when hitting power statistics were minimal around the National League, Kelly had a lifetime .308 batting average (hits / at bats) and a .428 slugging percentage (total bases / at bats) with 69 home runs (the average player might hit 5 home runs per season). His best season was 1886 when he had a .388 batting average with a .538 slugging percentage and 4 home runs.

Babe Ruth began his career with the Boston Red Sox in 1914, primarily as a pitcher. Indeed his pitching statistics for Boston through 1919 are impressive: an earned run average (ERA) of 2.2 runs per game. Ruth is most remembered for his hitting, which did not come to prominence until his sale to the New York Yankees in 1920 for the unheard of sum of $100,000. His power statistics are phenomenal, even by today's standards: a lifetime .342 batting average, 714 home runs (at a time when the average player hit about 10 home runs per season), 2,213 runs batted in (RBI) and a .690 slugging average. His best season was arguably 1927 when he hit 60 home runs with a .356 batting average and 164 RBI. Ruth's home run totals would have been higher except that, at that time, if a ball was hit past the foul pole in fair territory, but landed in foul territory, it was deemed a foul ball.

The Bureau of Labor Statistics has computed that the price level across the United States has increased roughly 10.2 times since 1920. A figure is not available for 1886. Babe Ruth's sale fee of $100,000 would be worth $1.02 million of purchasing power in 2006. This is not a huge sum in comparison to more recent player sales. Wayne Gretzky, a player of similar impact to Ruth in his league, was sold from the Edmonton Oilers to the Los Angeles Kings for $15 million in 1989. It could be that the Boston Red Sox drastically underestimated the value of Babe Ruth. Nevertheless his price would appear to be a bargain.

Comparisons of this sort can be deceiving since the average salary of a major-league baseball player is now much higher than it was in 1920, certainly more than 10.2 times higher. The average salary in 1920 is not available, however "Shoeless" Joe Jackson, a star player for the Chicago White Sox in 1919 earned $6,000 (Quirk and Fort (1997)) before his expulsion from the league on game fixing charges. Babe Ruth's sale price was roughly 16.5 seasons of pay for Jackson. It is thought that the salary earned by the best players at the time of Mike "King" Kelly was about $2,000, making his sale fee five seasons of pay. The salaries earned by the best baseball players in 2006 averaged around $12 million per season. Babe Ruth's sale fee in 2006 would then be a phenomenal $198 million ($12 million x 16.5) and "King" Kelly's fee would be $60 million ($12 million x 5). These figures give some indication of the impact these two players had on the game during their eras.

Mike "King" Kelly

Source: http://www.baseballhalloffame.org/

George Herman "Babe" Ruth

Source:

http://www.baseballhalloffame.org/

Chapter 3
Basic Principles II

This is the second of two chapters that reviews the basic economic principles needed to continue further in the text. The focus in this chapter is the economics of how firms behave in competitive markets and markets where competition is restricted. Although professional sports leagues do not operate in very competitive markets, it is useful to consider the case of competitive markets as many leagues operated competitively early in their histories. In order to show how professional sports benefit from restricting competition, it is necessary to understand how firms behave in competitive markets. We focus on a partial equilibrium model here but cover a two-team league model in Chapter 5.

The key concepts to learn in this chapter are listed below.

- The role of profit maximization for the firm. Where do firms set output to maximize profits? The concepts of total product, total revenue, marginal revenue and marginal cost.
- The characteristics of perfect competition and how the firm behaves in a perfectly competitive market.
- The characteristics of a monopoly and how the monopolist behaves. The deadweight loss to society due to the monopolist.
- The economic theory of cartels and why cartels are doomed to fail. This is especially relevant to the behavior of professional sports leagues, which are cartels.

- A simple model of a professional sports club that relies on the dominance of fixed costs.

3.1 The Role of Profit Maximization

Why are firms in business? What is it they are trying to do? The professional sports industry is no different than any other industry that is operated by business owners. They exist to earn profit and the ruthless accumulation of profit guides their business decisions. This makes the world sound like a greedy place, but as we shall see, it is that greed that produces outcomes that are generally good for businesses and consumers.[22] The world will not become a polluted cesspool caused by uncaring businesses if it is profitable to reduce pollution and produce environmentally friendly products. The difficulty is creating consumer demand for "green" products by pricing them competitively.

At the level of the professional sports league, we will assume that club owners set ticket prices so as to maximize *economic profit*. Economic profit is defined as total revenue (ticket sales) less total operating costs and the *opportunity cost* of the owner. The opportunity cost is the value of the next best alternative use of the owner's resources. If the owner could earn an income as a shipping magnate instead of running a professional sports team, that income is his or her opportunity cost and should be deducted from total revenue in the profit calculation. As we shall see in the next section, competition drives economic profit to zero in the long run, but it does allow the team owner to recoup his or her opportunity cost. If economic profit is negative, the owner should sell or disband the team and leave the industry. This is often not the case due to the presence of tax

---

[22] Some economists think of team owners as only caring about winning as long as they break even. The "win-maximizing" model will be covered in Chapter 5.

advantages (see the Veeck tax shelter in Chapter 4) that increase profits, or profits from holding the franchise and selling at a later time.

Analytical example: Calculating economic profit.

Question: The demand curve for tickets for the new Los Angeles Surfers NFL team is given by P = 145 − 0.001Q where P is the ticket price and Q is the number of tickets sold. The current average ticket price the owner is charging is $85. Other revenues include concession, parking and other local revenues totaling $15 million. Television revenues are $50 million. The current team annual payroll is $85 million and other annual operating costs total $15 million (the team pays no stadium rent to the city). The team plays 8 home games every season. The owner formally ran a real estate business that earned a profit of $5 million annually. What is the economic profit of the Surfers?

Answer: Ticket revenue is found from the demand curve equation. At a $85 ticket price, 60,000 tickets are sold every game. Total ticket revenue for the season is $85(60,000)(8) = $40.8 million. Accounting profit is total revenue less total costs: $40.8 + $15 + $50 - $85 - $15 = $5.8 million. Economic profit is accounting profit less opportunity cost: $5.8 - $5 = $0.8 million. Big deal.

This chapter will deal with two types of market structures that are on polar ends of the competition scale: perfect competition and monopoly. We will deal with the details of these two markets later in the chapter. However the rule each a firm in either market will use to find the profit-maximizing output and price is the same, therefore we can derive it here. Let's assume for now that the average ticket price does not fall as more tickets are sold - a violation of the law of demand at the market level, but useful as a simplification here. For a team, *total revenue* is just the average ticket price multiplied by the number of tickets sold. The total revenue schedule will be as given in Figure 3.1. In its simplest form, we define a revenue function as $R = R(Q)$.[23] With a fixed ticket price, the R schedule is a straight line with a slope just equal to the ticket price. Here we are measuring the number of tickets sold over an entire season and thus R is for the entire season. A team cannot sell any tickets if it reaches the capacity of its facility, so the R schedule is not defined past the full capacity number of tickets given by Q_{FC}.

Marginal revenue (MR) is defined as the change in total revenue for a given change in output, usually one ticket. If a team sells one more ticket, what is its increase in total revenue? It is the MR.

$$MR = \frac{\Delta R}{\Delta Q} = \frac{\partial R}{\partial Q} \qquad (3.1)$$

Since we are assuming that the ticket price is constant, the marginal revenue from the sale of one more ticket is simply the constant ticket price. Algebraically, $R = PQ$ and with P constant, $\partial R / \partial Q = P$. More generally, the marginal revenue can be measured by the slope of a line drawn tangent to any point on the total revenue curve.

The *total cost* (*TC*) schedule is also given in Figure 3.1. For most firms, we assume in economics that the total cost schedule rises at an increasing rate as more tickets are sold. This is because as more output is produced, factor prices rise due to their scarcity. *Marginal cost* (*MC*) is the change in total cost for a given change in output, again usually one unit.

---

[23] In fact revenue is a function of ticket sales Q, ticket sales are a function of winning percentage w, and winning percentage is a function of the team stock of talent t. This will give $R = R\left(Q(w(t))\right)$. We leave that for Chapter 5.

$$MC = \frac{\Delta C}{\Delta Q} = \frac{\partial C}{\partial Q} \tag{3.2}$$

The marginal cost can be measured by taking the slope of a straight-line drawn tangent to any point on the total cost curve. Due to the increasing slope of the total cost curve in Figure 3.2, marginal cost will rise as more tickets are sold. An example of a cost function that behaves this way is $C = cQ^2$ so $\partial C / \partial Q = 2cQ$. As Q increases, so does MC.

How many tickets should the team owner sell to maximize profits over the season? Profit is the vertical distance between the total revenue and total cost curves. At 2,000,000 tickets this vertical distance is maximized. How do we know? The slopes of the tangent lines just touching the total revenue and total cost curves are identical, implying that at 2 million tickets, $MR = MC$. The interpretation of this condition for profit maximization is straightforward. For every ticket sold up to two million, $MR > MC$ since the slope of the TR line is greater than the slope of the TC curve and thus profit is rising. For the last ticket sold at 2 million tickets, the contribution to profit is zero since $MR = MC$, and for every ticket sold beyond 2 million, $MR < MC$ so profit is diminishing.

Algebraically we can define the team profit function as $\pi = R - C = R(Q) - C(Q)$. We maximize profit by choosing the level of ticket sales such that the slope of the profit function is just equal to zero, that is, where $\partial \pi / \partial Q = \partial R / \partial Q - \partial C / \partial Q = 0$. The last two terms are just MR and MC. This is the level of ticket sales where $P = MC$ if the ticket price is constant.

Firms will maximize profits at the level of output where MR = MC.

104

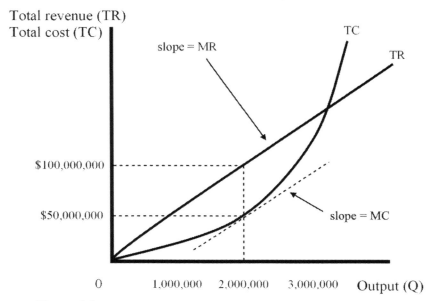

Figure 3.1
Profits are maximized by selling 2 million tickets where the difference between total revenues and total costs are maximized. The slope of the total cost curve at any point on it is the marginal cost (MC). The slope of the total revenue curve is the marginal revenue (MR). Only 2 million tickets do we have MR = MC.

This is the guiding economic principle for profit maximization and applies to any firm in any type of market structure. Do team owners actually *maximize* profits? Perhaps not since finding the right level of ticket output where *MR = MC* is complicated by the capacity of the stadium or arena. Some owners are more interested in winning at the expense of profit maximization. However we can assume that owners act as if they are trying to maximize profits since any owner would prefer more profits to less.

- We assume team owners set prices to maximize economic profit. Economic profit is total revenues less total operating costs and opportunity costs.
- The team owner maximizes economic profit by selling tickets up to the point where the marginal revenue (MR) just equals the marginal cost (MC) of running the club. Marginal revenue is the change in total revenue when an additional ticket is sold. Marginal cost is the change in total cost when an additional ticket is sold.

3.2 The Perfect Competition Model

Perfectly competitive industries are characterized as having many firms each producing an essentially identical product. Each firm must charge the same market price that is determined by the total output of the industry. Trying to charge a price that is higher than the market price will result in no sales. Also, the entry of new firms and the exit of existing firms is unregulated but not without some cost to them. That is not very representative of a modern professional sports league where the entry of new teams is restricted and the number of teams is not too large. Each team is free to charge its own ticket price that maximizes its own profit instead of facing a market price. So the perfect competition model is not a very good model of a professional sports league, however we begin with it so that we can see how the business practices of sports leagues require a lack of competition.

The early periods in most professional sports leagues can be thought of as nearly perfectly competitive. Before the development of the National League in 1876, baseball was a "barnstorming" tradition with transitional teams made up of some amateur players and some paid players. There were hundreds of teams with no formal schedule or championship.

At the turn of the century, local promoters organized basketball games as part of the entertainment for a dance or other activity. The promoter hired players and there was no fixed schedule or league. In these days, ticket prices were whatever a promoter could get and usually quite low and promoters were very competitive.

If each team must charge the same ticket price under perfect competition, how is this price determined? The market price for tickets is determined by the intersection of the market demand and supply schedules for all of the teams. The market demand schedule is the horizontal summation of the individual team demand schedules at various prices. So if the Surfers, Cowboys, Jets and Raiders are the only four teams in a competitive league and each can sell 1 million tickets over the season at a ticket price of $50, the market demand curve is set at 4 million tickets sold at a price of $50. This summing up is repeated for different ticket prices to trace out a market demand curve. The market supply curve is the horizontal summation of the ticket outputs that can be produced at each ticket price. The market ticket price is then determined where the market demand curve and market supply curve intersect. We have already seen that market forces will move the price to the equilibrium price from Chapter 2. At the equilibrium market ticket price of $60 in Figure 3.2, there will be no shortage or surplus of tickets.

No team can set a price higher than the market price without the prospect of losing all attendance since all teams produce an identical product. In the early period in baseball, ticket prices were typically ten cents. While the market demand curve is downward sloping, the demand curve each team faces is completely elastic (flat), as in Figure 3.2. In theory, the price elasticity of demand for the team is equal to minus infinity since, if the team owner increases the average ticket price by so little as ten cents, the quantity demanded of tickets will fall to zero and all sales will be lost. Since each team is a price taker, the only issue in maximizing economic profit is how many tickets to sell.

If new firms enter the industry and set up shop, the supply curve in Figure 3.2 will shift to the right since more output can be made available in the industry at the same price. This will cause the market equilibrium price to fall and reduce profits for all of the firms.

If the ticket price is constant no matter how many tickets are sold, the total revenue curve is shown as in Figure 3.1. The slope of the total revenue curve, the marginal revenue, is the constant ticket price ($P = MR$). *Average revenue* (AR) is revenue divided by the number of tickets sold.

$$AR = \frac{R}{Q} \tag{3.3}$$

With a constant average ticket price, $TR = P \times Q$, so from (3.3) $AR = P$, as well as equaling MR.

For the price taking firm, $P = MR = AR$ with a completely elastic demand curve.

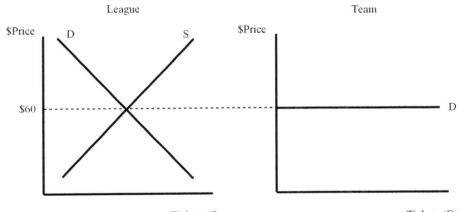

108

Figure 3.2
Firms in perfectly competitive industries are price takers. Changes in ticket sales for any one team will not affect the market price for tickets. The market price for tickets is determined by the intersection of the market demand and supply curves.

We have assumed that total costs rise as more tickets, and thus games, are sold. Costs may rise due to higher salary costs, transportation and other *variable costs*. Variable costs (VC) are costs that change as output changes. *Fixed costs* (FC) remain the same regardless of the level of output. The total cost curve in Figure 3.2 is assumed to rise with output at an increasing rate.

Total costs (TC) = Total variable costs (VC) + total fixed costs (FC) (3.4)

Average cost is total cost divided by the number of tickets sold.

$$AC = \frac{C}{Q} = \frac{VC+FC}{Q} \tag{3.5}$$

The total cost curve could intersect the vertical axis above zero in Figure 3.1 due to the presence of fixed costs. It is easy to show that the *AC* curve is U-shaped as ticket sales increase. Figure 3.3 draws a total cost curve that is upward-sloping with a positive amount of fixed costs. Let's say that the team is currently selling 25,000 tickets per game giving a total cost of $500,000 per game. The *AC* is easy to compute: $500,000 / 25,000 = $20 per ticket. In Figure 3.3, the *AC* is the slope of a line drawn from the origin to the point on the *TC* curve. Slope is given by rise over run which is just the calculation we did to get the *AC* of $20. We could start at a low level of ticket sales and draw a line from the origin through points on the *TC* curve. Initially the line will become less steep so the *AC* is falling. Eventually a level of ticket sales is reached where the slope of the line starts to increase and the *AC* is rising. So if we draw the *AC* curve with the quantity of tickets sold on the horizontal axis, it initially falls and then increases.

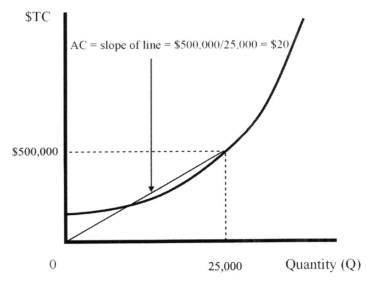

Figure 3.3
The Average Cost (*AC*) curve is found by computing the slope of a line drawn from the origin to any point on the Total Cost (*TC*) curve.

For the perfectly competitive team owner, profits are maximized at the level of ticket sales where *MR* = *MC*. For the last ticket sold, there is no contribution to profit since the increase in revenue (the ticket price) just equals the increase in total cost. However the owner earns a profit for all the tickets sold up to the last ticket sold. The *MC* curve is just the slope of the tangent lines of the *TC* curve at different levels of ticket sales (we showed this in Figure 3.1). Since the ticket price, *AC* and *MC* are all measured in dollars, we can put the demand curve facing the team owner, the *AC* curve and the *MC* curve all in the same diagram in Figure 3.4. It is important to draw the *MC* curve so that it cuts through the *AC* curve at the lowest possible *AC*. This can be shown to be true algebraically, but we won't show it here. The profit-maximizing amount of tickets to sell is where the *MC* curve just cuts through the team demand curve: where $P = MR = MC$. This is 20,000 tickets in Figure 3.4.

To determine the level of profit, we can note that average profit = $TR/Q^* - TC/Q^* = AR - AC = P - AC$. The average cost curve is U-shaped and marginal cost cuts through the minimum of average cost from below. The vertical distance between price and average cost at Q^* is the average profit per ticket. Total profit is $(P-AC)Q^*$, the shaded box in Figure 3.3. Entry of new teams into the local market shifts the industry supply curve to the right in Figure 3.2, reducing the equilibrium market price. The demand curve for each team shifts down to the new price, reducing profits. In the long run, entry of new teams will continue until $P = AC$ and economic profit is zero.

Consider the table below that describes revenues and costs for a hypothetical barnstorming basketball team at the turn of the last century, the Crosstown Rivals. If the market price for a basketball ticket is fifty cents, what will be the profit maximizing number of tickets per game that the team needs to sell (assume that the costs facing the team are the same for every game played)?

P($)	Q	TR ($)	MR ($)	TC ($)	MC ($)	AC ($)
0.50	0	0	-	$20	-	-
0.50	25	12.50	0.50	25	0.20	1.00
0.50	50	25.00	0.50	31	0.24	0.62
0.50	75	37.50	0.50	39	0.32	0.52
0.50	100	50.00	0.50	50	0.44	0.50
0.50	125	62.50	0.50	62	0.48	0.496
0.50	150	75.00	0.50	75	0.52	0.50

0.50	175	87.50	0.50	89	0.56	0.51
0.50	200	100.00	0.50	105	0.64	0.525

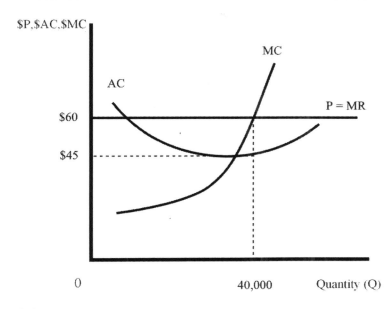

Figure 3.4
The profit maximizing amount of tickets to sell for the team owner is 20,000 tickets per game. This is where P = MR = MC. Profit is given by the rectangular area ($60 – $45)40,000 = $600,000.

At zero ticket sales, marginal revenue, marginal cost and average cost are undefined. Total cost is $20 which represents only fixed costs since at a zero output, there are no variable costs. If 25 tickets are sold per game, total revenue is $0.50(25) = $12.50 and marginal revenue is just $12.50/25 = $0.50. At any level of ticket sales, marginal revenue is the same as the ticket price since the ticket price is always $0.50. The total cost for the Rivals to sell just 25 tickets is $25 and the marginal cost is $5/25 =

0.20^{24}. the average cost is the total cost divided by 25 tickets, $25/25 = \$1.00$. If the team sells another 25 tickets, the total cost rises to \$31.00 and the marginal cost is the increase in the total cost divided by the increase in ticket sales, $6/25 = \$0.24$. The average cost falls to $31/50 = \$0.62$. You can continue doing the calculations up to the last row where the team sells 200 tickets. The profit maximizing number of tickets for the Rivals to sell per game is somewhere between 125 and 150 tickets where $MR = \$0.50$ equals $MC = \$0.50$ (and MC is increasing). The Rival's profit will be somewhere around \$1.50, the level of profit at say 125 tickets sold. Not much, but back in those days, the team organizer was lucky not to lose his or her shirt.

Analytical example: Calculating economic profit.

Question: The Burnaby Bandits are a soccer team playing in the low-level Pacific Coast Soccer League (PCSL). The league has imposed a standard ticket price of \$5 for each team in the league to keep prices reasonable for fans. The total cost equation for the Bandits (per game) is given by the equation $TC = 500 + 0.5Q + 0.01Q^2$. What is the AC equation for the Bandits? What is the profit-maximizing number of tickets to sell per game and what is the profit?

$MC = 0.5 + 0.02Q$ (use calculus)

Answer: The AC equation is just the TC equation divided by Q. This gives $AC = (500/Q) + 0.5 + 0.01Q$. The profit-maximizing number of tickets to sell is just Since the ticket price is fixed at \$5, $MR = \$5$. Now equate the MC equation to MR and solve for Q.

$$0.5 + 0.02Q = \$5$$
$$0.02Q = \$4.50$$
$$Q = 4.5/0.02 = 225$$

The Bandits should sell 225 tickets per game. The profit is total revenue less total cost.

$$\text{Profit} = \$5(225) - [500+0.5(225)+0.01(225^2)]$$
$$\text{Profit} = \$6.25 \text{ per game}$$

Spend it wisely.

3.3 The Long Run in the Perfect Competition Model

---

[24] This really an average of the marginal costs for each ticket from the first ticket sold to the 25th ticket sold.

Economics defines the long run as the length of time to wait until all the factor inputs are variable. Only labor can be changed in the short-run, but in the long-run, capital, land, energy and all the other factors that go into producing output can be changed. In the long-run, the firm can set all of its factor inputs to zero and go out of business if it wishes. Since Figure 3.4 is drawn for the short-run where all factors, except labor, are fixed, we need to draw a different picture to represent the optimal long-run position of the owner, that is, how many tickets to sell to maximize profits. By increasing the amount of capital the owner uses, say by expanding the stadium to seat more customers, the short-run MC and AC curves shifts to the right in Figure 3.5. Since these curves represent only the labor cost component of costs, more output can be produced when there are more of the fixed factors that are used with labor. Essentially adding more of the fixed factors to the labor that is already in place increases the size of the business. So the curve labeled $SRAC_2$ (short-run average cost where only labor is changing along the curve) is further to the right than $SRAC_1$ because the firm is using more capital and is getting bigger in size. When the firm achieves the curve labeled $SRAC_4$, it is using a large amount of capital and other fixed factors, besides its labor and is quite large.

In Figure 3.4, the long-run AC curve ($LRAC$) is drawn as the "envelope" of all the short-run AC curves, each drawn successively for a higher amount of capital. Any point on the $LRAC$ curve gives the average cost per ticket to produce a given amount of tickets when all the factors of production can be changed. In the long run, the team owner can choose to operate at any level of output along the $LRAC$ curve, since each point on the long run AC curve is the minimum average cost of a given short run AC

curve[25]. This is because with perfect competition, new clubs will enter the industry and ticket prices will be forced down to the minimum of each *SRAC* curve in the short-run. The owner will incur losses below this point since $P < SRAC$.

The *LRAC* curve is drawn as a bowl shape for a reason. It can be divided into three regions that determine the "returns to scale" of the team owner's business. The downward-sloping portion exhibits *increasing returns to scale* where output rises more quickly than total costs, hence average costs fall. Firms that engage in assembly line production typically exhibit increasing returns to scale. The founder of modern economics, Adam Smith, referred to this property as the "division of labor". By training each worker to specialize in a specific task, output can be increased far beyond the number of workers. By doubling the amount of labor input, output is more than doubled. As we shall see in the last section of this chapter, professional sports organizations typically operate with increasing returns to scale, which allows them to prevent entry of new, rival organizations.

> **The long-run AC curve (LRAC) connects the minimum points of each short-run AC curve.**

The upward-sloping portion of the *LRAC* curve is said to exhibit *decreasing returns to scale*, where total costs rise faster than output. By doubling the amount of labor input, output increases by less than double. This is usually due to the scale of the business. For instance, doubling the amount of labor that works a fixed size plot of farmland will probably not

---

[25] Years ago, an economist named Jacob Viner asked one of his students to draw a long run *AC* curve that connects the minimum points of each short run *AC* curve with a smooth curve. Of course, this cannot be done and is referred to as "Viner's error". However in theory, this is what the *LRAC* curve represents.

increase the crop yield by double when they are a lot of workers on the land. At the minimum of the LRAC curve is the point of *constant returns to scale*. Here total cost rises by the same factor as total output for small increases in output, so that the *LRAC* is constant. In other words, doubling the amount labor input just doubles the amount of output. Handcrafted industries typically operate with constant returns to scale since each piece of output requires one unit of labor input.

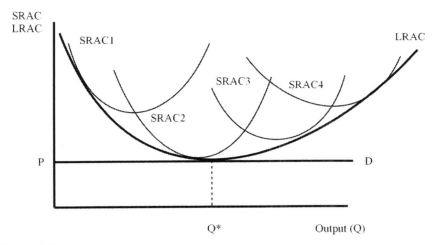

Figure 3.5
Each average cost curve is drawn for a higher level of capital, thus $SRAC_1$ has the smallest amount of capital and $SRAC_4$ has the largest amount of capital. The long-run *AC* curve connects the minimum points of each short-run *AC* curve. The efficient level of capital and output occurs at output Q^*. Competition as new firms enter the market will drive down the market price P to the minimum point of *LRAC*.

As long as positive economic profits is being made, new firms will continue to enter a perfectly competitive industry. This entry will drive down the market price (the market supply curve shifts to the right) and shift down the demand curve each firm faces, until the market price is just equal to the minimum of the *LRAC* curve. At this point, zero economic profit is being made and each firm is operating at their efficient scale or size. Average costs cannot decrease any lower than this. Since professional sports clubs typically do not operate at constant returns to scale, and can restrict the entry of new clubs, they will not reach their efficient scale but instead be at a level of output below Q^* in the long-run. Economists call this one of the inefficiencies of a lack of competition: costs will not be minimized and these savings will not be passed on to consumers.

Brief Review of Concepts

- A firm operating in a perfectly competitive industry faces a large number of competing firms, each selling an identical product, who can enter and exit the industry easily.
- Each firm is a price taker: the product price is determined by the interaction of demand and supply at the industry level. Price and marginal revenue are the same since any change in output does not affect the price. The demand curve for each firm is completely flat (elastic) where $P = MR = AR$.
- Fixed costs do not change with output while variable costs do change with output. Marginal cost (MC) is the change in total cost when output increases by one ticket. The average cost (AC) curve is U-shaped. The MC curve cuts through the AC curve from below at the minimum AC.
- Profit is given by the difference between price and AC at the profit maximizing level of output (where $P = MR = MC$) multiplied by the level of output.
- In the short run, labor is assumed to be variable but capital is fixed. In the long run, all inputs are variable. The long run AC curve is U-shaped and touches the minimum of each short run AC curve, for differing levels of capital. Increasing (decreasing) returns to scale are characterized by declining (increasing) long run AC.
- In the long run, positive profits will encourage new firms to enter the industry, driving down the ticket price to the minimum of long run AC. Firms earn zero economic profit in the long run.

3.3 The Monopolist

The monopolist is the only firm in the industry. In order to maintain this lofty position, the monopolist must prevent the entry of new firms into the industry, otherwise, as new firms enter, industry supply will shift to the right and the market price will fall towards the price that will minimize *LRAC*. We often think of the professional sports leagues as monopolies, although a single league is composed of many teams. While no one sports team is the only team in the industry, teams can be local monopolists within their league-assigned geographic areas. Any new team wishing to enter this protected area must receive the support of every team in the league and pay a large sum of money to the existing team as compensation for losing some market share. This has happened in some cases. When the American Basketball Association (ABA) New York Nets merged into the NBA in 1977, the team owner was required to pay compensation to the NBA New York Knicks of $4.8 million, on top of the $3.2 million expansion fee to join the NBA. To raise the money, the Nets owner sold his superstar player, Julius Erving, to the Philadelphia 76ers (NBA). The New York Islanders (NHL) paid a $4 million fee to the New York Rangers (NHL) when the new team moved into the New York area in 1972. This new franchise was established by the NHL to prevent the establishment of the new New York Raiders team of the rival World Hockey Association (WHA).

A professional sports league must restrict the entry of new teams in its sport and it can do this very effectively. However it has little control over the establishment of new rival leagues that establish teams in its geographic markets. We will have much more to say on rival leagues in Chapter 6. The monopolist team owner can choose an average ticket price that maximizes his or her profit, unlike the price-taking team owner operating in a competitive market. The demand curve for the monopolist owner is downward sloping, unlike the competitive market where it is flat. In order to sell more tickets, the average price for *all* tickets must be decreased. We will assume for now that the team owner cannot sell additional tickets at different prices, he or she must charge the same price for all the tickets sold. The former case is called price discrimination and is illegal, but occurs frequently in professional sports teams as it is hard to enforce. We will assume the team owner sells *N* number of tickets at a certain price. If he or she wishes to sell one more ticket, the price for each of the *N+1* tickets must be decreased. This is the Law of Demand in operation.

The owner's total revenue increases with higher ticket sales, but at a diminishing rate. This is because to sell more tickets, the ticket price on all tickets must be reduced. More tickets are sold (higher volume) but at a lower price so the effect on revenue is not as great as when the ticket price is always the same, such as in the competitive market case. Marginal revenue (*MR*) is the change in the team's total revenue when one more ticket is sold. In the competitive market case, *MR* was just equal to the ticket price, but *MR* will be less than the ticket price in the monopolist case since the price must be reduced to sell the additional ticket.

Algebraically we define revenue for the monopolist as $R = P(Q)Q$ since the ticket price will be a function of ticket sales. Marginal revenue is found by taking the derivative of revenue with respect to Q (use the product rule here).

$$MR = \frac{\partial R}{\partial Q} = P(Q) + Q\frac{\partial P}{\partial Q}$$

The term $\partial P/\partial Q < 0$ and is the slope of the ticket demand curve. We can derive a more interesting expression for MR by multiplying and dividing the last term by P. This is perfectly legal since $P/P = 1$.

$$MR = \frac{\partial R}{\partial Q} = P + PQ\frac{\partial P}{P\partial Q} = P + P\frac{\partial P}{P}\frac{Q}{\partial Q} = P(1 + \varepsilon^{-1})$$

The term ε^{-1} is the inverse of the price elasticity of demand from Chapter 2. It is negative since the demand curve for tickets slopes downward. The smaller (more inelastic) is the price elasticity of demand, the greater is the gap between the MR and P.

To make the distinction between the ticket price and MR clearer, consider the ticket price and ticket sales numbers per game given in the table below for the Big City Bulldogs, a hypothetical professional football team operating within a major league. The Bulldogs are the only team in the state and thus can be considered a local monopolist of professional football. How many tickets per game will the Bulldogs owner wish to sell to maximize profits? The profit-maximizing rule is the same as the competitive market case. Sell enough tickets to get to the point where MR = MC. The table below provides the calculations for the TR, MR, MC and AC numbers. You should be able to compute these yourself from the P, Q and TC numbers provided. From the table below, at an average ticket price of $50.00, the monopolist can sell 60,000 tickets per game. At this point MR and MC are very close. The maximum profit achieved is the difference between the TR and TC: $3,000,000 - $2,500,000 = $500,000 per game. Note that MR becomes negative sometime after 60,000 tickets, which means the stadium is at full capacity.

P ($)	Tickets (Q)	TR ($)	MR ($)	TC ($)	MC ($)	AC ($)

$200	0	0	-	$500,000	-	-
175	1000	175,000	175	600,000	100	600
150	3000	450,000	112.50	700,000	50	233
125	6000	750,000	100	800,000	33	133
100	12,000	1,200,000	75	950,000	25	79
75	25,000	1,875,000	51.90	1,300,000	26.90	52
50	60,000	3,000,000	32	2,500,000	34.30	41.70
25	70,000	1,500,000	-15	4,000,000	150	57

A stylized picture of the monopolist team owner is given in Figure 3.6. If the demand curve is a straight line (as drawn in Figure 3.6), the MR line is drawn with double the slope of the demand curve and the same vertical intercept.

Demand curve: $P = A - B \cdot Q$ $MR = A - 2B \cdot Q$

The owner will maximize profits at an average ticket price of P_m (m for monopoly) and the quantity of tickets Q_m. At this level of ticket sales, the MR and MC curves intersect so $MR = MC$. Total profit is given by the rectangle between the AC curve and the ticket price, since profit per ticket is just the ticket price less the AC.

The monopolist will charge a higher ticket price and sell fewer tickets than the perfectly competitive team owner. A price-taking team owner sells tickets up to the point where $P = MR = MC$, where ticket sales are Q_c and average ticket price is P_c. The pricing behavior of the monopolist may result in empty seats if Q_m is at less than full capacity of the arena. Nevertheless, it is profit maximizing for the monopolist to have empty seats[26].

Monopolists have the ability to practice *price discrimination*. Price discrimination is charging different prices to different consumers for the same good. Technically this is illegal in Canada and the United States under anti-trust laws, however it is very difficult to prove that a monopolist is practicing price discrimination in a court of law. Team owners can charge different prices for different seats in the stadium, which is a form of price discrimination. The owner will argue that more expensive seats have better sight lines, more amenities and give the fan a better "feel" for the action of the game. This argument may not justify the large price differentials between different seats at most major-league arenas and stadiums. Since team owners typically rent the stadium or arena, the rent is a fixed cost that must be paid regardless of how many tickets are sold. Hence the marginal cost of providing a seat closer to the action is no more than the marginal cost of providing a less desirable seat.

Analytical example: Monopoly profits.

Question: The Burnaby Bandits (of the previous Analytical example) have successfully joined a major professional soccer league that has guaranteed the team exclusive territorial rights. The total cost equation for the Bandits (per game) is given by the equation $TC = 1000 + 1.5Q + 0.02Q^2$. Costs have risen. The

Answer: $MC = 1.5 + 0.04Q$. The AC equation is just the TC equation divided by Q. This gives $AC = (500/Q) + 0.5 + 0.01Q$. MR is given by $MR = 45 - 0.1Q$ using the rule for a straight-line demand curve. Now equate the MC equation to MR and solve for Q.

$$1.5 + 0.04Q = 25 - 0.1Q$$
$$0.04Q = 23.5 - 0.1Q$$
$$0.14Q = 23.5$$

---

[26] The Carolina Hurricanes (NHL) averaged only 11,766 fans per game for the 2016-17 season, despite having an arena capacity of 18,692. In this case, the Hurricanes may have been minimizing losses rather than maximizing profits, yet the optimal price and ticket sales are the same.

team now faces a market demand curve for its area given by $P = 25 - 0.05Q$. What is the profit-maximizing number of tickets to sell per game and what is the profit?	$Q = 23.5/0.14 = 168$ The Bandits should sell 168 tickets per game. The ticket price is $P = 25 - 0.05(168) = \$16.60$. The profit is total revenue less total cost. Profit $= \$16.60(168) -$ $[1000+1.5(168)+0.02(168^2)]$ Profit $= \$972.32$ per game

In theory, the monopolist could extract the consumer entire surplus under the ticket demand curve and above the ticket price by charging a different price for every seat in the arena. The team owner could conduct an auction with each ticket going to the highest bidder. Fans would then reveal the maximum price they are willing to pay for seats of different "quality". This is too impractical to put into practice, yet some arenas have a vast array of seating sections, all with different prices[27].

Price discrimination is an effective way to extract consumer surplus if the resale of tickets is prevented. With resale, some fans will purchase tickets in low price sections and sell the tickets to fans that are willing to pay more for the same section. This is hard to prevent at sporting events, but teams make some effort using different strategies. One strategy is to lobby local governments to ban "ticket scalping" around stadiums. A second strategy is to offer some tickets only on a "walkup" basis, which limits the amount of time available for resale[28]

[27] The Toronto Blue Jays (MLB) play in the Rogers Center which has eleven ticket levels ranging from $14 to $268 for the 2016-17 season. Games designated as premium games have higher ticket prices as a further method to extract consumer surplus.
[28] Tickets for bleacher seats in baseball are typically only sold on a "walkup" basis.

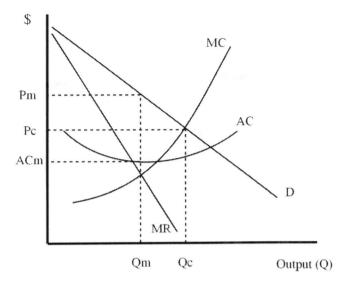

Figure 3.6
The monopolist has the ability to determine his or her own price since it is the only firm in the industry. It maximizes profits where $MR = MC$ at Q_m number of tickets sold. Profit is given by the area $(P_m - AC_m)Q_m$. Because the MR curve slopes downward, the monopolist will sell fewer tickets than the perfectly competitive team.

3.4 The Theory of Cartels

Professional sports teams form a *cartel* when they reach an agreement to act together when negotiating national and international broadcasting rights, player contracts, endorsement agreements, logos and apparel and so on. These are revenue sources that extend beyond a single team's market area and are generally shared equally by all teams in the league. Teams are still allowed to exploit their own market areas for some revenue sources that extend beyond ticket revenue, such as parking and concession revenue, stadium signage, and local radio and TV revenue. The loosest form of a cartel is a sort of gentleman's agreement, although the team owners seldom act like it. In professional sports, the formation of a league with common rules, scheduling, broadcast rights, etc. requires agreement and coordination among team owners. Owners are not allowed to move franchises, make endorsement arrangements or arrange their own national broadcast rights without permission of the other league owners. As we shall see, this sort of self-regulation is necessary to insure the cartel does not fall apart[29].

Here we will construct a simple economic model of a cartel that can be applied to any industry. Famous cartels in the past include the American steel cartel and the OPEC oil cartel. More recently most illegal drugs are grown and harvested through powerful cartels. Assume that there are N competitive teams in a professional league that have each maximized profit in the short-run and long-run.[30] Let's consider a different output the team is producing in addition to tickets: hats with the team logo embroidered on them. Assume that each team faces the same demand and cost curves shown in the left of Figure 3.7 (not realistic but simple). Teams will sell hats up to the point where $MR = MC$, resulting in q_c hats sold per team. The hat price for every team is P_c. The figure on the right displays the industry demand and supply curves that are the horizontal summations of the demand and marginal cost curves for hats for each team. The industry output is Q_C, which is $N \cdot q_c$. So far these monopoly teams operate without any cooperation in the setting of hat prices.

The teams now agree to form a cartel and each firm is assigned a quota of $(1/N)$ times total industry output of hats, which is now Q_M where

---

[29] The Oakland Raiders move to Los Angeles in 1982 and the San Diego Clippers move to Los Angeles in 1984 were done without league permission. The owners were sued by the leagues (NFL and NBA). The Raiders won a decision, but the Clippers lost and were forced to make a steep settlement payment to the league. Recently the Dallas Cowboys (Nike) and the New York Yankees (Adidas) entered into endorsement contracts without league permission.

[30] A monopoly owner will not produce output where constant returns to scale is achieved. Can you draw a picture that shows why?

$MR = MC$ for the industry. Each team is given an equal quota of industry output and agrees to produce only that amount and no more. Essentially a cartel is analogous to a monopoly for the industry with each team as a member. The hat price rises to P_M and hat output for each team is $q_m = Q_M/N$. Fewer hats are produced and this drives up the price for a hat. Instead of each team flooding its market with hats, hat production is restricted so hats are more scarce and exclusive.

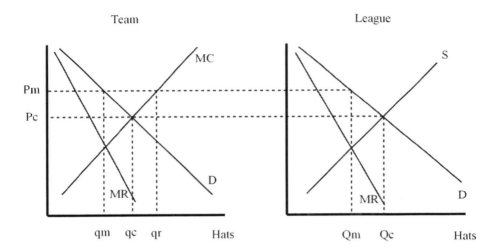

Figure 3.7
If all clubs act competitively, the market price will be P_c where demand and supply intersect in the market diagram on the right. If the clubs form a cartel and restrict output, a higher ticket price can be extracted from the consumer. This is so because all the clubs essentially form one firm, a league with rules governing what each club can and cannot do. The market then sets the ticket price where $MR = MC = S$ in the diagram on the right. The cartel price which maximizes league profits is P_m.

Cartels are inevitably doomed to fail (OPEC for example) since there exists an incentive for teams to leave the cartel, increase their own output, and reap higher profits since they can still charge the cartel price. In Figure 3.7, if one team owner decides to leave the hat cartel and produce his or her own hats, the team output of hats can be increased to q_r where the cartel enforced price intersects the marginal cost curve. The rebel team owner thus benefits from the cartel price enforced by the remaining cartel members, but is allowed to choose his or her own hat output. Since each team owner knows this, there is an incentive for all team owners to leave the cartel if they believe no other team owner will follow. The cartel then falls apart at the start.

Focus Box: American Needle vs. the National Football League

American Needle produces hats and other apparel that feature logos from professional sports teams. The company produces the apparel for large companies such as Adidas and Nike. Recently American Needle won a landmark anti-trust lawsuit against the NFL (2008), arguing that the NFL acts as a cartel in selling the rights to using team logos. The case began in the year 2000 when the NFL struck a new deal with Reebok International (now a part of Adidas AG) to be the exclusive purchaser of the logo rights. Prior to this, NFL teams each negotiated rights agreements with American Needle. American Needle sued the NFL arguing that the NFL violated anti-trust laws that protected consumers from unlawful cartels. The NFL responded by arguing that it is only a single business entity and that teams only compete on the field but not in business.

The Seventy Circuit court ruled in favor of the NFL in 2008, prompting an appeal from American Needle to the Supreme Court. The Supreme Court ruling in 2010 is worth quoting.

"Each of the teams is a substantial, independently owned, and independently managed business. Directly relevant to this case, the teams compete in the market for intellectual property. To a firm making hats, the Saints and the Colts are two potentially competing suppliers of valuable trademarks. When each NFL team licenses its intellectual property, it is not pursuing the "common interests of the whole" league but is instead pursuing interests of each "corporation itself," teams are acting as "separate economic actors pursuing separate economic interests," and each team therefore is a potential "independent center of decision making"

The court ruled that Section 1 of the Sherman Act applied to the NFL and that any unilateral decision made by the NFL on behalf of all the teams must be reviewed using the "rule of reason" provisions of the Act. The case was sent to a lower court for review.

Brief Review of Concepts

- The monopolist is the only firm in the industry and thus can charge any price along the demand curve. Major league clubs are assumed to act as local monopolists within their allotted geographical area.
- Since price changes with ticket sales, MR is less than the average ticket price. The monopolist maximizes profits where MR = MC.
- Ticket sales for the monopolist will typically be lower than ticket sales for the perfectly competitive firm. Ticket prices will be higher for the monopolist.
- Price discrimination involves charging a different price to different consumers for the same product. Team owners often practice price discrimination by charging a wide variety of prices for its tickets. Price discrimination is illegal, however team owners justify the different ticket prices by pointing out different viewing angles, food and beverage service and other amenities.
- Several local monopolists can agree to form a cartel. A common industry price is established that maximizes the joint profits of the cartel members. Professional sports leagues are good examples of cartels. Cartels are doomed to fail since there is always an incentive for a single cartel member to leave the cartel and reap higher profits.

3.5 A Model of the Professional Sports Club

We can now construct a partial equilibrium short-run model of the professional sports club that incorporates some of the unique economic aspects of the industry. Each club behaves as a local monopoly and participates in a league cartel. The cartel does not act to enforce an identical average ticket price for every club since clubs face different local demand and cost conditions. However the league cartel does provide identical broadcasting, apparel, logo, endorsement, and other revenues to each team by acting as the league's negotiator. The league cartel is enforced through restricted entry and exit provisions, which must receive unanimous approval of all team owners. The cartel also restricts the entry of new players through a drafting system and restricts the movement of players and salaries through a general agreement with the players.

The bulk of a club's total costs is assumed to be fixed costs. Fixed costs (costs that do not change as more tickets are sold) include stadium rental, if the club does not own the stadium, or principle and interest charges if the club does own the stadium. Player contracts are also a fixed cost, as well as administrative salaries. Transportation costs are fixed in advance once all the clubs agree upon the league schedule. Variable costs (costs that increase as more tickets are sold) are assumed to be small and not important to total costs. Total costs assumed to be constant regardless of how many tickets are sold over the season. Of course, fixed costs can become variable costs, and thus avoided, if the league does not play for a season. Discounting this possibility, the marginal cost of each ticket is zero until the point of full stadium capacity is reached. This is because all costs are fixed, so selling one more ticket does not increase the team's total costs. At full stadium capacity, the marginal cost becomes infinite unless the stadium is expanded or a new stadium is constructed. Selling one more ticket when all of the seats are taken requires adding additional capacity or even building a new facility. The addition to the total cost for this additional ticket could be very large.

Figure 3.8 illustrates the professional sports team model. The demand curve is the market demand curve that the monopoly owner faces in his or her protected metropolitan area and is downward-sloping. The MR line is drawn using the rule already given for straight-line demand curves. Marginal cost is zero, but is vertical at full stadium capacity. The MC curve is completely flat and traces along the horizontal axis until full capacity is reached. Let's assume the stadium capacity is 25,000 seats. Since total cost is constant with the existing facility (all costs are fixed), profit-maximization is equivalent to revenue-maximization for the owner. The owner simply seeks the highest revenue possible and then pays the fixed costs. Since selling additional tickets requires lowering the ticket price for all the tickets that are sold, maximizing revenue does not necessarily mean selling out the facility.

The optimal quantity of tickets sold in Figure 3.8 is 20,000 where $MR = MC = 0$. The optimal average ticket price is \$60, given by the demand curve at a ticket output of 20,000. The demand curve gives the maximum price consumers will pay for 20,000 tickets per game. The profit-maximizing rule is the same as the competitive market and the monopoly case with the additional wrinkle that all costs are fixed so the MC curve is L-shaped. Another curious characteristic of the model is that the AC curve is always downward-sloping – it is not U-shaped. This is because all costs are fixed so dividing a constant fixed cost by an increasing number of tickets sold results in a falling AC. The professional sports team operates in the area of increasing returns to scale at least over the short-run (a single season). The AC at 20,000 tickets sold is \$30, resulting in a profit for the team owner of (\$60-\$30)×20,000 = \$400,000 per game. This is the rectangular area in Figure 3.8.

Some interesting results from this model are worth mentioning. First, if a new larger stadium is built with public funds (zero cost to the team owner), the average ticket price will not change. If the new stadium has a large capacity than the old one, the marginal cost curve shifts to the right and become vertical at the full capacity of the new stadium. The idea of providing a new stadium to the team owner, or even subsidizing the team owner with public funds to build a stadium, does not affect the marginal cost of providing an extra ticket (zero) up to the point of full capacity. The optimal number of tickets, 20,000 in Figure 3.8, is unchanged. This means that total revenue, total costs and the resulting profit will remain the same and the owner will have no incentive to improve the quality of the team with more expensive players.

It is common that the demand curve and MR curve shift to the right due to higher demand for tickets as a result of a temporary curiosity to see the new facility. Clapp and Hakes (2005) refer to this as the "honeymoon effect" and they found that attendance does increase when a new facility is opened for a period of 3 to 7 years, depending on the sport.[31] With higher demand, the optimal number of tickets to sell increases where $MR = MC = 0$, however the effect on ticket prices is uncertain since the demand curve has shifted. There is much evidence to suggest that team owners raise ticket prices following the construction of new facilities, whether financed publicly or privately. This would require the demand curve to shift to the right substantially. Normally this would then result in much higher profits for owners since all costs are assumed to be fixed so AC is declining. Bloomberg reports that MLB team owners raised team payrolls by an

---

[31] Clapp, C. and J.Hakes. 2005. How long a honeymoon? The effect of new stadiums on attendance in Major League Baseball. *Journal of Sports Economics*, 6(3): 237-63.

average of 30% since the 2000 season after moving into new digs.[32] Unfortunately this increase in payrolls does not seem to translate performance on the field according to Clapp and Hakes (2005). The notion of subsidizing a team owner with public funds to build a new facility with the goal of lowering ticket prices is incorrect, but it might result in a better team on the field.

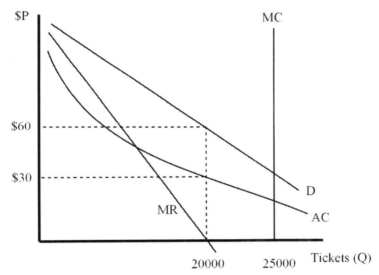

Figure 3.8
If most of the costs facing a professional sports club are fixed costs (salaries, transportation, stadium rental, etc.), the *AC* curve will diminish as more tickets are sold (*AC = FC/Q*) and the *MC* curve will be zero up to stadium capacity (total cost does not change as more tickets are sold). The profit-maximizing output is 20,000 tickets, which is also the revenue-maximizing output.

A second interesting result concerns when to expand a stadium, or build a new, larger stadium. Suppose the stadium is being filled to capacity so that every game is a sell-out. If the marginal revenue curve intersects the horizontal axis at zero marginal cost, just at 25,000 tickets in Figure 3.8,

[32] http://www.bloomberg.com/video/58830942-ticket-prices-payrolls-increase-with-new-mlb-stadiums.html

profits are maximized for the owner and the stadium need not be expanded. If the demand for tickets shifts further to the right so that the *MR* line intersects the horizontal axis to the right of 25,000 tickets, profits are not being maximized and the team owner may lobby to expand the stadium. Expansion should take place if at full stadium capacity, *MR* is greater than zero. A simpler rule for the owner is that, at full capacity, if the demand for tickets is elastic ($|\eta| > 1$), the stadium should be expanded. This is demonstrated in Figure 3.9. With $MR > 0$ at 25,000 tickets, total revenue will rise along the total revenue curve if more tickets can be sold because of the position of the ticket demand curve. When a reduction in the average ticket price to sell more tickets raises total revenue, we noted in Chapter 2 that the demand curve is elastic. At the profit-maximizing number of tickets $Q^* > 25,000$, the demand curve will be unit-elastic ($|\varepsilon| = 1$). For a very small increase in ticket sales, total revenue is unchanged at the top of the total revenue curve. This means the percentage drop in the ticket price to sell the extra tickets just equals the percentage increase in ticket sales. The profit-maximizing, or revenue-maximizing owner will want to sell enough tickets to reach the point where the demand curve is unit-elastic.

A third point concerns the possible entry of new teams from a rival league into the local area. Since all costs are assumed to be fixed costs, average costs exhibit *increasing returns to scale*, meaning that an increase in output (tickets) lowers the average cost. Existing teams in the league can take advantage of this by temporarily lowering the average ticket price from the profit-maximizing price and selling more tickets if new teams are considering entry into the local market. Profits will not be maximized but should not fall off dramatically. This will have the effect of capturing the additional market share that the new rival team was hoping to gain. After the rival threat has been removed, ticket prices can be increased back to the profit-maximizing price. Of course if the existing club is already operating at full stadium capacity, this sort of *predatory pricing* behavior is not possible. It may be in the interest of team owners, and the league, to maintain some number of empty seats to preclude entry of new leagues. This translates to higher average ticket prices for the existing league that might be above the profit-maximizing price, but allowing the entry of a new rival league could reduce profits by far more.

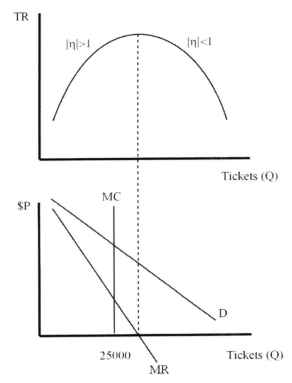

Figure 3.8
The team owner maximizes profit where $MR = MC$ at Q^* which is full capacity of the stadium. To maximize revenue, the team owner should expand stadium capacity to the point where $MR = MC = 0$, or where the price elasticity of demand just equals one.

3.6 Price Elasticity of Demand Again

In the last chapter, we noted that estimates of the price elasticity of demand for professional sports teams suggest that they operate in the inelastic portion of the demand curves they face (price elasticity $< |1|$). This is rather odd since profit-maximizing teams will set their ticket prices so as to operate in the elastic portion of their demand curve, while a revenue-maximizing team will set their ticket prices where demand is unit-elastic (see Figure 3.9). It would appear that professional sports teams are not maximizing profit, instead they are selling to many tickets at too low a price. Krautmann and Berri (2007) summarize eleven different research studies that estimated price elasticities of demand over different periods of time, most for major league baseball. [33] The estimated price elasticities range from –0.06 to –0.93 and tend to decrease in value over time.

What factors could account for these rather small price elasticity estimates? Krautmann and Berri (2007) make the following suggestions.

1. Team owners may not be as concerned over maximizing profit as they are concerned about maximizing their own satisfaction from winning (referred to as utility in economics). This so-called "sportsmen" hypothesis is difficult to model in economics and also very difficult to test.

2. Team owners might choose to keep ticket prices low in order to gain special treatment from local governments, such as large subsidies for new stadiums or special tax concessions, whose economic value outweighs the lost ticket revenue.

---

[33] Krautmann, A. and D. Berri, "Can We Find It at the Concessions? Understanding Price Elasticity in Professional Sports", *Journal of Sports Economics*, 8(2), 2007, 183-191.

3. Attending professional sporting events may become habitual for some fans. Temporarily setting ticket prices temporarily low might lose profit for the team owner in the short-run, but if fans become "addicted", might raise profit in the long-run as these fans by more expensive seats and become less sensitive to price increases.

4. Measurement problems might result in unreliable price elasticity estimates. For instance, every stadium contains a wide spectrum of ticket prices depending on how close the seat is to the playing surface. Ideally, every seating category possesses its own price elasticity of demand, but data for attendance by seating category is generally not available. Instead, an average ticket price is used across all seating categories. If the inexpensive seats are largely empty, as is often the case in major league baseball, using an average ticket price can seriously understate the true ticket price.

A very plausible explanation for the inelastic price elasticity estimates that persist in the economics literature is that team owners sell fans a package of goods who attend a game, not just a ticket. Fans also purchase concessions, such as food, drink and apparel. They might also purchase programs and parking. It might then appear that tickets are underpriced because tickets are not the only output that is being purchased. Figure 3.10 demonstrates this. Let the line $MR(T)$ be the marginal revenue from selling tickets and $MR(T+C)$ be the marginal revenue from selling tickets and concessions. Where MC is vertical determines the stadium capacity. The team owner will maximize revenue where $MR(T+C) = 0$ in the case where the majority of costs are fixed costs. The optimal number of tickets to sell is greater than the optimal number of tickets where $MR(T) = 0$ when concession revenue is ignored. Since $MR(T) < 0$ when $MR(T+C) =$

0, price elasticity estimates that ignore concession revenue will be in the inelastic portion of the team demand curve (the demand curves have been omitted to keep the figure clear). The only drawback to this argument is that not all professional sports teams receive the concession revenue from their home games. Whether they do or not depends on the lease arrangement with the stadium owner (usually the local government), if the club does not own its own stadium.

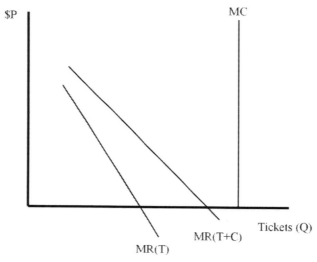

Figure 3.10
The price elasticity of demand can be estimated to be inelastic when $MR(T) < 0$ when $MR(T+C) = 0$. Concession revenue is being mistakenly ignored.

Brief Summary of Concepts

- The majority of a professional sports club's costs are assumed to be fixed costs. These are composed of player salaries, transportation and equipment expenses, stadium rental and administrative costs, which are invariable to ticket sales. The *AC* curve slopes downward.

- Marginal cost (MC) is zero up to the point of full stadium capacity since total costs are fixed. The club owner maximizes profit where $MR = MC = 0$. This is equivalent to maximizing total revenue.
- Changes in stadium capacity, or even a new, larger stadium, do not affect average ticket prices or ticket sales, if demand is unchanged.
- Stadium capacity should be increased if the price elasticity of demand for tickets is elastic at the average ticket price and sales.
- Predatory pricing involves temporarily lowering the average ticket price below the average cost of a new rival in order to prevent entry of the new club. Local monopolists can practice predatory pricing due to the downward sloping AC curve (increasing returns to scale).
- Price elasticity estimates are typically inelastic for professional sports teams when only ticket revenue is used.

Test Your Knowledge

1. This question refers to the *Report of the Independent Members of the Commissioner's Blue Ribbon Panel on Baseball Economics* found on my web page.

a) Describe the proposed competitive balance tax in the report. What problems does this tax attempt to address?

b) Using the model of the professional sports club in Chapter 3, explain what would happen to the ticket prices, number of tickets sold and profits of the rich clubs paying the tax. Explain with a diagram.

c) Do the same as in part b for the poor clubs.

2. The Haney Hustlers are a new Frisbee football team that plays in a rather unorganized league composed of a large number of teams that come and go every summer. To keep costs low, the players receive only small stipends to cover food and transportation costs. The team plays in a local high school football stadium and charges a nominal fee of $20 to watch a game. Tickets are sold on a web site and at the gate. The team is responsible for hiring a clean-up crew after each game and to provide security. The table below summarizes the team costs to sell tickets.

Tickets	Total costs	Tickets	Total costs

0	$2,000	250	$3,700
50	2200	300	4400
100	2450	350	5200
150	2800	400	6200
200	3200	450	7300

a) Calculate the Hustler's average cost and marginal cost for each level of ticket sales above zero. What is the amount of fixed costs?

b) What is the profit-maximizing number of tickets to sell? Calculate the profit.

c) If new teams enter the league, the ticket price the Hustlers can charge will fall. What is the lowest price the Hustlers can charge?

3. Each team in a hypothetical cartel poker league has identical demand and cost curves. Each team is free to produce sets of poker chips with its team logo printed on each chip and sell them to consumers in their local market. The demand curve each owner faces for a box of poker chips is given by $P = 9 - 0.0005Q$ where P is the price of a box and Q is the number of boxes sold. The MC curve for each team is $MC = 0.000625Q$.

a) How many boxes of poker chips will each team sell to maximize profit when the selling of logos is competitive? What will be the price of a box of chips? (Hint: use Figure 3.7)

b) Suppose the poker league teams form a cartel for selling the licensing rights to use their logos on poker chips and sell these rights to only one company. What will be the new quantity of boxes that each team is allocated to sell and what will be the cartel price? (Hint: use Figure 3.7)

c) If one poker team decides to exceed their quota of boxes of chips yet still charge the cartel price, how many additional boxes will it sell?

4. Consider an NHL club that faces a demand curve summarized in the table below. The capacity of the arena is 21,000.

Average ticket price	Quantity of tickets sold	Average ticket price	Quantity of tickets sold
$15	21,000	$40	17,000
$20	20,800	$45	16,000

$25	19,800	$50	15,000
$30	19,000	$55	13,500
$35	18,000	$60	11,000

a) Compute the total revenue (TR) and marginal revenue (MR) at each ticket price starting from $20.
b) Total salary costs are established at the start of the season and take the value of $500,000 per game. Assume there are no other costs. Compute the average cost at each quantity of tickets sold per game.
c) What is the profit-maximizing quantity of tickets to sell per game? Compute the total profit per game.
d) Suppose ticket prices and the demand curve remain unchanged for the next season, but payroll costs rise to $750,000 per game. What is the profit-maximizing quantity of tickets to sell per game? Compute the total profit per game. How does this result differ from the case of a monopolist facing mainly variable costs?

Focus box: Do Higher Payrolls Lead to Higher Ticket Prices?

The simple model of the professional sports club developed in the last section suggests that higher payrolls do not result in higher ticket prices. Higher payrolls shift the AC curve upward holding everything else constant. The profit maximizing ticket output for the team owner is left unchanged: $MR = MC = 0$ at the same ticket output. Higher payrolls are simply absorbed by team owners in the form of lower profits. However this ignores the potential increase in ticket demand if the performance of the team improves. If ticket demand increases substantially, ticket prices could increase. Figure 3.11 plots the team payroll and average ticket price for each of the 15 National League (NL) clubs operating in the 1998 and 2007 seasons. The payroll figures are for the end of the regular season, while the ticket prices are set at the beginning of the season, hence the comparison is not without some degree of error. Nevertheless, the figure reveals a clear positive association[34], suggesting that the simple model of the professional sports club may be correct but needs to include shifts in ticket demand that can result if team performance improves. Of course, many other variables that determine the average ticket price are not accounted for in this simple analysis.

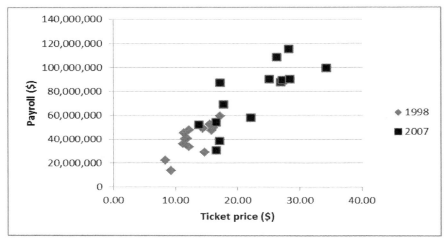

Figure 3.11
Average ticket prices and total payrolls for NL teams (1998 and 2007 seasons).
Source: https://sites.google.com/site/rodswebpages/code

---

[34] The correlation coefficient, which measures the degree of linear association between two random variables, is 0.768 for the 1998 season and 0.787 for the 2007 season, indicating a reasonably strong positive association.

Chapter 4
Profitability and Franchise Values

This chapter discusses the business of running a major-league sports organization. The nuts and bolts of annual operations are detailed to give the student an idea of the complexity of being a major-league owner. Also discussed is the long run return to the owner from selling the franchise and how this return is determined. The important points in this chapter are listed below.

- Sources of revenues, typical expenses and annual profits or losses.
- Types of taxes faced by owners and their effects on running the organization.
- A historical overview of franchise values.
- Theories of how franchise values are determined.

4.1 Sources of Revenue

Despite rapidly increasing costs during the last two decades, professional sports remain profitable for most clubs due to revenues that have increased even faster. This increase in revenues has been driven by higher demand for tickets to major league sporting events, higher ticket prices (partly justified by the incredible expansion in new stadiums and arenas over the last decade) and more lucrative national and local broadcast agreements. Financial statistics for professional sports teams are very difficult to obtain. Almost all clubs are privately owned and are not required to publish financial statements. A few publicly owned clubs do exist: the Boston Celtics of the NBA and the Green Bay Packers of the NFL. Baseball's Cleveland Indians have minority public ownership. Figure 4.1 provides a summary of the revenue picture for MLB from 1990 to 2016. The top and bottom lines show the revenues earned by the highest and lowest revenue clubs respectively, while the middle line shows the average revenue for all clubs.

Several important trends are revealed in Figure 4.1. First, average revenues increased throughout the 1990-2016 period, with the exception of 1994, a strike year. The last month of the 1994 regular season, as well as all playoff games, were cancelled due to a labor dispute. Average revenues increased by an annual average rate of 16.5% over the entire period. It is quite likely that this figure is similar in the three other major leagues. A second striking feature revealed in Figure 4.1 is the widening gap between revenues of the richest and poorest clubs. The gap was approximately $60 million for the 1990 season, but increased to approximately $225 million for the 2016 season. This provides some evidence of the increasing disparity in revenues in MLB. A luxury tax on the richest teams was introduced during the 1997 season to address this disparity. Revenues are taxed for a few of the highest revenue clubs but are not redistributed towards the remaining teams. Instead the tax collections are used to fund marketing projects for MLB. The competitive balance tax is still in place today, but it has not proven to be a very effective way to reduce the disparity in revenues. We will explore this tax in more detail later.

The most successful revenue-generating club during the period was the New York Yankees with $526 million in revenues for the 2016 season and average revenues of $290 million over the entire period. The least successful club was the Montreal Expos (now the Washington

Nationals) with revenues of only $80 million for the 2004 season and average revenues of just $68.4 million (excluding the expansion Florida Marlins, Colorado Rockies and Tampa Bay Devil Rays). The Expos moved to Washington, D.C. to be renamed the Nationals for the 2005 season.

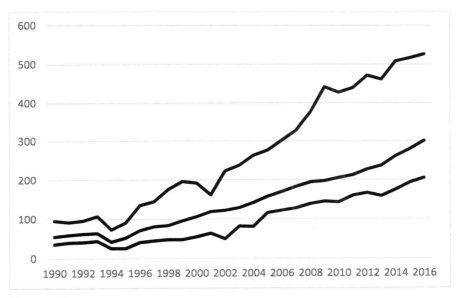

Figure 4.1
Total Revenues for Major League Baseball Clubs, 1990-2016.
Source: https://sites.google.com/site/rodswebpages/codes.

The biggest expense facing a professional sports team is salaries for its players, which usually take up over half of its total expenses. Figure 4.2 provides estimates of team payrolls for MLB clubs during the 1990-2016 period. Average team payrolls grew by an annual rate of 17.5%, outstripping revenue growth. A key feature is the rapid growth in payrolls for the richest clubs, 36% annually, versus the 15% annual growth in payrolls for the poorest clubs. The widening disparity in payrolls is far larger than the disparity in revenues. The relatively flat period of payroll growth during 1992-1996 was partly due to the expiration of a lucrative television contract with CBS, replaced by a far less profitable television contract with the FOX network. The biggest spender on salaries was the Los Angeles Dodgers with a payroll of $346 million for the 2015 season and the largest average payroll was the New York Yankees at $164 million over the sample period. The lowest payroll club was the Tampa Bay Devil Rays with a payroll of $27.2 million for the 2004 season. The lowest average payroll over the sample period of just $25.7 million was owned by the Montreal Expos.

Profit is determined by subtracting salaries and other expenses from revenues. This is not the same as economic profit, however we do not know what the opportunity cost of each owner is, so we must use accounting profit. The profit picture in Figure 4.3 is far less rosy than the revenue picture in Figure 4.1 for MLB. Profits barely changed at all on the average over the 1990-2016 period, but clearly suffered during the strike season of 1994. Profits finally increased above their pre-1994 levels in the 2005 season. Profits for the richest clubs increased by 26.2% annually and *fell* by a drastic 26.7% annually for the poorest clubs. The widening disparity in revenues and payrolls is also reflected in profits. The single highest loss was the Los Angeles Dodgers, who recorded a loss of $80 million in 2013, while the highest recorded profit was the St. Louis Cardinals who recorded a profit of $83.8 million in 2016.

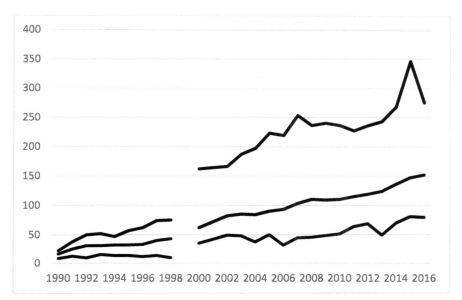

Figure 4.2
Total payrolls for major league baseball clubs, 1990-2016.
Source: https://sites.google.com/site/rodswebpages/codes.

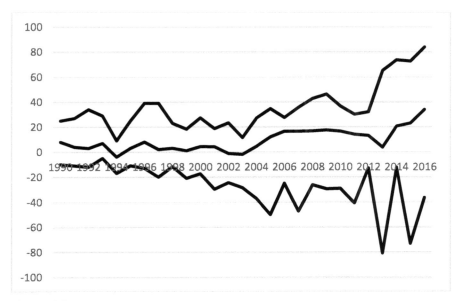

Figure 4.3
Total profits for major league baseball clubs, 1990-2016.
Source: https://sites.google.com/site/rodswebpages/codes.

4.2 Financial Statements

The nuts and bolts of the revenues and expenses facing a major-league club can be explored with the use of income statements for MLB's Pittsburgh Pirates. Teams generally do not make their financial statements available to the public, however the 2007 and 2008 statements for the Pirates were leaked to the press. The leak also included financial statements for the Los Angeles Angels, the Tampa Bay Rays and the Florida Marlins.[35] The Pirates income statements for the 2007 and 2008 seasons are presented in Table 4.1.

It is useful to study some of the revenue accounts for the Pirates in Table 4.1. The largest source of revenue for the 2008 season was revenue received from the other MLB clubs under the revenue sharing agreement. Each MLB club contributes one-third of local revenue (no national revenue) to a central fund that is then distributed evenly among all MLB clubs. The revenue sharing amount of just over $39 million is the net revenue take from the central fund for the Pirates. The Pirates contributed less to the fund from local revenue than the team received from the even split of the fund. This is typical of small market clubs in MLB and is the stated intent of the revenue sharing agreement according to MLB owners. The Pirates received only $30 million from revenue sharing in the 2007 season. Broadcasting is the next largest revenue source for the Pirates in 2008. This includes local television and radio revenue as well as the national broadcast revenue that is shared equally by all MLB teams. You may be surprised to know that home gate receipts contributed only 22% of total revenue for the Pirates in 2008. This may not be surprising since the

---

[35] http://deadspin.com/5615096/mlb-confidential-the-financial-documents-baseball-doesnt-want-you-to-see-part-1

Pirates did not perform well on the field and had among the lowest ticket prices in MLB.

	2008	2007
Revenues		
Home gate receipts	$32,129,368	$34,422,311
Broadcasting	$39,007,164	$40,326,222
Revenue sharing	$39,046,312	$30,302,652
Concessions	$8,283,870	$7,142,641
Signage and naming rights	$10,459,674	$10,022,346
Other revenues	$17,067,049	$16,420,174
Total revenues	$145,993,437	$138,636,326
Operating expenses		
Player salaries	$51,040,233	$50,871,186
Team operations	$12,604,510	$14,111,881
Player development	$23,182,677	$21,166,850
Broadcasting	$3,167,977	$2,746,577
Restructuring		$2,475,000
Ballpark and game operations	$17,092,460	$16,060,288
Marketing, administrative	$17,115,178	$15,006,990
Total operating expenses	$124,203,045	$122,438,772
Operating profit less interest expenses and taxes	$14,408,259	$15,008,032

Table 4.1.
Pittsburgh Pirates 2007-08 income statements

The bulk of the 2008 expenses for the Pirates were related to player salaries and player development (minor league operations) at 59.8%

of total expenses. Signing bonuses are not treated as salaries as these expenses represent an immediate cash outlay that is unrelated to the player's salary[36]. Nevertheless, the Pirates payroll ranked the fourth lowest in MLB in 2008, leaving little room for other expenses before turning an operating profit into a loss. Largely thanks to the revenue sharing agreement, the Pirates turned a nice profit of $14.4 million in 2008. This figure is close to the $15.9 million profit estimated by Forbes magazine and ranked the Pirates very close to the MLB average profit of $16.7 million in 2008.

The Florida Marlins are considered one of the smallest market teams in MLB, typically reflected in the team's on-field performance. Surprisingly, the Marlins were the most profitable team in MLB in 2008. How did they do it? Table 4.2 presents the income statements for the Marlins for the 2008 and 2009 seasons. The Marlins statements provide a little more detail than the statements for the Pirates. Home gate receipts contributed only a paltry 15% of total revenue in 2008. In fact, total local revenue accounted for only 37% of 2008 revenues. What makes the Marlins profitable is the large national revenues and the low payroll costs. Revenues from the revenue sharing agreement, the MLB central fund (national broadcasting) and MLB Properties, Inc. (team logos licensing) accounted for a whopping 63% of total revenue. One could surmise that the Marlins only survive in a revenue sense by relying on the rest of the league to generate revenues for them. Although the team moved into a new stadium in 2011, local revenues are still a small proportion of total revenue. Payroll costs accounted for only 29.6% of total expenses, among the lowest percentage in MLB to go along with the lowest payroll in MLB in 2008.

---

[36] Under previous tax laws, club owners could depreciate player salaries but not signing bonuses. See the Focus Box later in the chapter.

	2009	2008
Revenues		
Home gate receipts	$21,529,000	$20,985,000
Local broadcasting	$16,716,000	$15,900,000
MLB Central Fund	$31,592,000	$31,298,000
Revenue sharing	$43,973,000	$47,982,000
MLB Properties, Inc.	$7,620,000	$8,623,000
Concessions	$2,582,000	$2,268,000
Sponsorship and promotions	$3,343,000	$4,348,000
Other revenues	$8,176,000	$8,243,000
Total revenues	$135,531,000	$139,647,000
Operating expenses		
Player salaries	$43,002,000	$29,739,000
Team operations	$24,806,000	$23,646,000
Amateur players signing bonuses	$5,218,000	$6,324,000
Broadcasting	$747,000	$630,000
Other expenses	$20,374,000	$9,095,000
Ballpark and game operations	$7,847,000	$7,715,000
Marketing	$10,094,000	$11,543,000
Total operating expenses	$122,854,000	$100,433,000
Operating profit less interest expenses and taxes	$12,677,000	$39,214,000

Table 4.2.
Florida Marlins 2008-09 income statements.

The income statements for the Los Angeles Angels of Anaheim provide a stark contrast to the Florida Marlins and the Pittsburgh Pirates. The Angels operate in a relatively large market with over 15 million people in the greater Los Angeles area, although the Angels play in Anaheim, about a 40 drive from the Los Angeles metropolitan area. The Angels enjoyed success on the field in the 2008 and 2009 seasons, making playoff appearances at the end of each season, but not progressing to the World Series. The Angels fell slightly above the estimated average revenue for MLB clubs in 2008 of $194 million, ranking sixth highest. The club also had a greater than average payroll ($109.5 million), ranking seventh highest at an estimated $132 million (Forbes magazine). The 2008 and 2009 income statements for the Angels are presented in Table 4.3.

What distinguishes the Angels from the Marlins and the Pirates is that revenue sharing shows up as an expense. The Angels contributed just over $27 million more into the central fund that the team received in 2008. Without the burden of revenue sharing, the Angels owner would have almost tripled the operating profit for 2008 (ignoring tax considerations). This is typical of the large market teams in MLB and in other professional sports (NFL) that use revenue sharing: revenue is redistributed from the have teams to the have-not teams. Economics suggests that this could be a subsidy for small-market teams to stay small by not relocating to better markets or to fail to invest the revenue sharing proceeds into a better club on the field.

	2009	2008
Revenues		
Home gate receipts	$100,116,000	$103,209,000
Local broadcasting	$45,998,000	$42,967,000
MLB Central Fund and other	$37,774,000	$38,822,000
Concessions	$15,593,000	$16,516,000

Sponsorship and promotions	$16,730,000	$19,005,000
Other revenues	$12,491,000	$12,976,000
Playoff revenue	$12,122,000	$4,374,000
Total revenues	$240,824,000	$237,869,000

Operating expenses

Major league operations	$139,475,000	$142,138,000
Minor league operations	$8,031,000	$8,087,000
Scouting	$11,262,000	$8,252,000
Stadium operations	$16,671,000	$16,840,000
Revenue sharing and central fund	$27,318,000	$26,378,000
Marketing	$9,846,000	$10,080,000
Other expenses	$12,513,000	$12,502,000
Total operating expenses	$228,898,000	$226,615,000

Operating profit less interest expenses and taxes	$10,732,000	$7,088,000

Table 4.3
Los Angeles Angels of Anaheim 2008-09 income statements.

Brief Review of Concepts

- The chief sources of revenue for major league baseball clubs are ticket sales, suite rentals, broadcasting royalties (both local and national) and local merchandising. Differences in revenues among clubs can be largely attributed by differences in ticket sales, suite rentals and local merchandising, but perhaps most importantly, by revenue sharing. It is quite likely that these characteristics are shared by the three other major sports leagues.
- The single largest expense for major league baseball clubs is player salaries, which account for about half of total expenses for large market clubs. Operating expenses such as ticket operations and stadium rental make up the remainder.

154

Focus Box: The Road to Higher Profits

The income statements for the Pittsburgh Pirates, Florida Marlins and Anaheim Angels suggest that higher payrolls result in greater team success on the field and bigger profits. To achieve this, the revenue growth from team success on the field would have to be higher than the growth in payroll needed to improve the team. In the simple model of the professional sports team, the demand curve would have to shift out further to the right than the vertical shift in the AC curve that results with a higher payroll (draw this for yourself). Is this in fact the case? Some casual evidence can be found in the revenue, payroll and profit histories already discussed in Figures 4.1, 4.2 and 4.3. Figure 4.4 below plots a scatter diagram of the average win-loss percentage and real payroll (1991=100) for each baseball club for 1990-2013 (excluding the Colorado Rockies and Tampa Bay Rays). The association is positive: a higher total payroll tends to be associated with a higher average win-loss percentage. The correlation coefficient between total payroll and team success is 0.331, indicating a reasonable, but not strong, linear association[37]. As the old saying goes, "you get what you pay for".

Figure 4.5 below plots a scatter diagram of the average win-loss percentage versus real local revenue for 1990-2013. The association between revenue and winning is not strong. The correlation coefficient is positive, but weak at 0.295.

The evidence suggests that, on the average, higher payrolls lead to team success on the field, and that team success results in higher local revenue. Owners who argue that payrolls must be cut to raise profitability

---

[37] The correlation coefficient is a descriptive statistic indicating how close the scatter points form a straight line. It is bounded by −1 and 1, with zero indicating no linear association.

(the Florida Marlins of 1998, after winning the World Series in 1997) may be misguided.

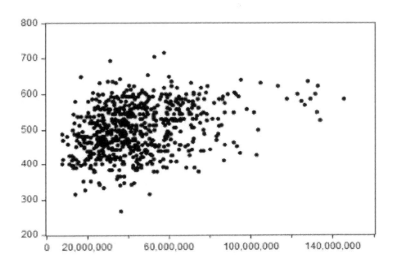

Figure 4.4
Average win-loss percentage versus real payroll (US$ millions) for MLB teams, 1990-2013.

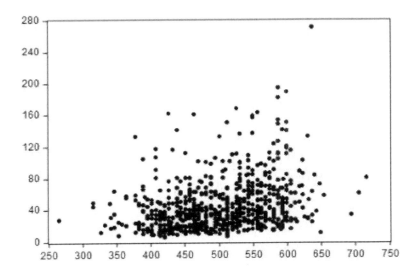

156

Figure 4.5
Average win-loss percentage versus real local revenue (US$ millions) for MLB, 1990-2013.

4.3 Taxation Issues

Team owner's face two different types of taxes, all of which reduce the profitability of running a successful professional sports franchise. These are taxes imposed by governments and taxes imposed by the league owners upon themselves. Taxes are imposed by governments to raise revenue to finance government expenditures. The two principles of taxation used by governments is *ability to pay* and *equality of taxation*. Ability to pay means that governments tax most heavily those with the greatest ability to pay taxes – those with higher incomes. This results in a *progressive tax system* where the tax rate on income rises as more income is earned. Professional major league players fall into the highest tax brackets since they have a great ability to pay taxes with their high incomes. The average salaries in the NFL, NBA, NHL and MLB for 2016 were $2.1 million, $6.25 million, $2.9 million and $4.4 million respectively.[38] Income tax for players is calculated and paid in the country in which the team operates (Internal Revenue Service in the U.S. and Canada Revenue Agency in Canada). Equality of taxation implies that all income earners be taxed at the same tax rate to share the burden of taxation. This results in a flat-tax system, which is not a feature of US or Canadian federal taxation. The province of Alberta utilizes a flat-tax rate of 10% on income earned by players on teams based in Alberta, other provinces use a progressive provincial income tax. A total of 43 U.S. states charge a state income tax and some local governments also collect an

[38] https://www.forbes.com/sites/kurtbadenhausen/2016/12/15/average-player-salaries-in-major-american-sports-leagues/#6a6a6e491050

income tax. The optimal income tax system is a blend of the ability to pay and equality of taxation concepts, but will not be dealt with here.

The tax treatment of profits from a major-league franchise depends upon whether the franchise is run as a separate corporation or as a personal business for the owner. In the latter case, the owner must pay personal income tax on all profits after allowable deductions. There are devious methods that owners can use to reduce the amount of profit showing on their income statements (see the Focus Box after this section) in order to reduce or even eliminate any tax owing. Profits can also be re-invested in building a new facility, acquiring new players, or other expenses that reduce taxable profits to zero. Personal income tax rates vary depending upon the income of the individual. A distinction must be made here between marginal tax rates and average tax rates. The *marginal tax rate* is the amount of tax paid on the last dollar of income earned stated as a percentage. The *average tax rate* is the amount of tax paid on all income as a percentage of all income. In a progressive tax system, the marginal tax rate rises more quickly than the average tax rate so that the average tax rate is "pulled up" by the increasing marginal tax rates. Marginal tax rates do not increase for each additional dollar of income earned, instead the marginal tax rate increases as individuals move into higher income brackets but stays the same within the same bracket. The average federal personal income tax rates are provided in Table 4.3 below for both the US and Canada.

Canadian average tax rates are higher than US average tax rates for roughly the same income brackets, although the difference is reversed at the highest income bracket where most team owners and players reside. On the face of it, professional players and owners in Canada will pay less federal income tax, however U.S. tax law allows for the deduction of many expenses that Canadian tax law does not. For instance, the interest portion of mortgage payments for principle dwellings can be deducted from taxable income in the U.S., whereas Canadian tax law does not allow this. This can be a distinct advantage for players and owners who choose to live in the US where housing prices are typically higher, particularly for the lavish homes many professional athletes live in. For businesses, the interest portion of mortgage payments can be deducted in both Canada and the U.S. The numbers suggest that it is not clear if professional athletes playing for Canadian teams have any distinct tax disadvantage, but one must also include Canadian provincial income taxes which are typically much higher than U.S. state income taxes.

Marginal tax rate U.S.	Single Income in excess of $10,000	Marginal tax rate Canada	Single Income in excess of $10,822
10%	$0 – $8,925	15%	$0 - $43,561
15%	$8,926 – $36,250	22%	$43,562 - $87,123
25%	$36,251 – $87,850	26%	$87,124 - $135,054
28%	$87,851 – $183,250	29%	$135,055+
33%	$183,251 – $398,350		
35%	$398,351 – $400,000		
39.6%	$400,001+		

Table 4.3
U.S. and Canadian marginal tax rates for 2013.
Sources: http://www.tax-services.ca/canadian-tax-brackets-2013-income-tax-rates-canada/ and http://www.forbes.com/sites/moneybuilder/2013/01/05/updated-2013-federal-income-tax-brackets-and-marginal-rates/

A team owner can incorporate the franchise in order to garner tax savings. A *corporation* is formed when the owner issues shares that are equal to the net worth of the team. The *net worth* is defined as the team's assets (things the team owns) minus the team's liabilities (things the team owes). The net worth is what the team owner could expect to receive if the team is sold to a buyer (but sale prices are typically far higher than the net worth). These shares can be sold by the owner to other investors, but typically the team owner remains the largest shareholder. All shareholders are entitled to a portion of the future team profits (a dividend). Businesses are usually incorporated when large amounts of funds are needed to finance new projects (like a new arena), amounts that exceed the amounts that can be borrowed from a bank. Corporations are entitled to deductions that personal team owners are not and also benefit from a significantly lower corporate tax rate. The corporation pays the income tax and the owner receives a dividend from the team that is subject to a very low tax rate (often zero after deductions). Owners might also pay themselves a salary from the team's revenue that is subject to the higher personal income tax rate. The average corporate tax rate, after reasonable deductions from income, for the service sector in the U.S. is 40% and 26.5% in Canada.[39] These rates include provincial or state corporate tax rates.

States and provinces levy income taxes, though these are usually much lower than federal taxes. Entertainment taxes are also levied at the state and provincial level. These taxes are computed as a percentage of the ticket revenue generated by the team and can be quite steep. The Ottawa Senators of the NHL claim that the Ontario entertainment tax costs the team just over $10 million per season. Property taxes are levied by civic governments and are based on the assessed value of the property owned by the club owner. Canadian NHL teams who own their own arenas (Toronto Maple Leafs, Montreal Canadians, Ottawa Senators and the Vancouver Canucks) pay significant property taxes. In fact, the property taxes paid by

---

[39] http://www.kpmg.com/global/en/services/tax/tax-tools-and-resources/pages/corporate-tax-rates-table.aspx

the Montreal Canadians for the Bell Center for the 2011-12 season were higher than all US based teams combined at $11.2 million.

4.3.1 Effects of taxes in theory

Team owners can react to having to pay higher taxes in a number of ways. The most obvious is to pass on the tax to the consumer by raising ticket prices. Using the simple model of the sports franchise developed in Chapter 3, it is easy to show that government imposed taxes have *no effect* on the ticket pricing decisions made by team owners, at least in the short-run. This might sound surprising, but a simple diagram is all that is needed. The bottom portion of Figure 4.6 displays the typically demand, marginal revenue, marginal cost and average cost curves for a team owner. Since all costs are fixed costs, the MC curve is flat at zero dollars up to the point of full capacity of the arena where it becomes vertical. The average cost (AC) curve is downward sloping since costs are fixed as output (tickets) increases. The team owner maximizes profits, or revenues, where $MR = MC = 0$. The profit-maximizing level of output is extended to the upper portion of the figure so that the revenue curve is at its highest point. Recall that with all costs being fixed costs, maximizing profit and maximizing revenue will occur at the same level of ticket sales. The total profit is computed as the difference between the ticket price and the average cost evaluated at the dotted line, over all previous tickets. Since ticket sales are less than where MC becomes vertical, the club is operating with some empty seats in the arena, but this is still profit maximizing.

The upper portion of Figure 4.6 displays the total revenue curve for given levels of output (tickets). It is hump-shaped because total revenue is maximized where $MR = 0$ (total revenue is unchanged for small changes around this point). Imposing a government income (profit) tax on the team owner reduces profits[40]. The total revenue curve shifts down by the amount of the tax that is collected by the government. The largest vertical drop in revenue is at the dotted line since the highest average tax rate will be charged when total revenues are the highest and that is this position. Thus the total revenue curve shifts down and becomes flatter, yet total revenue is still the highest at the same level of ticket sales. This means taxes will be paid out of profits after the maximum profit has been achieved. The AC curve in the bottom figure shifts upward by the amount of the tax divided by the number of tickets sold at each level of ticket sales. The largest increase in AC will occur at the dotted line since that is where the most tax is paid. Essentially, the team owner knows the demand curve and the fixed costs that he or she faces for the coming season. The profit-maximizing level of ticket sales is chosen and the ticket price is set. The profit and the amount of tax to be paid can then be computed. This does not change the profit-maximizing position for the team owner in comparison to paying no profit tax, but it does reduce the after-tax profit.

We can demonstrate this result algebraically. Profit for the team is owner is given by $\pi(Q) = R(Q) - C(Q)$ where Q is tickets sold. Without a profit tax, the team owner will maximize profit where $\partial R/\partial Q - \partial C/\partial Q = 0$ or where $MR = MC$ for the last ticket sold. Let the profit tax rate be $t = t(\pi)$. If $dt/d\pi = 0$ then the profit tax is a flat rate tax whereas if $dt/d\pi > 0$, the profit tax is a progressive tax. At what level of ticket sales will the team owner maximize after-tax profit? After-tax profit is given by $\pi^A = \pi(Q)[1 - t(\pi(Q))]$ so the first-order condition is given by

---

[40] The treatment of the profit tax here is sometimes referred to as a "cash-flow" tax in the public finance literature.

$$\frac{\partial \pi^A}{\partial Q} = \frac{\partial \pi}{\partial Q}\left[1 - t\big(\pi(Q)\big)\right] - \pi(Q)\frac{dt}{d\pi}\frac{\partial \pi}{\partial Q} = 0$$

$$= \frac{\partial \pi}{\partial Q}\left[1 - t\big(\pi(Q)\big) - \pi(Q)\frac{dt}{d\pi}\right] = 0$$

The term in the square bracket could be positive or negative, but as long as $\partial \pi / \partial Q = 0$, the first-order condition is assured. This means the team owner will sell tickets to point where $MR = MC$ for the last ticket sold, the same result as the case with no profit tax.

In the long run, higher government taxes *can* affect the profit position of the team owner. Suppose the full capacity constraint is reached and the team owner wishes to expand the arena or build a new one. The owner can choose between raising the needed financing through ticket revenues or taking a loan. Waiting for ticket revenues to rise sufficiently might take too long, and the presence of taxes makes taking a loan more desirable since the tax on ticket sales is avoided and the interest charges on the loan are deductible from taxable income. In this way, taxes introduce a distortion in the decision to finance capital projects out of ongoing income or debt. If all team owners behave the same way, the demand for capital will increase and the user cost of capital may rise. The user cost of capital is usually stated as an interest rate on the loan, but is a complicated function of the price of capital, depreciation, taxes and other factors. Since a loan is a fixed cost, the AC curve will shift upward and profits will be reduced further than just the taxes.

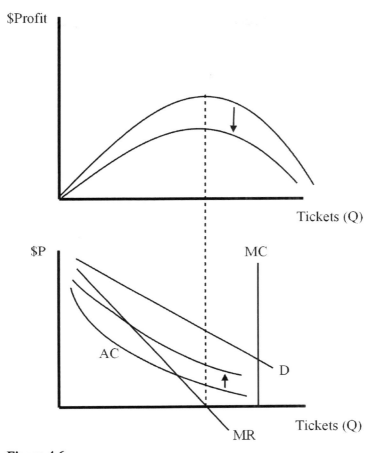

Figure 4.6
The monopolist team owner maximizes revenue and profit at Q* tickets sold at price P* in the bottom picture. The profit schedule reaches a maximum at Q* in the upper picture. A progressive tax on profits shifts the profit schedule down by the most at Q* since, at that position, the most tax will be paid. If the owner anticipates selling Q* tickets, then paying the profit tax, at the start of the season, the tax can be treated as a fixed cost over the season. This shifts the AFC curve vertically in the lower picture to reduce profits.

Some taxes are imposed team owners on themselves by way of a majority vote of owners. A recent example is the luxury tax used by MLB. A *luxury tax* (or competitive balance tax as coined by MLB) is imposed on the teams with the largest payrolls, and then redistributed to small market teams with smaller payrolls. The idea is to promote equity among all the cartel members. Major league baseball adopted a luxury tax in its 1996 collective bargaining agreement (CBA). The initial luxury tax was 35% of the excess team payroll over and above the mid-point of the fifth and sixth highest payrolls. Each total team payroll is computed using the annual average salary of each player over his entire contract, rather than the amounts actually paid to each player. The Baltimore Orioles paid a luxury tax of just over $3.1 million for the 1997-98 season. Despite the highest payroll in MLB, the Orioles floundered on the field. The New York Yankees paid $4.4 million in luxury tax after the 1996-97 season, but then reduced their tax to only $684,390 after the 1997-98 season. The Boston Red Sox paid the second largest luxury tax after the 1997-98 season at $2.1 million.

With every passing major league season, payrolls usually increase for all teams. This raises the mid-point between the fifth and sixth highest payrolls, the threshold where teams begin to pay the luxury tax. With the threshold increasing every season, the luxury tax is a relatively ineffective method to hold down spending on salaries. Of course, in the simple model of the professional sports franchise, a luxury tax would raise the AC curve (since salaries are a fixed cost) and reduce profits, but leave the optimal average ticket price unchanged. In fact, economics suggests that the players on those teams that pay a luxury tax will absorb some of the tax in the form of lower salaries. This discussion is left until Chapter 8.

Baseball altered its luxury tax system in its 2002 CBA, renaming it the competitive balance tax. The new system established absolute thresholds for club payrolls of $120.5 million for the 2004 season, $128 million for the 2005 season and $136.5 million for the 2006 season. Any team that exceeded the payroll threshold paid a tax of 22.5% of the overage to the Industry Growth Fund, an organization that operates independently from the MLB central office to promote baseball. The tax rate can escalate to as high as 50% for repeat offenders. The 2012 CBA raised the payroll thresholds for the tax to $178 million for the 2012 and 2013 seasons, and $189 million for the 2014 through 2016 seasons.

The NBA adopted a luxury tax system in 1999 in an effort to hold down player salaries. The team salary threshold is roughly equal to the average team salary of the league (approximately $54 million in 2003, increasing to $71.5 million for 2008). The tax rate is 100% so for every dollar the team exceeds the tax threshold, one dollar in tax is paid, yet in 2009 14 of the 30 NBA teams exceeded the tax threshold. Each season, 10% of player salaries are placed in an escrow account to ensure that the tax can be paid if owing by a club. Any amount in the escrow account not needed to pay the tax is refunded to the players. The luxury tax collected by the league office is redistributed to clubs below the average payroll using a complicated formula. In 2003, poorer clubs received payments of close to $20 million from the fund. This may create an incentive for poor clubs to remain poor, however the NBA's concern over cost control seems to override detrimental effects from the luxury tax system.

Brief Review of Concepts

- Tax systems are based on two concepts. Ability to pay means that governments tax most heavily those with the greatest ability to pay taxes. Tax equality means that all parties are taxed equally. Most tax systems are a blend of these two concepts.
- The marginal tax rate is the amount of tax, as a percentage of income, paid on the last dollar of income earned. The average tax rate is the amount of tax paid on all income as a percentage of all income. In a progressive tax system, the marginal tax rate rises more quickly than the average tax rate.

166

- Corporate taxes are generally less than personal income taxes in both the US and Canada. Canadian taxes are generally higher than US taxes, but the difference is slight at the highest income levels. The US tax system has more generous deductions from income than Canada, making ownership of a US based sports club more profitable.
- In the short run, profit taxes on sports clubs have no impact on the optimal average ticket price or the optimal number of tickets sold. The tax is born by the owner in the form of lower profits. In the long run, the tax makes debt financing more attractive, raising the user cost of capital. This may reduce profits further.
- A luxury tax is imposed by the league on the clubs who spend have the highest payrolls. In major league baseball, the luxury tax is computed as 35% of the excess payroll above the mid-point between the fifth and sixth highest payrolls. Luxury taxes reduce profits for those clubs that pay the tax.

Focus Box: Bill Veeck: Baseball showman and tax shelter genius.

Bill Veeck's first venture into ownership of a baseball club was in 1941. At the age of 28, Veeck purchased the minor-league Milwaukee Brewers of the American Association and turned the club from worst to first in one year. Veeck was a shrewd owner who knew how to turn a team's finances around as well. He was a master promoter who would use any gimmick to bring fans to the ballpark. In 1946, Veeck headed an ownership group that bought the Cleveland Indians. Using fireworks shows, bat days and other promotions, Veeck turned the Indians into one of the best drawing teams in the American League. In 1951, Veeck purchased the St. Louis Browns and attempted to move the franchise first to Milwaukee, then to Baltimore. Both times he failed to secure enough team owner votes to secure the move. In 1958, Veeck purchased the Chicago White Sox (which he later purchased again in 1975 and sold in 1981), achieved immediate success, and then sold the team in 1961.

Veeck's idea for a tax shelter to avoid paying more income tax came to existence while he was a co-owner owner of the Cleveland Indians. Let's use a hypothetical example to explain how the tax shelter works. Suppose a new owner purchases an existing franchise for the price of $10 million (not an absurd price back in 1946). The value of the team in the balance sheet of the new owner is then a $10 million asset. Physical assets, like new buildings or equipment, wear out over time and must be replaced, thus the tax authorities allow depreciation expense to be deducted from annual income. Veeck argued that players are assets to the team as well. Specifically, the new owner assigns a value to the player contracts of the team, which is no higher than the purchase price of the club. The owner can only assign a new value to the player contracts if the club is reorganized as a subchapter S corporation, otherwise the owner only receives the depreciated value of the player contracts from the previous owner[41]. Suppose the new owner assigns a value of $9 million to the existing player contracts and $1 million to the rest of the team's assets. Veeck convinced the Internal Revenue Service (IRS) to allow club owners to claim depreciation expenses on player contracts over five years (20% per year). Hence the new owner deducts the normal operating expenses (including player salaries) from revenues to arrive at his profit, then he is allowed to deduct a further $1.8 million (20% of $9 million) to arrive at his final profit. The new owner can claim the same deduction every year for five years. Let's assume the owner is in a 30% income tax bracket. The tax savings is thus $540,000 (30% of $1.8 million) every year for five years. Under the Veeck tax shelter, player expenses are double counted.

---

[41] A subchapter S corporation issues shares like a normal corporation, but all profits flow to the team owner. The team owner must acquire some minimum percentage of the existing shares, usually 70%.

168

What happens at the end of the five years when the player contracts are fully depreciated and carry zero value on the balance sheet? The tax shelter is lost, profit will increase by $1.8 million per season, and the taxes paid by the owner will increase, right? Well, not quite. The team owner of a subchapter S corporation is allowed to convert the team to a regular corporation once during the owner's tenure. Thus at the end of five years, the team is converted to a regular corporation and pays the much lower corporate tax rate. Ingenious? Absolutely, however the effectiveness of the tax shelter was reduced by tax law changes in 1986.

Analytical example: The Veeck tax shelter.

Question: The new NFL Los Angeles Surfers have just finished its first season of operations. The new owner purchased an existing NFL team for $400 million and moved the club to Los Angeles. The owner is currently allowed to value the player contracts at 50% of the purchase price. Total revenues from all sources (local and national) are $250 million, while player expenses totaled $125 million. Other expenses, including the stadium rental, administrative expenses and other expenses totaled $65 million. The owner declared a subchapter S corporation when the club was purchased and faces an income tax rate of 40%. Compute the owner's after-tax profit and compute the tax savings from the shelter.

Answer: The accounting profit is total revenue less total expenses. This is $250 million - $125 million - $65 million = $60 million. Taxes owing without the Veeck tax shelter would be $60 million x 0.40 = $24 million for an after-tax profit of $38 million.

The tax shelter allows the owner to claim 50% of the $400 million purchase price as the value of the player contracts. This amount can be depreciated evenly over five years, giving a depreciation expense of $40 million per year. The accounting profit is now $60 million - $40 million = $20 million. Taxes owing will be $20 million x 0.40 = $8 million. The tax savings is $16 million per year for five years, yielding a total tax savings of $80 million.

4.4 Franchise Activity in Professional Sports Leagues

For the professional sports team owner, there are two principle sources of profit. First, there is the annual profit from ticket sales, broadcast rights, concession sales, apparel contracts and other normal business operations. As have seen in this chapter and in Chapter 1, many teams earn zero profit or even lose money each season. More importantly, the larger source of profit is the appreciation in the value of the franchise from when the club is purchased to when it is sold. Often capital gains from the latter source completely dwarfs profit from normal operations. There are some spectacular examples of owners who have reaped the profits from appreciation in the value of their franchise[42]. Joan Payson purchased the franchise rights for the New York Mets from the National League in 1961 for $2 million, which she then sold in 1980 for $21 million. This yields an annual average rate of return of 50%.

$$r = \frac{\left(\frac{21-2}{2}\right) \bullet 100}{19} = 50\%$$

The Mets were subsequently sold again in 1986 for a price of $100 million, yielding an annual average rate of return of 53.7%. Any positive profit from normal baseball operations would seem to be gravy. This rate of return is fairly reflective of franchises in all leagues, but the rate of return is less for older franchises. Another example is the Washington Redskins in the NFL. The Redskins were purchased as an expansion franchise in 1932 for $7,500 and were owned for most of their existence by the Cooke family. The Redskins, and Jack Kent Cooke Stadium, were up for sale in 1998. The NFL approved the purchase of the franchise for $800

---

[42] Some of these examples are drawn from Quirk and Fort (1997) and Scully (1995).

million in July of 1999, yielding an average annual rate of return of 140%! This is somewhat misleading since most of the appreciation in the Redskin's value occurred after the 1950's, making the rate of return over the last three decades obscene. The Los Angeles Dodgers of MLB was purchased by Frank McCourt in 2004 for $430 million from NewsCorp. The new owner spent over $100 million on improvements to Dodger Stadium and adjoining properties, increased the team payroll and gave large donations to charities. Unfortunately McCourt filed for bankruptcy in 2012 when he couldn't meet the player payroll or pay bills after MLB Commissioner Bud Selig declined to approve a $3 billion agreement between FOX and the Dodgers to extend their television broadcast rights. The team was purchased in 2012 by a group of investors including basketball's Earvin (Magic) Johnson for a reported $2 billion, yielding an average annual return of 40.6%.

Of course, there are far more team owners who lost money on their franchises than made money. Almost all the teams that fold in any league have terminal franchise values that are zero or even negative. This is particularly true in the modern rival leagues (ABA, WHA, WFL, USFL) whose teams were not absorbed by an existing league, except for a few. Table 4.4 provides a partial listing of recent professional sports franchise sales. The average annual rates of return on franchise sales up to 1990 were 8% in baseball, 16% in basketball and 20% in football.

Excluding the Federal League (1914-15), MLB has not seen an expansion franchise go under since the 1903 National Agreement, although many have moved or changed ownership. The period of greatest expansion activity was the period from 1900 to 1920. No new expansion franchises were granted, however two franchises moved: the original Milwaukee Brewers became the St. Louis Browns in 1902 and the original Baltimore

Orioles became the New York Highlanders in 1903, renaming itself as the Yankees in 1913. During this period, the ownership of clubs changed 33 times and the median tenure of ownership was only seven years. The period of greatest stability for major league baseball was 1920-1950. Again no new franchises were awarded and no teams moved to new cities. Teams were sold to new owners 22 times over this period. The median tenure of ownership peaked in the National League at 21 years during the 1930's and fell to 6.5 years in the 1940's. In the American League, the median tenure of ownership peaked at 24.5 years in the 1940's and fell to eleven years by the 1950's.

The period 1950-1980 is notable as an unstable period with six teams moving to new cities in the American League and four teams moving in the National League (the most notorious being the Brooklyn Dodgers move to Los Angeles in 1958 and the New York Giants move to San Francisco in 1957). There were ten new franchises awarded (the most strategically important being the establishment of the New York Mets, the Houston Colt 45's / Astros, the new Washington Senators and the Los Angeles / Anaheim Angels to stave off the stillborn Continental League) and clubs changed ownership 30 times. The median tenure of ownership in the American League was around 9.5 years and about 18 years in the National League.

Over the period 1901-1990, seven MLB teams were sold due to bankruptcies, the most recent being the Texas Rangers in 2009, the Houston Astros in 1976 and the Seattle Pilots in 1970. Owners tended to sell their clubs following a losing year for the team although the evidence is not overwhelming: 53% of National League teams had losing records the year before they were sold, 54% of American League teams.

Team	League	Owner	Value
Los Angeles Dodgers	MLB	Mark Walter	$2 billion
Washington Redskins	NFL	Daniel Snyder	$1.1 billion
Dallas Cowboys	NFL	Jerry Jones	$923 million
Houston Texans	NFL	Robert McNair	$905 million
New England Patriots	NFL	Robert Kraft	$861 million
Philadelphia Eagles	NFL	Jeffrey Lurie	$833 million
Denver Broncos	NFL	Pat Bowlen	$815 million
Cleveland Browns	NFL	Randy Lerner	$798 million
Chicago Bears	NFL	McCaskey Family	$785 million
Tampa Bay Buccaneers	NFL	Malcolm Glazer	$779 million
Baltimore Ravens	NFL	Steve Bisciotti	$776 million
Miami Dolphins	NFL	Wayne Huizenga	$765 million
Carolina Panthers	NFL	Jerry Richardson	$760 million
Green Bay Packers	NFL	Public	$756 million
Detroit Lions	NFL	William Ford	$747 million
Tennessee Titans	NFL	Bud Adams	$736 million
New York Yankees	MLB	George Steinbrenner	$730 million
Pittsburgh Steelers	NFL	Dan Rooney	$717 million
Seattle Seahawks	NFL	Paul Allen	$712 million
Kansas City Chiefs	NFL	Lamar Hunt	$709 million
St. Louis Rams	NFL	Georgia Frontiere	$708 million
New York Giants	NFL	W. Mara/P. Tisch	$692 million
Jacksonville Jaguars	NFL	Wayne Weaver	$688 million
New York Jets	NFL	Woody Johnson	$685 million
Cincinnati Bengals	NFL	Mike Brown	$675 million
Buffalo Bills	NFL	Ralph Wilson Jr.	$637 million
San Francisco 49ers	NFL	Denise DeBartolo York	$636 million
New Orleans Saints	NFL	Tom Benson	$627 million
Oakland Raiders	NFL	Al Davis	$624 million
San Diego Chargers	NFL	Alex Spanos	$622 million
Indianapolis Colts	NFL	Jim Irsay	$609 million
Minnesota Vikings	NFL	Red McCombs	$604 million
Atlanta Falcons	NFL	Arthur Blank	$603 million
Arizona Cardinals	NFL	Bill Bidwell	$552 million
New York Mets	MLB	Fred Wilpon	$482 million

Los Angeles Lakers	NBA	Jerry Buss	$447 million
Los Angeles Dodgers	MLB	Frank McCourt	$435 million
Boston Red Sox	MLB	John Henry	$426 million
Atlanta Braves	MLB	AOL/Time Warner	$424 million
New York Knicks	NBA	C. Dolan/J. Dolan	$401 million
Seattle Mariners	MLB	Hiroshi Yamaguchi	$373 million
Cleveland Indians	MLB	Larry Dolan	$360 million
Texas Rangers	MLB	Tom Hicks	$356 million
Chicago Bulls	NBA	Jerry Reinsdorf	$356 million
San Francisco Giants	MLB	Peter Magowan	$355 million
Colorado Rockies	MLB	Jerry McMorris	$347 million
Dallas Mavericks	NBA	Mark Cuban	$338 million
Houston Astros	MLB	Drayton McLane	$337 million
Philadelphia 76ers	NBA	Comcast Corp.	$328 million
Baltimore Orioles	MLB	Peter Angelos	$319 million
Boston Celtics	NBA	W. Grousbeck/S. Pagliuca	$290 million
Chicago Cubs	MLB	Tribune Co.	$287 million
Detroit Pistons	NBA	William Davidson	$284 million
San Antonio Spurs	NBA	Peter Holt	$283 million
Phoenix Suns	NBA	Jerry Colangelo	$283 million
Arizona Diamondbacks	MLB	Jerry Colangelo	$280 million
Indiana Pacers	NBA	H. Simon/M. Simon	$280 million
Houston Rockets	NBA	Les Alexander	$278 million
Sacramento Kings	NBA	G. Maloof/J. Maloof	$275 million
Washington Wizards	NBA	Abe Pollin	$274 million
Portland Trail Blazers	NBA	Paul Allen	$272 million
St. Louis Cardinals	MLB	B. DeWitt/F. Hanser	$271 million
Detroit Red Wings	NHL	Michael Ilitch	$266 million
New York Rangers	NHL	C. Dolan/J. Dolan	$263 million
Detroit Tigers	MLB	Michael Ilitch	$262 million
Philadelphia Flyers	NHL	Comcast Corp.	$262 million
Cleveland Cavaliers	NBA	G. Gund/G. Gund	$258 million
Dallas Stars	NHL	Tom Hicks	$254 million

Table 4.4
Recent professional sports franchise sales

174

Since the establishment of the NBA in 1946, franchise activity has been much more turbulent than baseball. While 27 expansion franchises were granted over the period 1946-1990, fourteen teams were folded, 17 teams moved to new cities and ownership changed 58 times. The median tenure of ownership hovered around seven years. Owners sold a team after a losing season in 53% of all sales.

The NFL was the most turbulent of the four professional leagues up to 1940 with 39 abandoned franchises, 31 expansion franchises and nine teams relocating cities. Most of these clubs were located in small cities with little chance of survival. Since 1940, 21 expansion franchises have been granted (12 coming from the AFL-NFL merger) and only three franchises were abandoned. Some of the remaining clubs today have long histories of ownership stability: the Chicago Bears have been owned by the Halas family since 1922; the Green Bay Packers have been owned by the city of Green Bay since 1923; the Bidwill family has owned the Chicago - St. Louis – Arizona Cardinals since 1932; and the Pittsburgh Steelers have been owned by the Rooney family since 1933. Up to 1990, the median tenure of ownership was 25 years. The sale of clubs following losing seasons is much more evident in the NFL at 68%.

Despite some difficulties in the early period of the NHL (1920's), the league was a model of stability up the 1970's. Basically the NHL consisted of six teams (Montreal Canadians, Toronto Maple Leafs, Boston Bruins, Chicago Blackhawks, Detroit Red Wings, and the New York Rangers) between 1940 and 1967 with those teams finding new owners only eight times. The median tenure of ownership peaked in the 1960's at 21 years. The year 1972 saw the establishment of the World Hockey Association (WHA), a rival league that raided the NHL clubs for established players[43]. To compete with the WHA, the NHL added six new expansion teams, eventually absorbing four WHA teams in 1977. One team, the Cleveland Barons (formally the Oakland Seals), was abandoned and the Minnesota North Stars absorbed its players. The NHL is currently undergoing a period of rapid expansion with eight new expansion franchises granted in the last 15 years. Over the period 1917-1990, 59% of team sales occurred after losing seasons.

Brief Review of Concepts

- The rate of increase of franchise values up to 1990 were 8% in baseball, 16% in basketball and 20% in football, far larger than the annual average increase in profits.
- The NHL had the most stable ownership up to the 1960's, followed by the NBA and baseball. The NFL had the least stable ownership up to the 1960's. Since the 1960's all leagues have experienced unstable ownership and rapid increases in the number of franchises. All leagues, except baseball, have suffered from competition from rival leagues.
- Franchise owners tended to sell their clubs just as often after a winning season as a losing season, with the exception of the NFL, where clubs were typically sold after a losing season.

Focus Box: When is a Loss a Loss?

In March of 2002, Baseball commissioner Bud Selig testified before the U.S. Congress that baseball teams had an operating loss of just over $200 million at the end of the 2001 season, and that only two teams had earned a profit over the previous five years. Michael Ozanian, of

---

[43] The most notable of which is Bobby Hull who was paid $150,000 in his last season with the Chicago Blackhawks. He was signed by the WHA Winnipeg Jets and received a signing bonus of $1 million.

Forbes Magazine, computes annual estimates of profits and losses for major baseball, the NBA, NHL and NFL using data gathered from the clubs themselves, bankers, financial reports and valuation experts. His estimate of baseball's profit for the 2001 season is just over $75 million. Both sets of profit figures are shown in a scatter diagram in Figure 4.7. Selig called Ozanian's figures "pure fiction". Selig is right in that an owner can invent a profit or loss figure within a finite range, however his assessment of the Ozanian numbers is suspect. Why the difference in the numbers?

Baseball owners include expenses in their profit calculations that do not require any cash outlays. One example is depreciation on baseball stadiums, which owners claim if they have any ownership in the stadium where they play. This lowers the reported profit for tax purposes but is not a real cash outlay. Baseball owners also inflate costs by including all operating costs for their minor league affiliates, while not including minor league revenues. The correlation coefficient between the Ozanian numbers and the official numbers is 0.844, strong enough to conclude that the Ozanian numbers are probably computed using the right revenue and expense categories.

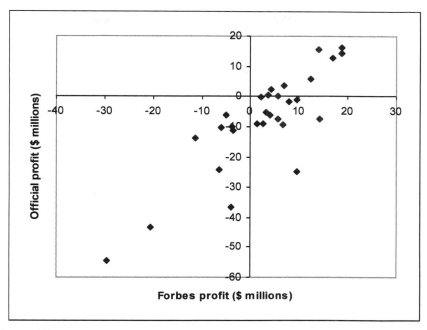

Figure 4.7

Source: Michael Ozanian, "Is Baseball Really Broke?",
http://www.forbes.com/2002/04/01/0401baseball.html

4.5 A Simple Model of Franchise Values

Table 4.4 provides a summary of market franchise values for all clubs in the four North American leagues. If the team owner were to sell the club, these numbers give an estimate of the price the owner could expect to receive. What determines these franchise values? A professional sports franchise is an asset to its owner, just as a stock or bond is also an asset to its holder. We can use the simple model of asset prices used to analyze financial instruments to investigate franchise values. Suppose future annual profits and interest rates are known with certainty. In this case, the current price of an asset must equal the present value of all future profits plus any terminal value. The *present value* of an asset is how much money would have to be invested today at a constant interest rate to earn the stream of known future profits plus the terminal value. Consider a simple example. Suppose a bond matures in one year's time paying $1,100 and carries an interest rate of 10%. The amount you would have to put in the bank today to earn the $1,100 in one year is

$$PV = \frac{\$1,100}{(1 + 0.10)} = \$1,000$$

Suppose you could purchase the bond for only $950? You could then make excess profits by borrowing the $950 at 10% interest, buying the bond and holding it until it matures. You would receive $1,100 and pay back $950(1.10) = $1,045 on the loan, for a riskless profit of $55. If everyone knows this, the current price of the bond will be bid up from $950 until the profit opportunity disappears[44]. If the current market price of the bond is above $1,000, those holding these bonds now could make excess profits by immediately selling their bonds and investing the proceeds for one year at the 10% interest rate. The price of bonds would fall until the bond price just reached $1,000. Hence the present value formula must hold to prevent excess profits.

More generally, if an asset earns a stream of known cash payments each year (y_t) for T years with a terminal value of z, at a constant interest rate of r per year, the present value of the asset is computed as

$$PV = \frac{y_1}{1+r} + \frac{y_2}{(1+r)^2} + \frac{y_3}{(1+r)^3} + \cdots + \frac{y_T}{(1+r)^T} + \frac{z_T}{(1+r)^T} \tag{4.1}$$

---

[44] This is called arbitrage in economic terms.

We shall treat professional sports franchises as having no terminal "scrap value" so $z = 0$. The price or present value of an asset can rise over time due to higher expected future cash flows or lower expected future interest rates. If cash flows grow at a constant rate of g per year, the present value formula becomes

$$PV = \frac{y_1}{1+r} + \frac{y_2(1+g)}{(1+r)^2} + \frac{y_3(1+g)^2}{(1+r)^3} + \cdots + \frac{y_T(1+g)^{T-1}}{(1+r)^T} \qquad (4.2)$$

In this case, the present value or price of the asset will also grow by g% per year. If the asset has an infinite life[45] (never matures), the formula for the present value reduces to $(r > g)$

$$PV = \frac{y_1}{r-g} \qquad (4.3)$$

Two interesting predictions arise from the simple present value model that are particularly applicable to professional sports franchises.

1) The only time an asset can increase in price (present value) at a faster rate than the rate of interest r is if, in some years, the cash flow is negative.

The total return to the owner of a franchise is the sum of the rate of return from annual profits and the rate of return from appreciation in the price of the franchise, which must equal the market rate of interest.

$$\frac{p_{t+1}^e - p_t}{p_t} + \frac{y_t}{p_t} = r \qquad (4.4)$$

---

[45] Some British bonds issued in the early twentieth century were called consols and had no maturity date. The British government has since retired these bonds.

Equation (4.4) is an arbitrage condition that must hold in a certain world. Suppose a potential owner knows a franchise will increase in price at a rate greater than the market rate of interest r. If the anticipated operating profit (y) over one year is positive, he could make a riskless profit by borrowing at the rate r to buy the franchise, hold it for one year, then sell it. If the first term in (3.4) is greater than r, then any positive operating profit over the year is a bonus. All potential owners will know this and the current franchise price p_t will be bid up until (4.4) just holds. In a certain world, the only way the appreciation in the franchise value can be greater than r is if operating profits show a loss for the year.

2) No asset can increase in price at a rate greater than the market rate of interest in the long run.

This prediction follows from the first prediction. In order for the franchise price to appreciate at a rate greater than r in the long run, annual operating profits would have to be negative every year in the future. Of course this cannot be true since the present value of the franchise, computed using (4.1) would be negative and nobody would hold the franchise.

The present value model predicts that franchise values should appreciate faster than the market rate of interest during the early years of a new franchise or league, when operating profits are typically negative. As the franchise and league become more established and attendance grows, operating profits should become positive and franchise values should increase at a rate less than the market rate of interest.

Period starting	MLB	NBA	NFL	NHL

in:				
1905	0.14			
1910	0.18			
1915	0.17			
1920	0.43			
1925	0.50			
1930	0.79		0.01	
1935	0.33		0.03	
1940	0.57			
1945	0.82		0.17	
1950	2.31		0.21	
1955	3.98	0.1		
1960	4.82	0.19		
1965	3.40	0.68	9.38	
1970	13.50	3.28	10.23	2
1975	12.00	4.7	13.03	6
1980	11.85	7.27	18.2	6
1985	23.89	13.38	60	
1990	100.00	48.7	81.88	
1995	124.30	125	182.6	50
2000	215.00	125	195	105

Table 4.6
Imputed Values of Sports Franchises ($ Millions)
Sources: Quirk and Fort (1997), Tables 2.7, 2.9, 2.11. Data for 1990's obtained from Table 4.4 and Associated Press.

Quirk and Fort (1997) provide average franchise values for the four professional sports leagues over their lifetimes up to 1990. These per team values were averaged over five year intervals and are given in Table 4.5. The evidence suggests that the period of greatest increase in franchise prices was the late 1980's and 1990's, contrary to the prediction of the present value model.

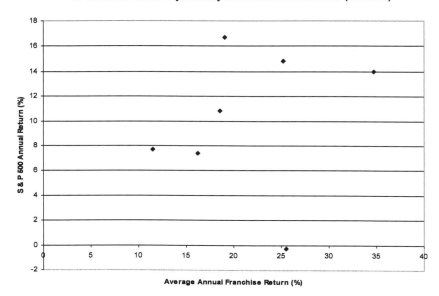

Figure 4.8
Standard and Poors index annual return versus average annual franchise return in MLB.

The present value model of franchise prices also predicts that there should be an inverse relationship between the market rate of interest and franchise values, *holding future profits constant*. This prediction is tested using data for the NFL taken from Quirk and Fort (1997). There they also compute the average rate of return from the Standard and Poors 500 stock market index over ten year periods, which is graphed against the average franchise price for each decade in Figure 4.8. Although the number of points is small, there is no evidence of the inverse relationship suggested by the present value model.

Brief Review of Concepts

- The certainty model of franchise values suggests that the value of a franchise at any point in time is equal to the discounted present value of the stream of all future profits.
- The rate of increase in the franchise value is also equal to the annual rate of increase of profits plus the market rate of interest. The franchise value can increase faster than the market rate of interest if the rate of increase of profits is negative. Of course, this cannot occur every period or the franchise will go bankrupt.
- The certainty model predicts that franchise should increase in value quickly during the early years of a league when operating profits are typically negative. Empirical evidence suggests that this is not the case.
- The certainty model also predicts that franchise values should be roughly inversely related with the market rate of interest. Empirical evidence suggests that this is not the case.

4.6 Uncertainty and Expectations

It is clear that the present value model of asset prices cannot explain the rapid rise in franchise prices during the last two decades, unless team owners were encountering tremendous losses, which was not the case. Future profits are not known with certainty and the model must be adjusted to incorporate what the owners think their future profits will be. Owners form expectations of future profits by using an information set that contains whatever variables owners can obtain and they think affect future profits. We could simply ask the owners what their expectations are for future profits, but this does not make the model general enough to use across different owners and leagues. Instead, economists assume that speculators form their expectations using a *process*. A process is a systematic method, which is assumedly known by all participants, and which yields a unique numerical expectation. There are two popular processes used by economists to form expectations: adaptive expectations and rational expectations. Rational expectations will not be covered here.

In an *adaptive expectation* process, a speculator will adjust his expectation of any variable by some fraction of the difference between the variable's actual value last period and what he was expecting it to be last period. He will raise his expectation this period if the actual value last period was higher than he was expecting, and he will lower his expectation if the actual value last period was below what he was expecting. If his expectation last period turned out to be correct, he will not adjust his expectation this period.

Adaptive expectations have some nice features that make them popular to use. First, speculators can be fooled temporarily if their expectations last period were incorrect, but they eventually catch on to the correct value of the variable. How long this takes depends upon the volatility of the variable: the more volatile, the longer it will take speculators to catch on. Second, the adaptive expectations process is completely general in that we could use it to form expectations for the future value of any variable, like future profits, interest rates, inflation, etc. Third, the process allows us to substitute for unknown values of future variables with their adaptive expectation. Hence we can relate known values of variables to unknown future variables in a simple way.

The adaptive expectations process is written formally as

$$y_t^e = \alpha y_{t-1} + (1 - \alpha)y_{t-1}^e \qquad (4.5)$$

where y_t^e represents the expected value of y in period t, y_{t-1} is the actual value of y in period t-1, and α is called the adjustment coefficient, which is between zero and one. It is not difficult to show that y_t^e is a function of all previous values of y through history with declining weights. Lag (4.5) by one period and substitute it for y_{t-1}^e in (4.5).

$$y_t^e = \alpha y_{t-1} + (1 - \alpha)(\alpha y_{t-2} + (1 - \alpha)y_{t-2}^e)$$
$$= \alpha y_{t-1} + \alpha(1 - \alpha)y_{t-2} + (1 - \alpha)^2 y_{t-2}^e$$

Equation (4.5) could be lagged two periods, and then substituted for y_{t-2}^e on the right side of the expanded form above. Successive substitutions will yield

$$y_t^e = \alpha y_{t-1} + \alpha(1 - \alpha)y_{t-2} + \alpha(1 - \alpha)^2 y_{t-3} + \cdots + \alpha(1 - \alpha)^{n-1} y_{t-n} \quad (4.6)$$

Since the adjustment coefficient α is less than one, the terms in front of the y's on the right side of (4.6) will diminish in size. This makes intuitive sense that the expectation of y today should depend most on recent past values of y. Values for y in the distant future have little effect on the expectation of y today.

For the purposes of explaining the tremendous rise in franchise prices in the last two decades, the important feature of adaptive expectations is that franchise prices can grow at a faster rate than the riskless market rate of return, even with positive profits. Consider a new television contract negotiated by the league cartel that promises higher televisions for each owner[46]. If television revenues increase each year by a constant rate for the owner, the franchise value will rise each year by the same rate. This result was demonstrated in the previous section. Assume the new TV contract raises TV revenues by a higher annual rate than the old contract. If owners immediately adjust their future profit expectations to take into account the higher TV revenues, franchise prices will increase immediately by the discounted value of all future revenue increases. The

---

[46] The NHL television contract for Canadian rights with Rogers Communications signed in 2013 garnered the league $5.23 billion (C$) over 12 years, the largest single media contract in NHL history.

rate of franchise price growth will also increase immediately to reflect the higher future rate of return.

Figure 4.9 demonstrates the adjustment in franchise prices[47]. With adaptive expectations, expectations of future profit growth adjust gradually to the news of a new TV contract. During the period of adjustment, franchise prices can rise at a faster rate than the new rate of profit growth if the adjustment coefficient α is close to one. The magnitude of α is affected by the historical behavior of profits. If profits are smooth and predictable, α will be close to one since expectations will be formed using the most current information. On the other hand, if profits are volatile and difficult to predict, α will be closer to zero since the most current values of profit will be unreliable.

Can the adaptive expectations approach explain the rapid increase in franchise values during the last two decades? It seems unlikely. Unexpected profits from TV contracts, endorsement deals and ticket sales would have to rise at a high rate for two decades, and still be rising in the near future. In addition, the adjustment coefficient α would have to be close to one, indicating smooth, predictable profits in the past. The period of the 1960's and 1970's was not a period of smooth, steady profits due to expansion and the emergence of rival leagues. Statistical methods using multiple regressions would be needed to make any firm conclusions.

---

[47] This figure is taken from Quirk and Fort (1997).

Franchise value ($)

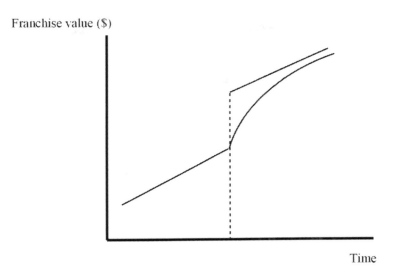

Time

Figure 4.9
With adaptive expectations, expectations of future profit growth adjust gradually to the news of a new TV contract. During the period of adjustment, franchise prices can rise at a faster rate than the new rate of profit growth if the adjustment coefficient α is close to one.

4.7 Bubbles in Franchise Prices

The explosive rate of increase of franchise values in the 1980's and 1990's is difficult to explain using the certainty model of asset prices, or the uncertainty model with adaptive expectations. A recent literature has developed to explain erratic movements of exchange rates and stock market prices using models of "speculative bubbles". A speculative bubble is a prolonged movement of an asset price above or below its "fundamental" value. The fundamental value of an asset is determined by underlying economic variables, which should determine an equilibrium price for the asset. The fundamental value of an exchange rate might be determined by its purchasing power parity value; the fundamental value of a common stock by the discounted value of future dividends.

Economics suggests three general requirements for the existence of a bubble.

1. Bubbles cannot occur for assets that have a known terminal value in the future.
2. Bubbles occur when the current price of the asset is a function of the expected future price of the asset.
3. All bubbles burst eventually.

To prove the first requirement, consider a common stock that will be retired in five years for a known price of $100. Next assume that the stock is traded once per year and the price is determined by demand and supply. At the end the fourth year, the last trade takes place before retirement of the stock. What will be the price of the stock? The last trader will only pay an amount equal to the discounted value of the terminal price (discounted by the market rate of interest for one year). She will not pay more, since that guarantees a loss on the trade. She will not pay less, since the seller will not accept less in payment. The argument can be extended back in time to the first trade at the end of year one. Hence the stock price will never deviate from the discounted present value of the selling price for the current buyer. A bubble cannot occur.

It is often the case that the current price of a financial asset reacts to changes in expectations of its future price. Sometimes this can cause drastic and sudden changes in current asset prices. A recent example is the popularity of so-called "pump and dump" stock market ploys by internet scam artists[48]. These scrupulous individuals set up web sites with realistic, well-researched, but bogus investor alerts concerning imminent price

---

[48] "Stock Scams Proliferate on the Web", J. Yaukey, USA Today, 2002.

changes to fairly unknown stocks. Innocent investors are encouraged to buy the stock immediately, driving up the stock price, while the scam artists sell their shares at the higher prices for large profits. This sort of false news is illegal according to Securities and Exchange Commission (SEC) laws in the United States. In economics, the increase in the stock price is described as self-fulfilling and is only driven by expectations that are incorrect.

Was the rise in franchise prices during the 1980's and 1990's due to speculative bubbles? Statistical tests exist for the presence of bubbles in asset prices, but they go well beyond the scope of this book. Detailed data for annual franchise values are not available either. It seems likely however, that bubbles account for at least some of the rapid appreciation in franchise values. Nominal riskless interest rates had either been falling or holding steady for most of the mid-1980's through the 1990's. Figure 4.10 plots the London Interbank Offer Rate (LIBOR), a sort of world interest rate, for the period 1970-95. For the 1981-95 period, LIBOR was falling, though somewhat erratically[49]. This would imply a rising value for r in (4.1). For instance, from a high value of $1/(1.16) = 0.86$ in 1981, to a low value of $1/(1.035) = 0.966$ in 1993. This is an annual appreciation rate in a of just less than one percent which is far short of the annual rate of franchise value appreciation.

Casual evidence of bubbles in franchise values can be found through inspection of the arbitrage condition (4.4). With r falling on the average through the 1981-95 period, and teams making positive profits for the most part, which increased through the period, franchise prices should

---

[49] LIBOR is a nominal interest rate. Real interest rates subtract some measure of expected inflation. This is not done here since the rate of increase of franchise prices is also nominal and subtracting the same inflation rate from both would make no difference.

have been falling. Only a speculative bubble could account for the rapid increase in franchise values, although formal statistical testing is needed to add more evidence.

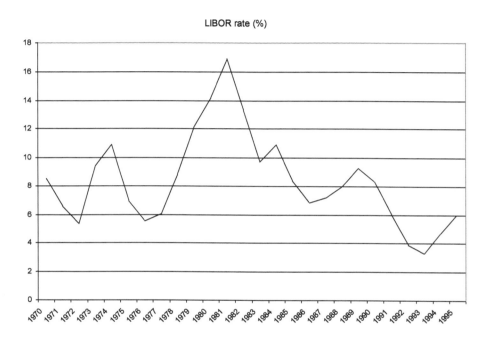

Figure 4.10

London Interbank Offer Rate, 1970-95. Source: World Bank.

Brief Review of Concepts

- In an adaptive expectation process, expectations of current variables adjust gradually to changes in the variable last period. The larger the adjustment coefficient, α, the faster expectations adjust.
- Franchise values could increase rapidly if expectations adjust in an adaptive way. A lucrative new TV contract raises future profits,

but expectations of future profits do not rise by the same amount immediately.

Focus Box: Anatomy of a Failure: The Phoenix Coyotes.

The Winnipeg Jets of the World Hockey Association (WHA) joined the National Hockey League in 1978 along with three other successful WHA clubs. Playing in the small and antiquated Winnipeg Arena proved profitless for the Jets, although the team enjoyed some success on the ice. The unwillingness of the city of Winnipeg to build the club a new arena resulted in the relocation of the club to Phoenix in 1996 and a new name, the Coyotes. The club played its games in the America West arena in downtown Phoenix to decent crowds, but never above the league average. The club accepted a free lease agreement in a new arena constructed in the city of Glendale, a suburb of the Phoenix area. Things went from average to worse. The club enjoyed little success on the ice and crowds were sparse, despite the partial ownership and coaching of Wayne Gretzky. At the end of the 2008-09 season, the Coyotes ranked 28th out of 30 teams in the NHL in attendance, drawing 14,875 per game.

On May 5, 2009, Coyotes owner Jerry Moyes filed for Chapter 11 bankruptcy without consulting with the NHL Board of Governors. The NHL promptly dismissed Moyes as owner of the club and took over daily operations. Moyes claimed that the club had lost over $60 million over the previous five seasons and the NHL did not dispute this. With Moyes effectively out of the picture, Judge Redfield T. Baum ordered that the club be put up for sale to pay off its creditors. Initially the NHL took little interest until an old foe entered the bidding. Jim Balsillie, CEO of Research in Motion, Inc., tendered a bid of $212.5 million under the condition that the club be relocated to the city of Hamilton. Balsillie had previously bid on the struggling Nashville Predators under the same condition and lost his case at the objection of the NHL. Forbes reports an estimated value of the club at $142 million in 2008 making Balsillie's offer very attractive. The NHL rejected the relocation condition by a 26-0 vote of its owners, and seeked its own bidders for the club, including Chicago White Sox and Bulls owner Jerry Reinsdorf, the Aquilini family that owns the Vancouver Canucks, movie mogul Jerry Bruckheimer, oil tycoon Max Chambers, former Montreal Canadiens owner George Gillett and a half-dozen or so others. All stops had to be pulled out by the NHL to prevent relocation of the club, yet Balsillie increased his offer to $242 million on September 7, 2009. That offered was rejected in favor of ownership by the NHL. The club was finally sold in 2013 to Renaissance Sports and Entertainment, a group of Canadian investors for $170 million.

Why did the NHL elite oppose the relocation to Hamilton so vehemently? The club is still losing money and will continue to do so in Phoenix, but the NHL brass is more interested in promoting the league in the US, already having a solid foundation in Canada. One more Canadian team will not move a major television deal forward in the US, which the NHL so desperately needs.

Test Your Understanding

1. Consider three teams that operate in the new 30 team North American lacrosse league: the Los Angeles Hackers, the Minnesota Bulldogs and the Winnipeg Threshers. After its first year of operations, total local revenue from all 30 teams is a modest $150 million. The local revenues for the Hackers, Bulldogs and Threshers are $15 million, $5 million and $2 million respectively. The new league owners voted at the inception of the league to use a revenue sharing system where each team contributes one-third of its local revenue into a central fund that is distributed evenly among all 30 clubs at the end of the season.

a) What will be the amounts contributed by the Hackers, Bulldogs and Threshers? What will be the size of the central fund and how much will each of the three teams receive back from the fund?

b) What is the average local revenue in the league? Considering your results in part a, can you think of a rule to determine if a team will be a net payer into the fund or a net receiver?

2. Calculate the annual rates of franchise value appreciation for the hypothetical purchases and sales given in the table below.

Team and owner	Purchase price	Sale price
St. Louis Robins, Evelyn Cash	$80 million, 1995	$250 million, 2006
Baltimore Nitro, Steve Sample	$125 million, 2001	$190 million, 2010
Edmonton Riggers, Joe Johnson	$60 million, 1990	$180 million, 2005

a) Which of the owners had the highest annual return?

b) Suppose each of the owners could have earned the following annual returns in their next best investment opportunities: Cash – 8%, Sample – 10%, Johnson – 12%. Which of the owners did the best investing in the sports team now?

3. Monique Diamond-Barnes inherited $350 million from her late husband Biff Barnes and has decided to use some of the money to purchase an NBA team so that she can use the team to market her line of expensive perfumes. She is considering purchasing a team in Sacremento for an asking price of $300 million. As her accountant, Monique has asked you to estimate her potential profit from the club over the first five years of operation. You anticipate that annual revenues will be $200 million and annual operating costs will include $95 million in player expenses, $30 million in administrative expenses and $35 million in rental for the arena. The corporate tax rate on net income is 40%.

a) Compute the annual expected net income for the team before and after taxes. What is the annual rate of return as a percentage of the purchase price?

b) Monique doesn't think that the team will earn quite enough profit for her flailing perfume business. Can you think of a way to increase her after-tax annual rate of return? If so, compute it.

c) At the end of the first five years of operations, Monique is growing bored of being a basketball team owner, but might be convinced to have her spoilt son take over the team operations with Monique still retaining ownership. What are the options open to her son to do with the team?

4. Steve Stunning wants to purchase an MLS (Major League Soccer) team badly but he is trying to determine a good price to offer for a club. The club he is interested in buying has been earning a modest profit of $2 million per year for the last five years and this is expected to continue for the next five years. Steve has taken a course in sports economics and knows that the real money to be made is in selling the club at the end of the fifth season of his ownership. He thinks he can sell the club for $20 million in the future.

a) If the market rate of return is just 5%, what is the maximum price that Steve should offer to purchase the club?

b) If Steve defers the purchase for one year and sells the club after just four years for $20 million, what should be his maximum bid?

c) MLS just negotiated a new TV deal that promises to increase annual profits by $500,000 for each club. What price should Steve offer now assuming the scenario in part b?

Chapter 5
Maintaining the Appearance of Competition: Parity in League Play

For the true sportsperson, the notion of "fair play" rises above all other pursuits in playing sports. The spectacle of a powerful team beating up on a weak team seems unfair and not in the best interests of sport. Others do not share this belief, particularly those fans that benefit from a home team with a long record of victories. But for those fans who suffer with watching a perennial loser, interest will wane and the team could go broke. This makes the league itself unstable, jeopardizing its future profitability, particularly from television, media and promotions revenue. Economics does not have much to say on the notion of fairness. There are strands of economics that focus on the equity of taxation, earnings differentials among the sexes, and income distribution between the rich and poor, among other topics in welfare economics. Since the fairness of a sporting contest is just a characteristic of a leisure good that consumers buy (tickets), the sorts of economic analyses used for the traditional topics in welfare economics do not apply.

Instead we focus on the economics of encouraging evenly matched teams in a professional sports league in order to insure the stability of profits for the team owners. Is it in the owner's best interests to promote parity in a sports league? Obviously this will depend upon whether promoting parity increases profit. One may surmise that promoting parity is not profit-maximizing since the efforts to achieve parity, through luxury taxes, revenue sharing and other schemes discussed in the previous chapter, are usually only half-hearted attempts to help teams struggling at the gate, not on the field. However under certain conditions, the twin objectives of parity in play and profit-maximization go hand in hand. The important concepts in this chapter are listed below.

- Different casual measures of parity and some evidence through championships.

- A statistical measure of parity called the "idealized standard deviation" and the theory behind its use. This measure of parity is computed for the four professional sports leagues over the last two decades.

- A simple model of a two-team league is developed to explore efforts to promote parity. These include revenue sharing, a reserve clause, free agency, cash player sales, a salary cap and a luxury tax.

5.1 Casual measures of parity

Parity can be described as insuring that a small minority of teams do not dominate the results in a league in terms of winning contests. Nobody enjoys watching the same team win the league championship over and over again. Part of the attraction of professional sports is that the "underdog" team can beat the heavily favored team once in a while. If the outcome of the contest is a foregone conclusion, attendance will be sparse, even in the heavily favored team's home field. An informal measure of league parity is the number of different teams that have won the league championship over a period of time. Table 5.1 provides the two teams participating in the World Series since 1981. In the 1980's, no single team won the World Series more than once, although St. Louis appeared three times in the fall classic, while Oakland, Los Angeles and Philadelphia each appeared twice. In the 1990's, the New York Yankees and the Toronto Blue Jays each won the World Series twice, while Atlanta appeared four times and Cleveland appeared twice. Since the 2000 season, the New York Yankees and the St. Louis Cardinals each appeared four times with the Boston Red Sox and the San Francisco Giants each appearing three times. This might suggest some weak evidence that baseball is moving away from parity.

Team	World Series appearances
New York Yankees	2009, 2003, 2001, 2000, 1999, 1998, 1996, 1981
St. Louis Cardinals	2013, 2011, 2006, 2004, 1987, 1985, 1982
Atlanta Braves	1999, 1996, 1995, 1992, 1991
Philadelphia Phillies	2009, 2008, 1993, 1983
San Francisco Giants	2014, 2012, 2010, 2002, 1989
Boston Red Sox	2013, 2007, 2004, 1986
Oakland Athletics	1990, 1989, 1988
Detroit Tigers	2012, 2006, 1984
10 teams	2 appearances
10 teams	1 appearance

Table 5.1
World Series participants, 1981-2016. Source: www.baseball-reference.com

Table 5.2 provides the teams participating in the Stanley Cup final (NHL) since 1981. Judging by the number of multiple winners of the Stanley Cup, parity is much less evident in the NHL than in MLB. Since 1981, only ten teams have won the Stanley Cup with the Edmonton Oilers winning five championships, the New York Islanders winning four consecutive championships, and Detroit, Montreal and Pittsburgh each winning twice. In fact, if the list is extended back to 1970, the Montreal Canadiens won the Stanley Cup six times during the 1970's and the Philadelphia Flyers and Boston Bruins each won the cup twice.

Team	Stanley Cup appearances
Edmonton Oilers	2006, 1990, 1987, 1988, 1987, 1985, 1984, 1983
Detroit Red Wings	2009, 2008, 2002, 1998, 1997, 1995
New Jersey Devils	2012, 2003, 2001, 2000, 1995
New York Islanders	1984, 1983, 1982, 1981
Philadelphia Flyers	2010, 1997, 1987, 1985
Pittsburgh Penguins	2015, 2009, 2008, 1992, 1991
5 teams	3 appearances
9 teams	2 appearances
7 teams	1 appearance

Table 5.2
Stanley Cup champions, 1981-2016. Source: www.hockey-reference.com

Table 5.3 provides winners of the NBA championship since the 1981 season. During the decade of the 1980's, only four teams won the NBA championship: Los Angeles four times, Boston three times, Detroit twice and Philadelphia once. In fact, only seven teams participated in the NBA finals. The lack of parity indicated in the 1980's was worsened during the 1990's. Only 3 teams won the NBA championship, while ten teams participated in the finals. Since the 2000 season, three teams have appeared at least three times in the finals with the Los Angeles Lakers winning four championships and the San Antonio Spurs winning three. As we shall see later, the NBA is the worst offender of the four major North American leagues when it comes to promoting parity.

The number of championship winners provides evidence of who the elite teams are, but does not give any indication of how consistently the other teams in the league perform. In Table 5.4 data is provided for the NFL concerning the performances of all teams in the league. A team is classified according to its winning percentage (the number of games won as a percentage of all games played) as successful, poor or average. Parity would be indicated by a large number of average teams. After the NFL-AFL merger in 1970, parity did not exist with only five average teams. Gradually the number of average teams has increased to 13 by 1995, partly due to a change in scheduling in 1978, which pitted equally matched teams against each other, based on results from the previous season. By the 2010 season, the NFL had 32 teams with only six teams appearing in the average category. Yet the NFL is considered to have the most parity of the four professional North American leagues using statistical measures.

Team	NBA Finals appearances
Los Angeles Lakers	2008-10, 2004, 2000-02, 1991, 1987-89, 1982-85
Boston Celtics	2010, 2008, 1984-86, 1981
Chicago Bulls	1996-98, 1991-93
Detroit Pistons	2005, 2004, 1990, 1989, 1988
Houston Rockets	1995, 1994, 1986, 1981
Miami Heat	2013, 2012, 2011, 2006,
San Antonio Spurs	2007, 2005, 2003, 1999
3 teams	3 appearances
5 teams	2 appearances
6 teams	1 appearance

Table 5.3
Winners of NBA championship, 1981-2016. Source: http://www.basketball-reference.com

Season	Number of successful teams (0.600 or more)	Number of poor teams (0.400 or less)	Number of average teams ((0.401 – 0.599)
2014	12	10	10
2010	13	13	6
2006	8	9	15
2002	9	8	15
1995	8	7	13
1990	9	12	7
1985	11	8	9
1980	10	10	8
1975	9	12	8
1970	11	10	5

Table 5.4
Team success by winning percentage in the NFL Source: www.profootball-reference.com

5.2 A Formal Definition of Parity

We can define parity more formally using a bit of statistics. Exact parity is achieved if the probability of any team beating any other team in the league is 0.5. In this case, predicting the victor of any game is like tossing a coin. It may not be in the best interests of team owners to aim for this extreme form of parity, and certainly not in the best interests of odds-makers. However any movement towards a 50-50 chance is a movement towards parity and thus we can use it as a working definition.

To operationalize this definition of parity, consider a random variable called X that can only take on two possible values, zero or one. A random variable means that it is impossible to accurately predict the outcome of X from a single draw – its result is random. This is called a Bernoulli random variable when only two outcomes are possible, after the famous statistician Jacob Bernoulli who first considered this type of problem and published his results in 1713 (after his death). Our Bernoulli random variable can be easily defined for our purposes. Suppose that a team receives a one for a victory and a zero for a loss (it makes no difference if these values are reversed) for a single game.

$$X = \begin{matrix} 1 \, for \, win \\ 0 \, for \, loss \end{matrix}$$

Let P be the probability of a team winning a game where $0 \leq P \leq 1$. If we exclude tie games, the probability of losing the game is just $1 - P$. Suppose we took one game from a season (the population in statistical language), and wanted to guess whether one of the teams will win or lose. This is called the *expected value* of the random variable X. The expected value is simply your best guess of the outcome of an experiment, in this case the experiment being the playing of the game. The expected value of a random variable, denoted $E(X)$, can be found by finding the weighted sum of the possible outcomes, the weights being the probability of each outcome occurring. In our case, the expected value of X for a single game is just equal to P, even though the actual value for X can only be a 0 or a 1.

$$E(X) = (1 \times P) + (0 \times (1 - P)) = P \qquad (5.1)$$

So if $P = 0.5$, then our best guess is just a tie game (even though we have excluded ties). Of course, we will make mistakes often since most games do not end in ties. The error in our guess is just the difference $X -$

$E(X)$, where X is the actual outcome of the game (0 or 1). For a single game, the error can take on the values 0.5 or -0.5 for a win or a loss.

A professional sports team plays many games over the course of a season and we would like to know how well we can predict game outcomes over many games, not just one game. The *variance* is a measure of the average squared error over many games. The larger the variance, the greater the variability in actual game outcomes from what is expected. The variance of a random variable X over N games is given below.

$$VAR(X) = \sum_{i=1}^{N}\big(X_i - E(X_i)\big)^2 \times P_i \qquad (5.2)$$

To understand (5.2) a little better, let's consider the variance of guessing the outcome of only one game, so $N = 1$. Remember that in a single game, X can only be 0 or a 1 and the probability that the team wins the game is just P.

$$VAR(X) = (1 - P)^2 \times P + (0 - P)^2 \times (1 - P) = (1 - P)(P(1 - P) + (0 - P)^2)$$

The second part of the above equation is found by factoring out the $(1 - P)$ term. The last bracketed term reduces to just P if you multiply everything out to eliminate the brackets. So the variance of the random variable X for a single game is just $P(1 - P)$. We refer to the *standard deviation* as the average prediction error, found by taking the square root of the variance.

$$SD(X) = \sqrt{P(1 - P)} \qquad (5.3)$$

If we assume that there is so much parity that the outcome of a single game is unpredictable, then $P = 0.5$ and $SD(X) = 0.5$. This makes sense since the standard deviation is the average prediction error for X, which for a single game is plus or minus 0.5 from the expected value of 0.5. Whether a league comes close to parity is based on an entire season of games, not just one, so we need to extend the analysis to a full season of games. The expected value of a random variable over N repeated trials, or games, is given by $E(X) = NxP$. So if a league had a 20 game season with exact parity (no ability to predict which team will win a single game), the expected number of wins for each team would be $NxP = 20x0.5 = 10$. However in the real world, injuries, weather and other unpredictable events can influence the outcomes of games so that each team wins more or fewer than 10 games, even though the teams are evenly matched. How much of a deviation from parity can we expect due to random occurrences? The average error in predicting winners can be found by finding the standard deviation of X over a season of N games for one team in the league.

$$VAR \left(\sum_{i=1}^{N} X_i \right) = P(1-P) + P(1-P) + P(1-P) + \cdots + P(1-P)$$
$$= N \times P(1-P)$$
$$SD(X) = P(1-P) \tag{5.4}$$

For a 20-game season, the standard deviation of wins or losses for all teams should be $\sqrt{20(0.5)(0.5)} = 2.24$ games. So, on the average, each team is expected to win between 7.76 and 12.24 games if the league has achieved perfect parity.

Winning percentages over a season are a more accurate measure of team performance when we are comparing leagues that play a different number of games in a season. What if we want to predict the winning percentage for a team over a season? The winning percentage for team i, w_i, is the number of wins for the season, $\sum_{i=1}^{N} X_i$, divided by the number of games, N, so $w_i = \sum_{i=1}^{N} X_i/N$. We already know that, over the course of a season of N games, the expected number of wins is just NP.[50] Substituting for X in the winning percentage, we find $E(w_i) = NP/N = P$. This is not a surprising result. If a team has a probability of 0.5 of winning any one game, it should win half of all of its games, so it's winning percentage for the season will also be equal to P. What will be the average error in predicting a team winning percentage for a season? It will be the standard deviation of the winning percentage, taken as the square root of its variance.

$$VAR(w_i) = VAR\left(\frac{\sum_{i=1}^{N} X_i}{N}\right) = \frac{1}{N^2} VAR\left(\sum_{i=1}^{N} X_i\right) = \frac{1}{N^2} NP(1-P) = \frac{P(1-P)}{N}$$

$$SD(w_i) = \sqrt{\frac{P(1-P)}{N}} \tag{5.7}$$

Equation (5.7) is often referred to as the *idealized standard deviation*. The idealized standard deviation for the season winning percentages of the four professional sports leagues, based on $P = 0.5$ and N = number of games in a regular season for one team is given in Table 5.4.

NFL	N = 16	0.125
NHL	N = 82	0.055
NBA	N = 82	0.055
MLB	N = 162	0.0393

Table 5.4

---

[50] For convenience we now drop the multiplication symbol "x" from our equations. When two variables appear beside each other, the assumption is they are multiplied.

Idealized standard deviation of winning percentages

These idealized standard deviations can be compared to the computed actual standard deviations of winning percentages for each league using historical data.[51] By taking the ratio of the actual to the idealized standard deviation (parity ratio), we can form a measure of the deviation from parity for each league. The higher the ratio above one, the larger is the actual standard deviation of winning percentages relative to what is ideal in the parity sense and the worse is league parity. An example how to do this is given in the practice problem below.

Analytical example: Measuring parity in the Canadian Football League (CFL).

Question: The final standings for the 2013 CFL season are given below.

Team	W	L	w_i
Calgary Stampeders	14	4	0.778
Saskatchewan Roughriders	11	7	0.611
B.C. Lions	11	7	0.611
Toronto Argonauts	11	7	0.611
Hamilton Tiger Cats	10	8	0.556
Montreal Alouettes	8	10	0.444
Edmonton Eskimos	4	14	0.222
Winnipeg Blue Bombers	3	15	0.167

Answer: The actual standard deviation of the winning percentages is computed using the formula for a variance.

$$VAR(w) = \frac{1}{8}[(0.778 - 0.5)^2$$
$$+ (0.611 - 0.5)^2$$
$$+ \cdots (0.167$$
$$- 0.5)^2]$$
$$= 0.0386$$
$$SD(w) = \sqrt{0.0386} = 0.1965$$

The idealized standard deviation is:

Compute the parity ratio for the CFL.

---

[51] The actual variance of the winning percentages (not a single winning percentage as in (5.6) is computed using $VAR(w) = \frac{1}{K}\sum_{i=1}^{K}(w_i - 0.5)^2$. This makes use of the property that all of the winning percentages must average to 0.5. The constant K is the number of teams in the league.

208

$$\sqrt{\frac{0.5(1-0.5)}{18}} = 0.1179$$

So the parity ratio is $0.1965/0.1179$ = 1.667. Since the ratio is above 1, we can surmise that the CFL had far from perfect parity.

A parity ratio for a single season for only one professional league is not very informative. Things become more interesting when parity ratios are compared across the four North American professional sports leagues for different decades. These numbers are presented in Table 5.5. The worst offender by far is the NBA with the highest average parity ratio for all of the three decades by quite a wide margin. This is despite the use of soft salary caps in the NBA. The NFL has achieved the greatest level of parity with the NHL and MLB in between. The NFL uses a hard salary cap and revenue sharing to contain player costs and redistribute local revenues to small market teams.

	Idealized SD	Average parity ratio		
		1980-89	1990-99	2000-2009
MLB (AL)	0.039824	1.753	1.739	2.026
MLB(NL)	0.039824	1.687	1.757	1.683
NBA	0.05522	2.766	2.909	2.726
NHL	0.05522	2.040	1.829	1.606
NFL	0.125	1.506	1.502	1.581

Table 5.5
Average parity ratios by decade.

Brief Review of Concepts

- League parity can be casually measured by the number of distinct champion teams, the number of poor, average and good teams, etc.
- A better measure of parity is the idealized standard deviation and the parity ratio. The NFL seems the closest to achieving parity, while the NBA is the farthest.

Focus Box: The NBA Anomaly

The NBA has consistently demonstrated far less parity in winning percentages than the other three professional sports leagues in North America. Why is this? Recent evidence suggests that a lack of parity is inherent in the rules of the game of basketball.[52] Each shot is a scoring opportunity with a probability of scoring points (three points for a 3-point shot, two points for a field goal and one point for a free throw). NBA teams averaged 80 field goal attempts per game, 18 3-point shot attempts and 24 free throw attempts in the 2010-11 season. NHL teams averaged only 30 shot attempts in the same season. The law of large numbers (LLN) hypothesis suggests that with so many more scoring attempts, NBA games will have far fewer unexpected results – that is, the better-quality team will tend to win a contest with greater frequency than for NHL teams. The upshot is that the distribution of season winning percentages in the NBA will much more closely approach its "true" distribution of team qualities compared to the NHL.

When reducing the number of scoring attempts in the NBA to those observed in the NHL using a simulation model, the parity ratio for

---

[52] D. Rockerbie, "Exploring Inter-League Parity in North America: the NBA Anomaly", *Journal of Sports Economics*, 17(3), 2014, 286-301.

210

the NBA closely matched the parity ratio in the NHL. The results suggest that it is tricky to use parity ratios to make comparisons across different sports.

5.3 Policies to Promote League Parity: A Simple Model of a Two-Team League

This section sets up a simple model of a two-team league that will be useful in analyzing league imposed policies to promote parity, such as salary caps, revenue sharing and a reserve clause system. The original paper[53] is El Hodiri and Quirk (1971), however the exposition here is greatly simplified from the original paper. Call the two teams team A and team B. Team A is situated in a high revenue area where attendance is strong and fan interest is high. Team B is situated in a low revenue area where attendance and fan interest is significantly weaker. We will assume that each team can keep all of the revenues for its home games, but receives none of the opponent's revenues for its away games. That is, the two teams do not share revenues in any way. We will also ignore any revenues that are received from national agreements such as television and licensing. Our assumption will be that total revenue increases as a team's winning percentage increases, but at a diminishing rate. In our previous chapters, a team's output was considered to be ticket sales, but here we will redefine output as a winning percentage. Higher ticket sales are the result of higher team output, but tickets are not the output themselves.

Its smaller market puts Team B at a disadvantage in terms of its total revenue curve, depicted in Figure 5.1. Total revenue for Team B is increasing with winning percentage based on the assumption that team

---

[53] El-Hodiri, Mohamed and James Quirk, "An Economic Model of a Professional Sports League", *Journal of Political Economy*, 79, November 1971, 1302-1319.

success generates higher revenues, however the payoff to success is much higher for Team A since its total revenue curve lies above the total revenue curve for Team B. Competing for revenues is a zero-sum game for the two teams: if one team wins more games and receives more revenues, the other team must lose more games and receive less revenues.

In Figure 5.1, the slope of both total revenue curves is positive but decreasing, meaning that the marginal revenues of both teams, MR_A and MR_B, must be positive but falling. The MR curves reach zero when the total revenue curves have zero slope, or, are flat at their peaks. Since the total revenue curve for Team A is steeper than that for Team B at any winning percentage, $MR_A > MR_B$ at any winning percentage.

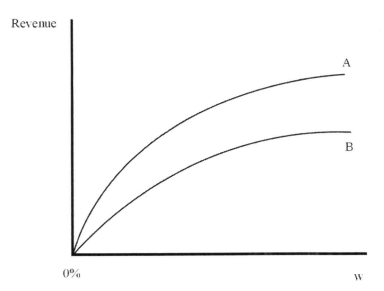

Figure 5.1

Team A faces a higher total revenue curve than Team B since Team A's home city is a higher revenue market than Team B. Output is winning percentage in the long run.

There is an optimal winning percentage for each team that maximizes its total revenue given the negative effect of its winning on the other team. This winning percentage also maximizes total revenue for the league. To find this optimal winning percentage, we must consider the marginal revenue curve for each team, shown in Figure 5.2. Recall that the marginal revenue of Team A (MR_A) is the change in its total revenue when it's winning percentage (output) rises by 1 percentage point (one unit of output). It is the slope of the total revenue curve for Team A at every winning percentage.

To find the optimal winning percentage for both teams, Figure 5.3 reverses the axes for Team B so that the marginal revenues intersect. The winning percentage for Team A increases as we move to the right on the horizontal axis, while the winning percentage for Team B increases as we move to the left on the horizontal axis. This is so because the two winning percentages must add up to 1: as one team loses, the other team wins.

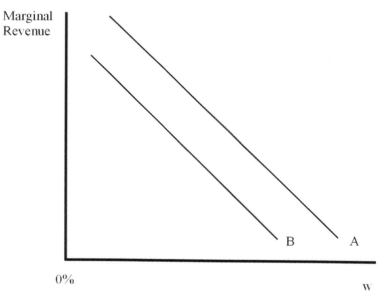

Figure 5.2

Since the slope of the total revenue curve for Team A is everywhere steeper than the slope for Team B, Team A's marginal revenue curve lies above Team B's marginal revenue curve.

The two teams will compete for and hire quality players up to the point where the marginal revenues are equated. The optimal winning percentage for Team A is w_A* and the optimal winning percentage for Team B is $w_B* = 1 - w_A*$. The marginal cost of acquiring players will be the same at $MC*$ for both teams. This is because both teams are monopolists in their local markets so they maximize profit where their marginal revenue just equals their marginal cost and both marginal revenues will be the same. In fact, the optimal winning percentages will always be w_A* and w_B* regardless of the initial allocation of quality players to each team[54] Why is this so? Suppose $w_A < w_A*$ so that Team A wins fewer games and Team B wins more games. Since $MR_A > MC* > MR_B$, Team A will buy quality players from Team B to improve its winning percentage and total revenue until w_A* is achieved. If $w_A > w_A*$ then $MR_B > MC* > MR_A$ and Team B will purchase quality players from Team A, improving its winning percentage until w_A* is again achieved. This will occur regardless of which team starts out with the better players.

The higher revenue teams will generally end up with the best quality, and highest salary, players. Of course, for the model to work, player sales by owners must be allowed in the league so that owners can freely move players around. North American sports leagues generally do not approve of player sales, except for minor league players or players of lesser talent. European soccer leagues do allow player sales subject to court

---

[54] This is called the Coase Theorem in economics. The original paper is Ronald Coase, "The Problem of Social Cost", *Journal of Law and Economics*, 3, October 1960, 1-44. The Coase Theorem is often cited when discussing pollution, crime and other negative externalities in economics. Interestingly, the idea appeared first in J. Rottenberg, "The Baseball Players' Labor Market, *Journal of Political Economy*, June 1956, 253-256.

imposed restrictions and conditions in the players bargaining agreement with each league.

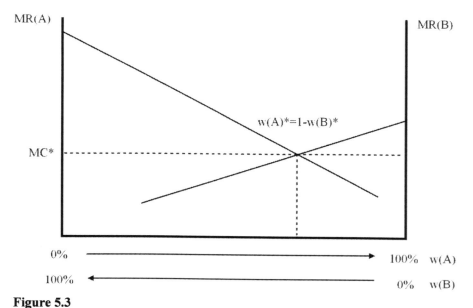

Figure 5.3

The optimal winning percentage for Team A and Team B is found where the two marginal revenue curves intersect. Marginal cost of player salaries is the same for both teams at *MC**. Total league revenues are maximized.

Player sales were never common in baseball, but were tolerated over its history. Mike "King" Kelly was sold to Boston from the Chicago White Sox for $10,000 in 1887; Dizzy Dean was sold to the Chicago Cubs from the St. Louis Cardinals for $150,000 in 1938. Player sales by the Philadelphia Athletics in the 1920's and 1930's devastated the team's performance but made money for the owner. The team moved to Kansas City in 1952, then to Oakland in 1968. Charlie Finley, then owner of the Oakland Athletics, tried to sell Joe Rudi and Rollie Fingers to the Boston Red Sox in 1975 for a total of $2 million, then he tried to sell Vida Blue to the New York Yankees for $1.5 million in 1976. Bowie Kuhn, the then commissioner of baseball, vetoed both of the sales arguing that they were not in the best interests of baseball. This ruling effectively ended large player sales in baseball and set the trend for the other sports leagues[55].

Player sales are commonplace in Europe under the transfer system, but rare in North America. This could be due to the differences in the tax treatments of player sales between North America and Europe. In the United States and Canada, capital gains tax must be paid on the difference between the player's cash value and the player's depreciated book value (see chapter 4). This makes a player trading system more attractive since tax need not be paid when a player is traded (the book value of the player drops to zero for the old team and rises to the new salary level for the new team).

It is even more efficient in North America for team owners to trade quality players for draft choices since this allows the owner to draft the right player for the empty position (avoiding a "double coincidence of wants"). Can a reverse order of finish draft promote league parity? In this system, the highest draft positions are awarded to the teams that have the lowest winning percentages from the previous season. Successful teams receive low order draft picks and unsuccessful teams receive high draft picks with the intent to make the league more competitive. To prevent teams from using strategic behavior on their order of finish, some leagues (NBA, NHL) use a lottery system for assigning draft picks where the poorer performing teams have a higher probability of obtaining high draft picks in the lottery since they have more "balls in the urn" from which team names are drawn. Regardless of the method of assigning draft picks, if draft picks can be easily traded by owners, economics predicts that any sort of draft system that favors poorer performing teams will have no effect

---

[55] The only exception being the sale of Wayne Gretzky from the Edmonton Oilers to the Los Angeles Kings of the NHL for $10 million in 1988.

on league parity. Drafted players will be eventually playing for the teams that value them the most since those teams will trade for them or sign them as free agents.

The model also works if players are allowed to move freely between teams in search of the higher salary, rather than have owners sell them to other owners. Under such a system of complete free agency, players receive the surplus from their superior abilities instead of the owners under cash sales. In the transfer system in Europe, the owners keep the surplus revenue generated by the players and use it buy players. In this way, the surplus is kept among the owners. One would think that European soccer players could negotiate a free agency system closer to that used in North America, however players in Europe have difficulty organizing due to the large number of leagues and countries in which they can play, each with its own soccer association.

Brief Review of Concepts

- The simple two-team league model predicts that teams and the league will maximize profits where marginal revenues are equated. This determines an optimal team quality and winning percentage for each team. Any deviation from this position reduces team and league profits.
- Cash sales of players insure that the optimum winning percentages are reached. Large market teams will have higher winning percentages than small market teams.
- The model predicts that players will eventually be allocated to the teams that value them the most. This is an efficient outcome, but will not promote league parity.

5.3.1 A Simple Algebraic Model

Let's assume that a club's revenue is determined by its local market size (m) and its winning percentage (w) in the revenue function below.[56] We refer to team A throughout but the revenue function for team B is the same form.

$$R_A = m_A[(1 - \beta)w_A + \beta w_A(1 - w_A)] \qquad (5.8)$$

An increase in the local market size shifts the revenue function upward for a given winning percentage due to the ability to draw more fans and charge higher ticket prices. Inside the square bracket, revenue is a weighted average ($0 \leq \beta \leq 1$) of the team A winning percentage and the closeness of the contests it plays against team B. Generally, fans are drawn to games where the outcome is more uncertain or when teams' A and B are evenly matched. No fan of team A one wants to pay to see a lop-sided game in favor or against team A. Since $w_B = 1 - w_A$, the product of the two winning percentages reaches a maximum when $w_A = w_B = .5$ and the contribution of uncertainty of outcome to revenue will be the highest.

After collecting the w_A terms, (5.8) can be rewritten as

$$R_A = m_A w_A - \beta m_A w_A^2 \qquad (5.9)$$

We will assume that each team maximizes its profit by choosing a team stock of talent that results in a winning percentage given by the logistic function introduced in Chapter 2 $\left(w_A = \frac{t_A}{t_A + t_B}\right)$. The marginal

---

[56] The exposition here follows S. Kesenne, "Revenue Sharing and Absolute League Quality; Talent Investment and Talent Allocation", *Scottish Journal of Political Economy*, 62(1)" 2015: 51-58.

revenue for team A is given by $MR_A = \frac{\partial R_A}{\partial w_A}\frac{\partial w_A}{\partial t_A} = m_A(1 - 2\beta w_A)\left(-2\beta\frac{t_B}{(t_A+t_B)^2}\right)$.[57] Likewise the marginal revenue for team B is given by $m_B(1 - 2\beta w_B)\left(-2\beta\frac{t_A}{(t_A+t_B)^2}\right)$. Let's assume for simplicity that $\beta = 0.5$ for both teams.[58] We have already shown that league revenue is maximized where $MR_A = MR_B = c$ Simplifying this gives the league equilibrium condition below.

$$-m_A(1 - w_A)\frac{t_B}{(t_A + t_B)^2} = -m_B(1 - w_B)\frac{t_A}{(t_A + t_B)^2}$$

$$m_A w_B^2 = m_B w_A^2 \text{ or } \frac{w_A}{w_B} = \sqrt{\frac{m_A}{m_B}} \tag{5.10}$$

The extent to which the winning percentage for team A rises above 0.5 simply depends upon the square root of the ratio of the market sizes. The ratio of the winning percentages is referred to as the competitive balance ratio. What will be the distribution of talent? Using the logistic contest success function in (5.10) gives

$$\frac{t_A}{t_B} = \sqrt{\frac{m_A}{m_B}} \tag{5.11}$$

The ratio of the profit-maximizing talent stocks is just equal to the square root of the ratio of the local market sizes.[59]

---

[57] Maximizing profit by choosing a winning percentage alone implicitly assumes that $\frac{\partial w_A}{\partial t_A} = 1$. This is not true with the logistic contest success function.

[58] If $\beta = 0.5$, then $MR_A = 0$ when $w_A = 1$ or 100%. This thought to be a desirable property.

[59] This result assumes an open talent market where each team can acquire all the talent it desires without increasing the market wage rate for talent. The closed

Analytical example: Determining profit-maximizing winning percentages.

Question: The revenue equations for two teams, A and B, in a two-team league are given below.

$$R_A = 150w_A - 150\beta w_A^2$$
$$R_B = 100w_B - 100\beta w_B^2$$

Solve for the optimal winning percentages of team that maximize both team and league profits. Also compute the marginal cost of winning.

Answer: Using the equilibrium condition in (5.10) assuming $\beta = 0.5$ gives

$$\frac{w_A}{w_B} = \sqrt{\frac{150}{100}} = 1.225$$

Now solve for the optimal winning percentage for Team A.

$$w_A = 1.225w_B = 1.225(1 - w_A)$$
$$w_A + 1.225w_A = 1.225$$
$$2.225w_A = 1.225$$
$$w_A = \frac{1.225}{2.225} = 0.551$$

Team B plays in the smaller market. Its winning percentage is $1 - 0.551 = 0.449$. Marginal cost can be found using the marginal revenue equation for either team from (5.10).

$$MC = m_A w_B^2 = 150(0.551^2) = 45.5$$

5.3.2 Promoting League Parity with a Reserve Clause

A reserve clause used to be part of the standard player's contract in MLB and was adopted by the NHL, NBA and NFL upon their creation. During the early years of these leagues, it was common for players and owners to agree on one-year contracts that were renegotiated in between seasons. The clause stated that if a player and an owner could not reach an

---

talent market result is more difficult to derive, and we do not cover it here. See R. Driskill and J. Vrooman, "It's Not Over Till the Fat Lady Sings: Game-Theoretic Analyses of Sports Leagues", *Journal of Sports Economics*, 17(4), 2016: 354-376.

220

agreement on the player's salary for the upcoming season, the player could be "reserved" by the owner to play the upcoming season at the salary earned in the just finished season. The reserve clause effectively bound the player to the owner for the player's career and prevented competitive bidding by owners for the player. Since player movement is not allowed, the player's salary can be kept well below the market value of the player to other teams. The reserve clause was removed in 1976 in MLB and the other three leagues quickly followed.

In Figure 5.4, the adoption of a reserve clause in our two-team league will lower salaries and have the effect of reducing the marginal cost of winning game from MC^* to MC^{**}. The marginal revenue lines are not affected since we will assume that fans are indifferent towards the reserve clause – they only care about the quality of the team on the field. If cash sales of players are allowed by the league, we can use some economic reasoning to show that w_A^* and w_B^* will still be the optimal winning percentages for Team A and Team B. Since Team A values talented players more than Team B, based on its higher marginal revenue from winning, Team A will find it profitable to purchase valued players from Team B. Team B will be happy to sell the players to Team A since the cash from the player sale is greater than the player's contribution to Team B's revenues (marginal revenue again).

Initially profits to each team will rise with lower salary costs but the optimal allocation of players will ultimately be identical to having no reserve clause with cash sales or unrestricted free agency. The marginal cost of winning will increase back to MC^* and excess profits will be dissipated. If cash sales are not allowed in a reserve clause system, there is no reason that w_A^* will be achieved by Team A. Perennial powerhouse teams could exist alongside perennial also-rans for long periods of time.

Players could be reallocated in the long run through sales of entire franchises if the divergence in revenues across teams is great enough.

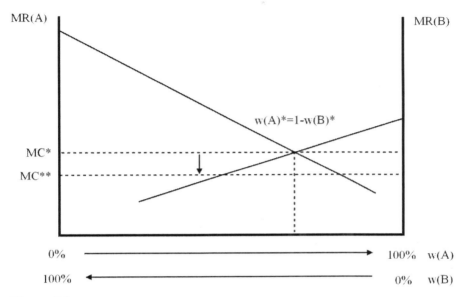

Figure 5.4
A reserve clause with cash sales, which reduce salaries in the long run, will still result in the same allocation of players as a system with no reserve clause.

5.3.3 Promoting League Parity with Revenue Sharing

In a revenue sharing system, home teams and visiting teams split the gate revenues using a league imposed percentage. The current revenue sharing systems in the NFL and MLB are pooled systems, whereas the old systems were gate revenue splits. Under the old system, in the NFL, the split was 60–40 in favor of the home team, while in MLB, the split was 80-20 in the American League and 95-5 in the National League. The NBA and the NHL use pooled revenue sharing systems that do not activate unless certain payroll conditions are met. Regardless of the type of system, revenue sharing is touted as allowing low revenue teams to compete for players with high revenue teams by redistributing revenues from high to low revenue teams. There is no doubt that revenue sharing helps leagues to maintain marginal teams. The two-team league model can be used to investigate if revenue sharing improves league parity. We will show that generally league parity will not improve but salaries may drop, increasing team profits.

In our two-team league model, it does not matter if the revenue sharing system we use is an old-fashioned gate sharing system or a modern pool type system, since with only two teams, each team will wind up with the same amount of revenue after sharing. We will use the pooled type system since it is what has been used for several decades. Suppose that the home team keeps a share α of its local revenues[60] and contributes the rest $(1-\alpha)$ to a central pool maintained by the league office.[61] The total revenue after revenue sharing for Team A (a superscript S denotes after revenue sharing) then depends partly on its own local revenue as well as the local revenue of Team B, and vice-versa. We will assume that the central fund is paid out evenly between the two teams.

$$R_A^S = \alpha R_A + \frac{(1-\alpha)(R_A+R_B)}{2} = \frac{1+\alpha}{2} R_A + \frac{1-\alpha}{2} R_B \qquad (5.12)$$

$$R_B^S = \frac{1+\alpha}{2} R_B + \frac{1-\alpha}{2} R_A \qquad (5.13)$$

The marginal revenue lines for Team A and Team B will change from those in Figure 5.2.

---

[60] Local revenues include all revenues that are not received from revenue sharing and sharing of league media revenues.

[61] In MLB each team contributes 31% of its local revenue to a central pool. In addition, contributions are made to a supplemental pool based on local market size. The contribution rate is 34% in the NFL and 50% in the NBA. Only the top ten revenue teams contribute to the central pool in the NHL with varying percentages that are small.

$$MR_A^S = \frac{1+\alpha}{2} MR_A + \frac{1-\alpha}{2} \frac{\partial R_B}{\partial w_B} \frac{\partial w_B}{\partial t_A} \qquad (5.14)$$

$$MR_B^S = \frac{1+\alpha}{2} MR_B + \frac{1-\alpha}{2} \frac{\partial R_A}{\partial w_A} \frac{\partial w_A}{\partial t_B} \qquad (5.15)$$

Why does $\frac{\partial R_B}{\partial w_B} \frac{\partial w_B}{\partial t_A}$ appear in (5.14)? If Team A increases its winning percentage by acquiring more talent, it will increase its total revenue by $(1+\alpha)/2\ MR_A$, its share of the its higher local revenue. However the local revenue for Team B will fall since its winning percentage falls by the same amount as the increase for Team A.[62] When Team A increases its winning percentage, it must absorb $(1-\alpha)/2$ of the fall in Team B's local revenue with revenue sharing. This means the marginal revenue for Team A (and Team B) is always less than it is without revenue sharing. This situation is depicted in Figure 5.5.

What happens to the optimal winning percentages when the league imposes revenue sharing, w_A* and w_B*, depends upon the magnitudes of the downward shifts in the marginal revenue curves for both teams. The team whose marginal revenue curve shifts down by less will increase its winning percentage from its winning percentage without revenue sharing. As drawn in Figure 5.5, both marginal revenue curves have shifted down by the same amount, leaving the optimal winning percentages unchanged. This is not a general result.[63] In fact it is easy to show in our algebraic model that revenue sharing *worsens* parity.

---

[62] Technically $\partial w_B / \partial w_A = -1$ due to the adding up property of the winning percentages.

[63] This so-called invariance proposition can be found by assuming that a one-unit increase in talent increases the team winning percentage by 1 percentage point. Algebraically, $\partial w_A / \partial t_A = 1$. See R. Fort, "Cross-Subsidization, Incentives, and Outcomes in Professional Team Sports Leagues", *Journal of Economic Literature*, 33(3), 1995, p. 1265-99 for this result. A good rebuttal is S. Szymanski,

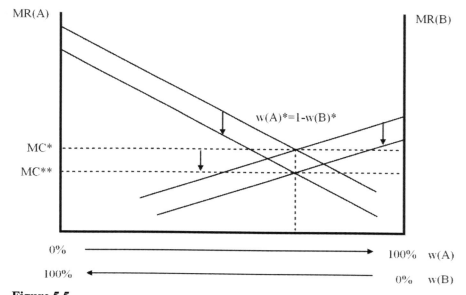

Figure 5.5
Revenue sharing lowers player salaries in general, but does not affect the optimal winning percentage for either team as drawn here.

Rewrite the revenue functions for Team A and Team B as $R_A = zw_A$ and $R_B = w_B$ where $z = m_A/m_B$ and $z > 1$ for simplicity (this will still result to (5.11)). Without revenue sharing, we can easily show that $t_A/t_B = z$, as before. We can use (5.12) and (5.13) to express team revenues after revenue sharing. The team owner will maximize profit after revenue sharing by choosing a stock of talent. The marginal revenues for Team A and Team B after revenue sharing are given below.[64]

$$MR_A^S = \frac{1+\alpha}{2} z \frac{\partial w_A}{\partial t_A} + \frac{1-\alpha}{2} \frac{\partial w_B}{\partial t_A} = \frac{1+\alpha}{2} z \frac{t_B}{(t_A+t_B)^2} - \frac{1-\alpha}{2} \frac{t_B}{(t_A+t_B)^2}$$

"Professional Team Sports are only a Game: The Walrasian Fixed-Supply Conjecture Model, Contest-Nash Equilibrium and the Invariance Principle, *Journal of Sports Economics*, 5, 2004, P. 111-26.
[64] You will need to use the quotient rule to differentiate the logistic contest success function. Don't worry, I will do it in class.

$$MR_B^S = \frac{1+\alpha}{2}\frac{\partial w_B}{\partial t_B} + \frac{1-\alpha}{2}z\frac{\partial w_A}{\partial t_B} = \frac{1+\alpha}{2}\frac{t_A}{(t_A+t_B)^2} - \frac{1-\alpha}{2}z\frac{t_A}{(t_A+t_B)^2}$$

Now set the marginal revenue equations equal to each other since they will both equal the common constant marginal cost of talent (assuming an open talent supply).

$$\frac{1+\alpha}{2}z\frac{t_B}{(t_A+t_B)^2} - \frac{1-\alpha}{2}\frac{t_B}{(t_A+t_B)^2} = \frac{1+\alpha}{2}\frac{t_A}{(t_A+t_B)^2} - \frac{1-\alpha}{2}z\frac{t_A}{(t_A+t_B)^2}$$

Simplifying gives

$$\frac{1+\alpha}{2}zt_B - \frac{1-\alpha}{2}t_B = \frac{1+\alpha}{2}t_A - \frac{1-\alpha}{2}zt_A$$

$$t_B\left[\frac{1+\alpha}{2}z - \frac{1-\alpha}{2}\right] = t_A\left[\frac{1+\alpha}{2} - \frac{1-\alpha}{2}z\right]$$

$$w_B\left[\frac{1+\alpha}{2}z - \frac{1-\alpha}{2}\right] = w_A\left[\frac{1+\alpha}{2} - \frac{1-\alpha}{2}z\right]$$

$$\frac{w_A}{w_B} = \frac{z(1+\alpha)-(1-\alpha)}{(1+\alpha)-z(1-\alpha)} \qquad (5.16)$$

It is easy to show that the ratio of the optimal winning percentages with revenue sharing in (5.16) is greater than that in (5.11) without revenue sharing. Hence competitive balance has worsened. The logic is simple. With greater revenue sharing, both teams must absorb some of the other team's losses in revenue when increasing talent, and hence winning percentage. The small market Team B must absorb a lot more since Team A is a large revenue team and loses a lot of revenue, so Team B marginal revenue shifts down by a lot.[65]

---

[65] Algebraically you can show that $\partial MR_A^S/\partial\alpha < \partial MR_B^S/\partial\alpha$ if $w_A > w_B$.

The two-team model assumes that revenue for each club is a positively associated with the quality of the home team only. In that case, the highest attendance and revenue should be garnered when the best team plays the poorest team at the better team's home stadium. Thus the model assumes that fans love a very lop-sided contest in favor of their home team. However, recent evidence[66] suggests that the opposite is usually the case: attendance and revenues are the highest when high quality teams play each other. Fans like to see a balanced contest where the outcome is not a sure thing.

We showed already that revenue sharing in the two-team model worsens parity. If revenue sharing does not shift the marginal revenue line for each club by the same amount, competitive balance will be improved for the team with the *smaller* downward shift. Is there ever a case where revenue sharing improves parity? Yes. If attendance and revenues are a positive function of the quality of *both* teams instead of just the home team, revenue sharing can lead to an improvement in quality and revenues for the small market team[67]. Suppose we consider a club that operates in such a small market that increases in team quality improves road attendance more than they increase home attendance.[68] Revenue sharing allows the small market club to receive a percentage of the road revenue that it's talent generates at the expense of giving up the same percentage of its smaller home revenue to the visiting club. In this case, total revenue

---

[66] T. Bruggink and J. Eaton, "What Takes Me Out to the Ball Game? A Game-by-Game Attendance Model for Major League Baseball" in Baseball Economics: Current Research, J. Fizel, L. Hadley and E. Gustafson, eds., Greenwood Publishing Group, 1996.

[67] D. Marburger, "Gate Revenue Sharing and Luxury Taxes in Professional Sports", *Contemporary Economic Policy*, April 1997, 114-123.

[68] We might refer to this as the Expos situation after the Montreal Expos of MLB. A more recent example might be the Tampa Bay Rays of MLB. Despite the Rays being in playoff contention for the last five seasons, attendance is among the lowest in MLB.

curve for Team B in Figure 5.1 *shifts up* for the small market club causing its marginal revenue curve to *shift upward*. The result is that the optimal winning percentage for the small market club will *increase* since it will acquire more talent to benefit from its large effect on road revenues. The league will move towards parity. Unfortunately for the players, salaries will still decrease since the shift down in marginal revenue for the large market club will overwhelm the upward shift in marginal revenue for the small market club.

There is a growing literature of research that considers team owners with objectives that differ from profit-maximization. It could be that owners only care about winning and will acquire expensive talent to do so as long as the club breaks even financially. Kesenne (2000) built a two-team model with this assumption in mind and found that revenue sharing improved league parity.[69] Vrooman (2009) used the same assumption with a slightly different revenue model and found that the invariance proposition still held.[70]. Unfortunately the economic models of sports leagues still do not offer any firm conclusions on the effects of revenue sharing.

Analytical example: Determining profit-maximizing winning percentages with revenue sharing.

Question: Consider the same two-team league as in the previous example. Each team contributes 30% of its local revenues to a pooled revenue sharing plan that is

Answer: Using the equilibrium condition in (5.16) assuming $\beta = 0.5$, $\alpha = 0.7$, and $z = \frac{150}{100} = 1.5$ gives

---

[69] Kesenne, S. (2000). "Revenue sharing and competitive balance in team sports", *Journal of Sports Economics*, 1(1), 56-65.
[70] Vrooman, J. (2009). "Theory of the perfect game: Competitive balance in monopoly sports leagues". *Review of Industrial Organization*, 34(1), 5-44

228

distributed evenly at the end of the playing season.

$$\frac{w_A}{w_B} = \frac{1.5(1 + 0.7) - (1 - 0.7)}{(1 + 0.7) - 1.5(1 - 0.7)} = 1.8$$

Solve for the optimal winning percentages of team that maximize both team and league profits. Also compute the marginal cost of winning.

Now solve for the optimal winning percentage for Team A.

$$w_A = 1.8w_B = 1.8(1 - w_A)$$
$$w_A + 1.8w_A = 1.8$$
$$2.8w_A = 1.8$$
$$w_A = \frac{1.8}{2.8} = 0.643$$

Team B plays in the smaller market. Its winning percentage is $1 - 0.643 = 0.357$. Marginal cost will be equal to either team's marginal revenue at the league equilibrium. Using the equation for marginal revenue one line prior to (5.16) gives

$$w_A \left[\frac{1 + \alpha}{2} - \frac{1 - \alpha}{2}z\right] = MC$$
$$0.643\left[\frac{1 + 0.7}{2} - \frac{1 - 0.7}{2}1.8\right] = 0.373$$

Multiply MC by $m_B = 100$ to make it comparable to the previous example.

The empirical evidence on whether revenue sharing improves, worsens or leaves parity unchanged is mixed with no firm conclusions. Solow and Krautmann (2007) estimate the effects on revenue sharing on parity by estimating marginal revenue functions for each club in MLB.[71] This was made possible by the release of club revenue data in the Blue Ribbon Panel report (Levin et al (2000)) originally convened by MLB Commissioner Bud Selig. They concluded that the expanded 1996 revenue sharing agreement that significantly increase the share of local revenue that

[71] Solow, J and A. Krautmann. (2007). Leveling the playing field or just lowering salaries? The effects of redistribution in baseball. *Southern Economic Journal*, 73(4), 947-58.

each club contributed to the central fund did not affect league parity despite significantly reducing the marginal revenue for each club. They also found that the same revenue sharing system did lower player salaries significantly. These results are consistent with the so-called *invariance proposition* that can be found in some theoretical models which states that revenue sharing will leave parity unaffected.

5.3.4 Promoting League Parity with a Salary Cap

The NBA, NHL and NFL use salary caps to insure a minimum level of profit for each team so the league can survive. The NBA has used a "soft cap" system since 1984. In this system, there is a league imposed maximum limit on the annual salary of each player, but there are many exemptions that allow clubs to exceed these salaries. The maximum limit increases the more seasons the player is employed in the league. Teams that exceed their salary cap after all of the exemptions are accounted for are subject to a 100% tax on the overage. The NBA salary cap for each team was $94.1 million for 2016-17, but almost every team spends more than the cap. The NFL has used a "hard cap" system since 1994. Each team faces a league imposed total payroll maximum, although any one player can earn any amount as long as the team payroll falls under the cap. The ceiling for the NFL cap is determined as a fixed percentage of projected league revenues for the coming season. For the 2017 season, the NFL has set a cap of $167 million for each team. The NHL also uses a hard salary cap for team payrolls, as well as a cap for individual salaries. The team payroll cap was $73 million for the 2016-17 season.

One often cited justification for a salary cap system is that smaller market teams will be able to compete for quality players in the free agent market. This should improve parity for the league. Using the simple two-team model, it can be shown that league parity may improve with a hard salary cap, but at the expense of lower team profits. In this case, the league may choose not to use salary caps to promote parity if it is trying to maximize profits.

In Figure 5.6, the optimal winning percentage of Team A is above 0.50 at w_A*. The marginal cost of winning is identical for both teams at $MC*$. The league now imposes a hard salary cap on each team, lowering the marginal cost of player salaries to $MC**$. Let's suppose that the general manager of each team acquires quality players until the salary cap $MC**$ is reached, so that each team has identical payrolls. This should distribute quality players fairly evenly across the two clubs so that league parity (a .500 winning percentage for each club) is reached at point A. However several problems exist at point B. First, neither team is maximizing profits where $MR_A = MR_B = MC**$ at point B. Team B, the lower revenue team, could raise its profits by spending *less* on quality players, losing more games, and moving to point A. Team A would win more games but would not be able to acquire the quality players given up Team B since it is already spending up to its salary cap, even though it would purchase talent from Team B since its marginal revenue is higher than Team B's at point B (point C is Team A's marginal revenue). This introduces inefficiencies in both the team market and the players market. A second problem is that league revenues are not being maximized at point B. All this brings into question why a hard salary cap would be enforced in the first place.

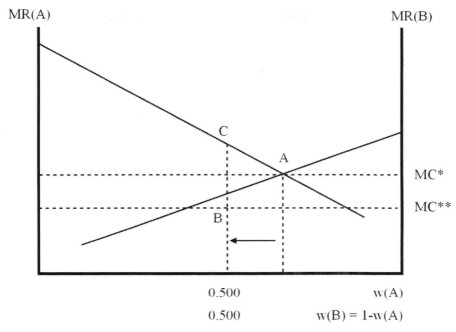

Figure 5.6
A league imposed salary cap at MC** does move Team A and B closer to, or just to, a 0.500 winning percentage. The cost is that league revenues are not maximized.

5.3.5 Promoting League Parity with a Luxury Tax

A luxury tax attempts to redistribute revenues from the richest clubs to the poorest clubs by imposing a tax on payrolls. Major league baseball adopted a luxury tax system in the early nineties and the NBA uses a similar system today. The computation of the luxury tax in baseball is quite straightforward. Any excess team salary over the threshold salary set out in the MLB collective bargaining agreement is subject to a tax paid to the league. The current systems sees that the tax rate escalates for repeat offenders, from 17.5% for first-time offenders to 50% for repeat offenders. The New York Yankees are the only team to be a repeat offender, so the tax is often referred to as the Yankees tax. As an example of the calculation of tax, the salary threshold in the 2013 season was $178 million. The New York Yankees total payroll for the 2013 season was $234 million. The tax owed by the Yankees owner was $28 million ((234 − 178)0.5). Since the luxury tax was instituted in its current form in 2003, the Yankees paid just over $250 million in tax through the 2013 season. The Los Angeles Dodgers had a slightly higher payroll than the Yankees in 2013 at $243 million, however the Dodgers were a first-time offender and paid a luxury tax of only $11.4 million. Computations for the luxury tax are deceiving since average annual player salaries are used for multi-year contracts, rather than the actual salaries paid. A player whose salary escalates or declines over the life of his contract will never actually receive the average in any year of the contract. Since the tax threshold increases every season along with escalating player salaries, the tax is relatively ineffective at holding team spending down.

In the two-team model, the effects of a luxury can be modeled by assuming that every team faces a payroll tax after the team reaches the league-imposed payroll threshold. To see how this affects parity in the two-team model, consider the large market Team A in Figure 5.7. To move down its marginal revenue line and increase its total revenue, Team A must increase its winning percentage. The only way to do this in the model is to acquire more talent and increase its payroll. At a threshold winning percentage we call w_A^T, the team payroll passes the payroll threshold and Team A pays a luxury tax on every dollar spent over and above the threshold, but not on any previous payroll spending up to the threshold. This will shift down the marginal revenue line for Team A since part of the revenue gained by increasing its winning percentage by one percentage point must be paid to the league as a tax. This creates a discontinuity in the marginal revenue line – the higher the tax rate, the greater the downward shift in the marginal revenue line.

Team B faces the same salary threshold as Team A, but it operates in a smaller market. What ultimately happens to league parity depends very much on at what winning percentage Team B hits the salary threshold. Since it is a small market team, it will not pay the same salaries as Team A for the same amount of talent – it cannot afford to. So it might hit the salary threshold at a much higher winning percentage than Team A, labelled as w_B^T in Figure 5.7. The tax has the effect of promoting league parity at the new point where the marginal revenues intersect, albeit at the cost of lower player salaries for Team A (its total area under MC^{**} is lower than under MC^*.

Despite lowering player salaries, player's associations are usually in favor of luxury taxes instead of salary caps to promote league parity. This seems counterintuitive, but the reason is that the tax is actually paid by only the top payroll teams. These teams usually collect the best players, hence the star players on the top teams will have to shoulder the greatest burden of the luxury tax by accepting lower salaries than would otherwise be the case without the luxury tax. The average player who makes up the bulk of the players on the remaining teams does not have to bear any part of the tax. Since players vote for highly paid representatives for their player's associations, it is not surprising that player representatives appeal to the average player and support the luxury tax system.

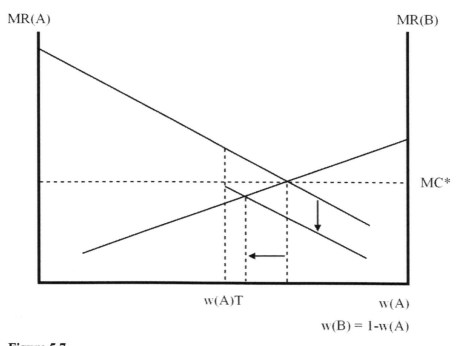

Figure 5.7
A luxury tax that improves league parity if only the rich club pays the tax and the tax is not redistributed to the other team.

In general, the two-team model predicts that players will always end up playing for the teams that value their services the most in the long run. Professional sports leagues always reach an optimal allocation of players if players are free to move among teams, by free agent status, or if cash sales of players are allowed. Powerhouse teams and poor teams will persist, however, this is the optimal distribution of success based on local and national market conditions. Salary caps can be used to achieve a more equitable distribution of team success at the cost of player mobility. An optimal allocation of players will not be achievable. The model predicts that revenue sharing will have no effect on promoting league parity, but will have the effect of lowering player salaries. This result rests on the assumption that attendance is a function of the home team's quality, usually measured as winning percentage, only. A more general model, where attendance depends on the total quality of the home and visiting team's quality, predicts that revenue sharing will promote league parity. Finally, a luxury tax system will not promote league parity, but will lower player salaries.

Brief Review of Concepts

- A reserve clause does not promote league parity if cash sales of players are allowed. Team payrolls will be lower than without a reserve clause.
- Revenue sharing does not promote league parity but can keep small market franchises from folding. This result relies on a simple specification of consumer demand for games. If consumers consider total game quality across both home and visiting clubs, revenue sharing can promote league parity.
- Soft or hard salary caps can promote league parity, but at the expense of reduced team and league profits. Of course, player salaries are reduced.
- Luxury taxes on team payroll can promote league parity. Player's unions prefer luxury taxes since the burden of the tax falls only on the richest players.

Test Your Understanding

1. Suppose we have a two-team league where team A plays in a large market area and team B plays in a small market area. The revenues of both clubs increase as their respective winning percentages increase. Assume that $m_A = 100,000$, $m_B = 50,000$, $\beta_A = 0.5$ and $\beta_B = 1$.

a) Solve for the optimal winning percentages for teams' A and B assuming there is free mobility of players and cash sales are allowed.
b) Solve for the optimal winning percentages if $\beta_A = \beta_B = 0.5$.
c) What is the level of marginal cost using your answer from part a?

d) If a reserve clause was instituted that lowered marginal cost to 15,000, what would be the resulting optimal winning percentages for A and B using your answer from part a? Why?

e) Suppose the team league institutes revenue sharing using $\alpha = 0.6$ and $\beta_A = \beta_B = 0.5$. Solve for the new optimal winning percentages for A and B with revenue sharing. What do you notice? Do you think this result is always true?

Focus Box: The Problems Facing Canadian Teams in the NHL

Canada's national game was facing an economic crisis. Since 1990, average player salaries increased from $276,000 to $1.2 million (US) by 1999. Canadian clubs lost a total of $113 million in the last 2000-01 and 2001-02 seasons trying to compete with their American counterparts. Canadian clubs typically face much higher property taxes than American clubs. Finally, the low value of the Canadian dollar relative to the US dollar (1C$ = $0.67US) in the late 1990's made it difficult for Canadian clubs to compete for quality free agents. Several Canadian clubs relocated to US cities in response to persistent losses: the Quebec Nordiques became the Colorado Avalanche; the Winnipeg Jets became the Phoenix Coyotes. The remaining six clubs played in relatively small markets, with the exceptions of Toronto and Montreal.

The NHL implemented several policies to redistribute revenues from wealthy US clubs to the revenue poor Canadian clubs. The Supplemental Currency Assistance Plan redistributed $45 million to the Canadian clubs, excluding Toronto and Montreal, during the 1996-2000 seasons. The Canadian Assistance Plan compensated Canadian clubs for the US dollar currency exchange differential when Canadian clubs signed Group II free agents. These two plans were cancelled by the NHL Board of Governors for the 2000-2001 season.

Things came to a head at the end of the 2003-04 NHL season. According to NHL owners, player salaries had reached 75% of league operating revenues, compared to the managed 56% for the NFL and NBA under their salary cap systems. According to Forbes, 16 of the 30 NHL clubs were losing money with only Toronto and Minnesota earning reasonable profits. The Levitt report, commissioned by the NHl, claimed that the league lost a total of $273 million in the 2002-03 season and that player costs had spiraled out of control. The owners initiated talks with the NHLPA to construct a new collective bargaining agreement (CBA) for the 2004-05 season with no success. For the first time since 1919, the NHL did not play a season.

During negotiations, the NHLPA fought for a luxury tax system based on the system used in MLB. The owners rejected this idea in favor of a salary cap system. The owners eventually won out and the new CBA, approved by 87% of the NHLPA members, included a lengthy, complicated and comprehensive salary cap system. Players were guaranteed 54% of league revenues, a salary floor was established and all contracts were guaranteed. Since the 2005-06 season, ticket prices have increased dramatically and the Canadian Dollar appreciated by over 25% relative to the US Dollar for a number of years, although falling back to the 75 cent range recently. Profits for NHL clubs have increased by over 50% and the league is back to viability. In fact, Canadian NHL clubs have fared much better than their American cousins.

Chapter 6
The Threat of Entry and Exit

The brief history of professional sports leagues has been peppered with episodes of the formation of new leagues, most of which died a quick death. Baseball has witnessed the threat to the National League by the Players League in 1889 (lasted one season), the American League in 1903, the Federal League in 1917 (lasted one season) and the Continental League in 1960 (never played a game). Only the American League survives today. The first serious rival league to the NFL was the All-America Football Conference (AAFC) which operated from 1946 to 1949. The NFL merged with the rival American Football League (AFL) in 1970 (the AFL began operations in 1960), then was threatened by the World Football League (WFL) in 1974 (lasted one season), then the United States Football League (USFL) in 1984 (lasted three seasons). The NBA absorbed four rival American Basketball Association (ABA) teams in 1977, but has not been credibly threatened by a rival league since.[72] The NHL absorbed four rival World Hockey Association (WHA) teams in 1979 and has not been credibly threatened since.[73] The number of rival leagues and the teams involved is vast among the four professional sports in North America and is summarized in Quirk and Fort (1997). The historical pattern is that rival

---

[72] These teams included the Denver Nuggets, the Indiana Pacers, the New York Nets (now Brooklyn Nets) and the San Antonio Spurs.
[73] These teams included the Edmonton Oilers, the Hartford Whalers (now Carolina Hurricanes), the Quebec Nordiques (now Colorado Avalanche) and the Winnipeg Jets (now Phoenix Coyotes).

leagues do not survive long, and either are merged or absorbed into the existing league, or disappear altogether. However their brief presence has sometimes changed the economic landscape for the remaining leagues.

There is no doubt that the formation of a rival league drives up player salaries, however this is usually a short-lived windfall for the players since salaries fall after the rival league fails or merges with the incumbent league. Table 6.1 provides average player salaries the season before and after the arrival of a new rival league.

Incumbent league	Rival league	Year	Average salary before	Average salary after
NL (baseball)	AL	1901	$2,000	$3,000
MLB	Federal League	1914	$3,000	$5,000
NBA	ABA	1967	$20,000	$143,000
NHL	WHA	1972	$25,000	$96,000
NFL	USFL	1982	$55,288	$102,250

Table 6.1. Source: Che and Humphreys (2015).

The important concepts covered in this chapter are listed below.

- Economics suggests that rival leagues will maximize joint profits by merging. However factors such as labor agreements and rules of play may prevent leagues from merging.
- Game theory models are used to predict the consequences of two leagues competing when they must consider the actions of the rival league when making decisions. A simple Cournot model is used as an example.
- A league's conjectural variation can be used to determine how credible the existing league believes the threat of entry of a new

league is. The optimal response to a credible threat is to temporarily lower ticket prices and search for new franchise cities to stave off the new entrant.

6.1 The Benefits of Merging

This section will use the short run model of the professional sports team developed in Chapter 3 to show that merging can result in higher profits for the leagues involved.[74] Let's assume there are two leagues of equal size, but the new league faces lower demand for its games, perhaps because it's teams play in lower revenue cities. Figure 6.1 demonstrates the initial profit for each league assuming each league faces identical fixed costs. The emerging league will charge an average ticket price of P_E and sell Q_E number of tickets, while the existing league will charge an average ticket of P_X and sell Q_X number of tickets. The existing league is earning higher profits than the emerging league, but may wish to merge with the new league if it can increase its profitability. As we will show below, the newly merged league must be able to reduce its fixed costs by enough in order to make the merger profitable. This can be achieved by taking advantage of economies of scale.

---

[74] An algebraic exposition is given in X. Che and B. Humphreys, "Competition Between Sports Leagues: Theory and Evidence on Rival League Formation in North America", *Review of Industrial Organization*, 46(2), 2015, 127-143.

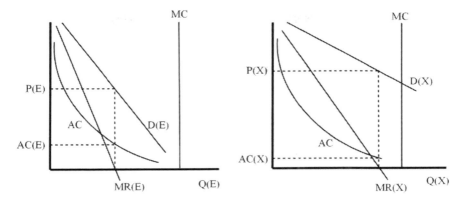

Figure 6.1
The new rival league faces lower demand than the existing league. With identical costs, the existing league earns higher profits than the new rival league.

Profit for the new entrant league is given by $(P_E - AC_E)Q_E$ and profit for the existing league is $(P_X - Q_X)Q_X$ in Figure 6.1. To demonstrate the importance of fixed costs, we need to assume some specific demand functions. Let's assume that the demand curve for tickets faced by the existing league is given by $P_X = 400 - 0.001Q_X$ and the demand curve for the new league is $P_E = 200 - 0.001Q_E$. The demand curve for the new league has a smaller vertical intercept of 200, so it faces a smaller than the existing league. Using our rule to find the marginal revenue equations, the marginal revenues are $MR_X = 400 - 0.002Q_X$ and $MR_E = 200 - 0.002Q_E$. Each league is assumed to face a fixed cost of $8 million at the start of the season, so $MC = 0$ up to the full capacity of tickets for each league (which we will assume is very large).

Each league is assumed to act as a cartel, so each sets the total ticket output for its league where $MR = MC$. For the existing league, $400 - 0.002Q_X = 0$ and $Q_X = 200,000$ tickets. The league will impose a ticket price for each team charge equal to $P_X = 400 - 0.001(200,000) = \$200$. The total profit for the existing league is just revenue minus cost, or $200(200,000) - \$8$ million $= \$32$ million. The profit-maximizing ticket output for the new league is found where $200 - 0.002Q_E = 0$, or 100,000 tickets. The cartel ticket price will be $P_E = 200 - 0.001(100,000) = \$100$ and the profit will be $\$100(100,000) - \$8$ million $= \$2$ million. Operating as separate leagues, the total profit for both is \$34 million.

If both leagues merge, the total demand curve is found by horizontally summing the demand curves at each price. To do this, must sum the quantity of tickets for each league sold at each price, but the demand equations have prices on the left-hand side. We can remedy this by solving the demand equations to place the quantity of tickets sold on the left-hand side. Doing this, we find that $Q_X = \frac{400-P}{0.001}$ and $Q_E = \frac{200-P}{0.001}$. Summing the quantities together gives $Q_X + Q_E = \frac{600-2P}{0.001}$ as the demand curve faced by the newly merged league. Now reverse the process and solve the merged demand equation for the ticket price on the left-hand side to get $P = 300 - 0.0005Q$ where we have now dropped the E and X subscripts since the new league contains all of the original teams from both leagues. It is now straightforward to find the profit-maximizing number of tickets to sell for the merged league by setting $MR = MC$.

$$MR = 300 - 0.001Q = 0, Q = 300,000$$
$$P = 300 - 0.0005(300,000) = \$150$$
$$Profit = \$150(300,000) - \$16\ million = \$29\ million$$

In this case, it is preferable for the leagues to not merge since the total profit falls by \$5 million after the merger. To make the merger profitable, fixed costs must fall more than \$5 million in total for the two leagues. This could be achieved by taking advantage of economies of scale (average costs must decline faster than without the merger) in operating the combined league. Fixed costs could be reduced by combining the administrative operations of the two leagues and negotiating a new collective bargaining agreement that lowers player expenses (since there is only one buyer of talent instead of two). Merging might also give the new league more bargaining power in revenue sources other than tickets, such as television and licensing agreements.

A number of problems may prevent two rival leagues from merging.

- The two leagues may operate under different conditions, which neither league wishes to change in order to merge. These conditions might include labor agreements, revenue sharing, ticket pricing, television rights and organizational structure. Sometimes even agreeing on a common set of playing rules is difficult.
- In any cartel, there is an incentive to be a renegade firm and leave the cartel. This is because the renegade firm can charge the cartel price, but increase output up to the competitive solution where $P = MC$. In order for the cartel to produce less than the competitive level of output, the cartel must enforce a quota system that controls output per firm and the number of firms in the cartel. The cartel with fixed and variable costs is demonstrated[75] in Figure 6.2. Historical instances of renegade teams are virtually non-existent, implying that league enforcement of output and membership is strict.

---

[75] The average cost curve is drawn as U-shaped here since starting a new league is a long-run decision.

244

Economies of scale can also prevent two rival leagues from merging if cost conditions dictate that there is only enough room in the marketplace for one league. In Figure 6.3, the demand curve facing the new rival league D_E is everywhere below the long-run average cost curve for the industry. The new league cannot make a profit at any level of output and thus will decide to go out of business, or perhaps, not enter the industry in the first place. With increasing returns to scale, the existing league could simply increase its output by playing a longer season, granting new franchises, or both, force the new rival league out of business.

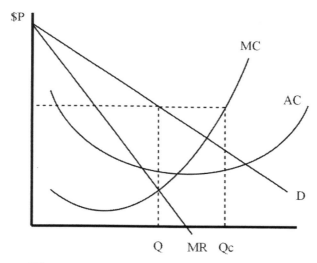

Figure 6.2
The league cartel charges an average ticket price P and earns a total profit of (P-AC)Q. This profit and output Q must be rationed among the member clubs to maintain the monopoly output level Q. The renegade club who starts a new league can also charge a ticket price of P, but can increase output its own output to its cartel rationed amount plus (Q$_c$-Q).

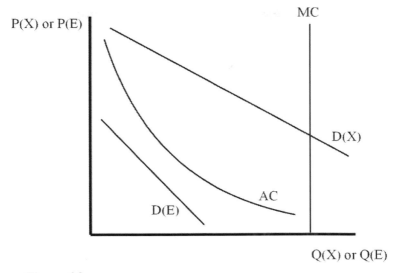

Figure 6.3
The demand curve facing the new rival league, D_E, is everywhere below the long-run average cost curve facing the industry. The new league will not be profitable at any level of output.

Brief Review of Concepts

- Two rival leagues can merge to become one league and realize far greater profits than the sum of each league individually.
- Leagues may find it difficult to merge due to different cost conditions, labor agreements, playing rules, etc. When teams merge to become a common league, they form a cartel. There is always an economic incentive to become the lone renegade in the cartel and raise output.

Focus Box: The World's Richest Game

At the end of every season, seven clubs in the Championship Division of the English Football Association (FA) play a knockout tournament to determine a winner. The top three teams in this division are promoted to the next upper division, while the bottom three teams of the top division are relegated to the next division down. The winning prize is promotion to the English Premiership Division for the next season, the top division in England. Moving from a division with little television broadcasting to the most heavily broadcasted football league in the world means a huge financial gain for the winning team, about £170 million per season over the television royalties from the Championship Division.[76] Of course a good portion of this new money must be spent on acquiring star players in order to ensure that the winner stays in the Premiership Division for seasons to come, otherwise back to the lesser division. No other single game has so much money riding on the result (at least legal money).

6.2 Conjectural Variations and Game Theory

Game theory is a branch of economics that explores how firms in an oligopoly industry compete strategically with one another. In an industry with only a few firms, the pricing and output decisions of one of the firms affects all of the other firms in the industry. When making these decisions, each firm must consider how the other firms will react, if at all. A firm's *conjectural variation* is its assessment of how the other firms in the industry will react. Usually the other firms can make one of three choices: follow the lead of the single firm, do nothing, or do the opposite of the single firm. Let's call these the collusive, Cournot and competitive conjectural variations respectively.

In an oligopoly with firms that collude, each firm will contact the other firms regarding price changes or changes to outputs that it would like to make. A frequently cited example is gas stations. Usually a lead gas station will increase its price and then is quickly followed by all of the other gas stations. This can occur due to outright collusion, which is illegal

---

[76] http://www.skysports.com/football/news/11689/10295845/the-price-of-championship-play-off-promotion-the-richest-game-in-football

under the Sherman Act in the United States and the Competition Act in Canada, or they follow each other's pricing decisions innocently, without contacting each other in a planned price change. It is difficult to prosecute firms that collude on pricing since simply observing all prices going up is not sufficient evidence of tacit collusion. The important point is that each firm will maintain its market share when all agree to increase the price at the same time, but sales for the industry will fall. You might be thinking that price elasticity of demand has something to do with this -if so, you are right. Figure 6.4 demonstrates. Increasing the price will decrease total revenue if the demand curve is in the elastic portion; lowering the price will decrease total revenue if the demand curve is in the inelastic portion. So we often draw a firm in an oligopoly with a rather odd demand curve that has a kink in it at the current market price. If a lead firm increases its price and all the other firms follow, total revenue will drop for every firm. If a lead firm decreases its price in the hope of increasing market share, all of the other firms follow and total revenue for each firm drops. So the kinked demand curve predicts that firms in an oligopoly will tend to have pretty rigid prices that change only infrequently, like gas stations.

Cournot was the first to model the oligopoly problem in 1838. He assumed that each firm considers the price and output of the other firms as staying constant when making decisions. A very simplified example follows. Assume that two firms, A and B, face an identical inverse demand curve given by $P = 100 - Q$. Let's also assume that each firm faces zero costs for simplicity. To start the model, suppose that firm A decides to set its output at 40 units, resulting in a price of 60 (it does not matter what the initial output and price are as long as they lie on the demand curve). Firm B then decides its output by assuming that Firm A's output is given. This is shown in the first panel of Figure 6.5. The marginal revenue for Firm B

248

cuts through the horizontal axis half way between 40 and 100, resulting in a profit-maximizing output of 70 for the industry and 30 for firm B. The market price falls to 30.

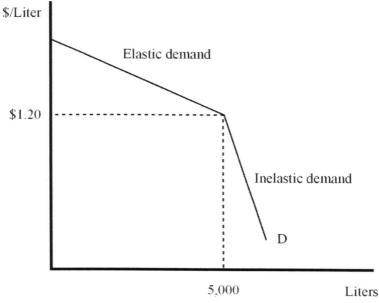

Figure 6.4
The firm in an oligopoly industry must consider the responses of other firms. If it raises its price for a liter of gas from $1.20, all the other firms will follow and revenue decreases for all of them. If it lowers its price, all of the other firms will too and revenue will fall. The kink in the demand curve occurs at the rigid market price.

In the next round, Firm A responds by changing its output to 35, given Firm B's output of 30. This is demonstrated in the second panel of Figure 6.5. Total market output is 65 units. The market price rises to 35. In the third round, Firm B responds by changing its output to 32.5 since the marginal revenue curve of Firm B is equal to zero marginal cost at an industry output of 67.5 (half way between 30 and 100). The market price falls to 32.5. Eventually the game ends when output is 33.3 for both firms and the market price is 33.3. In this way, total industry profits are maximized given the Cournot conjecture.

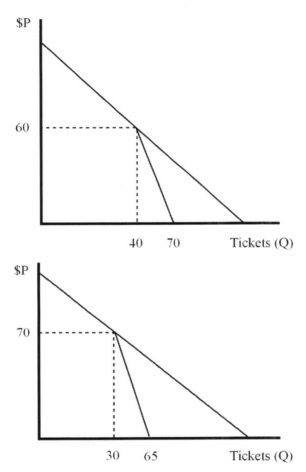

Figure 6.5
Each firm sets output where MR = MC = 0 by assumption, assuming the output of the other firm is constant. In the first panel, Firm B sets its profit-maximizing output at 30, given that the output of Firm A is 40. This lowers the market price to 30. In the second panel, Firm A responds by changing its profit-maximizing output to 35, given the output of Firm B. The game ends with output of Firm A and B both equal to 33.3 and a market price of 33.3.

Algebraically, the profit function for Firm A is given by $PQ_1 = (100 - Q_1 - Q_2)Q_1$ since we have assumed zero marginal costs, or $PQ_1 = 100Q_1 - Q_1^2 - Q_2Q_1$. Firm A chooses its output to maximize its profit giving rise to the first-order condition $100 - 2Q_1 - Q_2 = 0$. Solving this for its output gives the reaction function, or best response function, for Firm A. Since both firms are identical, each will have a best response function.

$$Q_1 = 50 - Q_2/2$$
$$Q_2 = 50 - Q_1/2$$

We can substitute the second equation into the first equation and solve for Firm A output which is 33.3. Firm B output will also be 33.3.

It should be easy for you to figure out that the monopoly price with only one league will be 50 and output will be 50 units, hence the non-cooperative oligopoly produces more output than the monopolist and at a lower price.

The Cournot conjecture might be reasonable when one considers the geographical separation of most professional sports teams operating in the same league. It's not likely that the pricing and output decisions of the Los Angeles Dodgers will affect the pricing and output decisions of the New York Yankees, due to the distance and the protected markets they play in. There are instances of teams that play in the same geographical market in the same sport: the Chicago Cubs and the White Sox; the New York Yankees and the Mets; the San Francisco Giants and the Oakland A's; the Los Angeles Dodgers and the Anaheim Angels. Perhaps these clubs do compete, at least with ticket prices[77], however most baseball fans that live on the south side of Chicago would not think of traveling to the north side to cheer for the Cubs. Even at a city level, geographical separation is significant in some cases. An interesting case to investigate would be the NFL New York Giants and New York Jets who play in the same stadium.

Focus Box: Bidding Among Rival Broadcasters

English football provides a good example of how rival broadcasters develop bidding strategies for valuable television rights. In 1992, the new FA Premier league offered the exclusive broadcasting rights for 60 of its 380 matches per season at auction. There were two bidders, ITV and British Sky Broadcasting (BSkyB). BSkyB outbid ITV by being allowed to submit a bid higher than ITV's by 30 million pounds at the last minute. The FA Premier League does not sell rights to any single game. If you wish to broadcast only one, or a few matches, you must purchase rights to all matches. We have just seen using economic theory how packaging broadcasting rights as a league cartel extracts a higher price for the rights. BSkyB broadcasts matches on its exclusive Sports Channel over its satellite network across Europe. These broadcast rights have been particularly lucrative for BSkyB as over 90% of subscribers purchase its Sports Channel.

BSkyB successfully outbid rivals for FA Premier League broadcast rights again in 1996, but felt nervous about the coming auction in 2001. In 1999, BSkyB made an attempt to acquire the Manchester United football club for the staggering sum of 1 billion pounds. The Monopolies and

---

[77] Firms that assume that the prices of other firms are given, are said to possess Bertrand conjectures. More complicated game theory models assume one dominant firm with all other firms following. This is the Stackelberg conjecture.

Mergers Commission (MMC) reviewed the bid and blocked the acquisition on the basis that BSkyB would obtain an unfair toehold in the market for broadcast rights. In the game theory literature, a "toehold" is a slight asymmetry in a competitive bidding auction that gives an advantage to one of the bidders. To describe the nature of the advantage, it is necessary to understand the "winner's curse". At a competitive auction, bidders ideally will bid just up to the maximum value they place on the good being auctioned, but no more. The winning bidder places a higher valuation than all other bidders on the good, but knows that the market value of the good is probably less than his bid. Thus by winning the successful bidder has lost.

Revenues from broadcast rights are shared unevenly between all of the FA Premier League clubs, unlike typical North American leagues. The more successful the club on the field and at the box office, the greater the share of broadcast revenues it receives. In 1999, the largest share at 8% went to Manchester United, which if acquired by BSkyB, would then revert back to BSkyB. Thus a significant portion of broadcast revenue has run full circle from BSkyB to the FA Premier League to Manchester United and back to BSkyB. This extra revenue could allow BSkyB to outbid other bidders for broadcast rights and not suffer the "winner's curse". The MMC decision effectively bars broadcasters, or any other companies, from obtaining large shares in any FA Premier League club. Broadcasters have reacted by acquiring small toeholds in clubs to try to outbid their rivals. In 1999, BSkyB maintained a small shareholding in Manchester United as well as a 9% stake in Leeds United, a 5% stake in Sunderland and a 9.9% stake in Manchester City. Similarly, NTL had increased its stake in Newcastle United to 9.8% and Granada acquired a 9.9% stake in Liverpool FC.

Source: David Harbord and Ken Binmore, "Toeholds, Takeovers and Football", *European Competition Law Review*, Vol. 21(2), 2000.

Test Your Understanding

1. Suppose that an existing European soccer league faces a market demand given by P = 400 − 0.0001Q and currently sells a total of 2 million tickets per season. All costs are fixed at the start of each season. A rival league is considering entering the industry and would like to estimate how many tickets it will sell and its average ticket price. Assume that both leagues possess Cournot conjectures concerning each other's output (ticket sales). Compute the average ticket price and ticket sales for each league at the Nash equilibrium.

2. Two minor hockey leagues, the International League and the American League, are considering a merger that will retain all of the teams from each league. Each league faces a total fixed cost of $2 million. The demand curve for tickets for the International League is given by $P = 100 − 0.0005Q$ while the demand curve for the American League is given by $P = 80 − 0.0005Q$.

   a) Compute the profit-maximizing ticket prices, ticket sales and level of profit for the two leagues before merging.
   b) Compute the profit-maximizing ticket price after the two leagues merge. What is the total profit after the merger? If the merged league could achieve a reduction in its fixed costs of $0.5 million, how would this help the bottom line?

3. Instead of competing with ticket sales, it would seem more realistic to think of professional sports teams (or any sort of business firms) as competing with ticket prices. This is called Bertrand competition in the economics literature. Suppose that two firms with identical prices and costs start to compete with each with price reductions under a demand curve that is not kinked. Where would the market price end up with both of the firms still staying in business? Why do you suppose we do not model strategic behavior as competing in prices?

6.3 The Threat of Entry

Sometimes a new rival league does not need to enter the industry in order to have an effect on the business decisions of the existing league. If the threat of entry is credible, it can be shown that the existing league will react by lowering ticket prices and seeking new franchise cities in order to prevent the new league from entering the industry. To set up the model, we will assume that the rival league faces higher costs than the existing league and that the total cost increases at a constant rate as ticket sales increase for both leagues. The total cost curve is a straight line with a positive slope equal to the marginal cost. Since the slope is constant, so is the marginal cost so the marginal cost curve is a horizontal line. We have seen the cases where the marginal cost curve is an upward sloping curve (Figure 3.4) and an L-shaped line (Figure 3.8). Here we assume a flat marginal cost line at some positive level of marginal cost only for the reason that it keeps the diagram simple and that it is also the average cost curve (figure this out for yourself by drawing a picture of the total cost curve).

In Figure 6.6, the demand curve for tickets that the existing league faces is the downward sloping line $D(X)$. The marginal revenue line is drawn using the simple rule for a linear demand curve and is the line $MR(X)$. The flat marginal cost line is $MC(X)$ which is also the average cost $AC(X)$. Without any threat of entry by a new league, the existing league cartel will maximize profit where $MR(X) = MC(X)$ and the result is Q_1 number of tickets sold at a ticket price equal to P_1. Profit is the area $(P_1 - AC_1)Q_1$.

If the existing league sets its ticket output at Q_1 tickets, ignoring the potential entry of the new league, the new league will enter and capture some of the market of the existing league. We will assume that the new league faces higher costs than the existing league since it has not yet achieved economies of scale. The marginal cost and average cost curve for the new league is $MC(E)$ and $AC(E)$ which is everywhere above the cost curves for the existing league. The existing league can react to the entry of the new league by selling additional tickets and charging a price of P_2. This price is just equal to the average cost facing the new rival league; hence the rival league will not be profitable. Unfortunately this price does not maximize profits for the existing league since that price was P_1.

At any price above P_1, the rival league can enter the industry profitably since the price will be higher than its average cost. The higher the price is above P_1, the larger the scale of entry of the new league and the less market share is left for the existing league. The demand curve facing the existing league, if the new league enters, can be found by subtracting the output of the new league from the market demand curve. This is labeled $D(X-E)$ in Figure 6.6. The marginal revenue curve of the existing league, $MR(X-E)$, is also plotted using our rule for plotting marginal revenue curves from demand curves. Given the credible threat of entry of the new rival league, the profit maximizing ticket output of the existing league is found where $MR(X-E) = MC(X-E)$. The model predicts that the existing league will respond to the credible threat of entry of the new league by lowering the average ticket price from P_1 to P_3, and increase ticket sales from Q_1 to Q_3. The existing league might also increase sales by granting new franchises.

If the average cost curve of the new league is below that of the existing league, such as at $AC(E')$, then it is optimal for the existing league to deter entry to survive, and set the ticket price at P_2. The new league will not be maximizing profit, but will be successful in deterring entry.

256

In 1960, Branch Rickey, former general manager of the Brooklyn Dodgers, gathered investors together to form the new Continental baseball league. The league never got off the ground, but it did elicit a large response from the National and American Leagues. The Houston Colt 45's (Astros), New York Mets and Los Angeles Angels (Anaheim) were granted expansion franchises to ward off new franchises in the same areas from the Continental League.

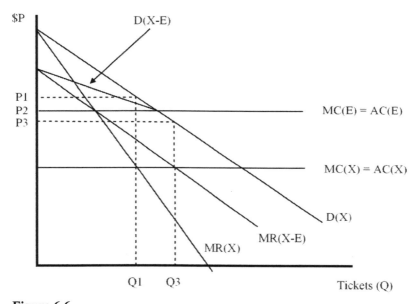

Figure 6.6
The new rival league faces higher costs (MC(E)) than the existing league (MC(X)). Normally the existing league maximizes profit at sales of Q_0 tickets and ticket price P_0. With the credible threat of entry of the new rival league, the existing league faces the dashed demand curve and maximizes profit at price P_2 and ticket sales Q_2. The credible threat of entry lowers ticket prices and may cause the existing league to grant new franchises.

Brief Review of Concepts

- Game theory is a branch of economics that models how firms operating in an oligopoly compete with one another. The Cournot

257

model assumes that firms take the output of the other firms as remaining unchanged when considering price and output changes. Under this framework, teams reach a Nash equilibrium where profits are maximized.

- Teams generally compete with price rather than output since the league fixes playing schedules. This rules out the Cournot model. The Bertrand model assumes teams take the prices charged by other teams as remaining unchanged. This might be a realistic model in markets that are geographically close.
- The credible threat of entry of a new league is sometimes enough to elicit a response from the established league. Generally, economics predicts that existing leagues will respond by raising output (granting new franchises) and lowering ticket prices. The rival Continental baseball league never got off the ground, but forced baseball to respond by granting new franchises.

Focus Box: Gary Davidson and his Stable of Rival Leagues

Gary Davidson graduated from law school at UCLA and immediately went to work as a tax lawyer in Los Angeles. He had no interest in sports but saw a profitable opportunity in helping establish the American Basketball Association (ABA) in 1967. The new league challenged the monopoly status of the long-established NBA by luring star players away from NBA teams and by offering a more exciting style of play[78]. Davidson was a promotional wizard with Robert Redford good looks. The rebel leagues he helped establish were pushed as a "mod" alternative to the boring established leagues. Indeed, the ABA played with a red, white and blue basketball. The World Hockey Association (WHA), established by Davidson in 1971, played with a dark blue hockey puck, and sported garishly colorful uniforms. The short-lived World Football League (WFL) played with a gold football with red stripes.

---

[78] The three-point shot and the 25-second shot clock were ABA innovations eventually adopted in the NBA.

Each league was given credibility by signing star players from the established leagues. The ABA signed star player Rick Barry, who enjoyed many successful seasons in the new league. The WHA signed Bobby Hull to an unheard of $1 million contract to play with the Winnipeg Jets of the new league. His salary with the NHL's Chicago Black Hawks was $150,000 per season. Hockey legend Gordie Howe and his two sons played for the same team in the WHA. The WFL signed Miami Dolphin's stars Paul Warfield, Larry Csonka and Jim Kiick.

The new rebel leagues were loosely organized and poorly run. Most teams made large losses and did not last more than one season. To insure a fresh supply of new franchise cities, Davidson and partner Dennis Murphy would travel from city to city searching for new owners. Their tag line was "Would you rather be known as the owner of the Detroit Wheels or as a manufacturer of brassieres?" New franchises could be had for as little as $500,000, although many of the checks bounced. Creditors always followed the antics of the rival leagues closely. Following the first and last World Bowl (WFL) in 1974, creditors confiscated player's uniforms and equipment and the league collapsed. Many players had not been paid for most of the season.

What is the legacy left by the antics of Gary Davidson? In some ways, Davidson had the most profound effect on professional sports since turn of the century. His raiding of star players from the established leagues probably speeded the adoption of free agency and the repeal of the hated reserve clause. Player salaries increased significantly as the rebel leagues competed with the established leagues for star players and rookies[79]. The establishment of the rebel leagues also led to the granting of new franchises in the existing leagues to compete. Eventually four ABA and

---

[79] In the nine seasons of existence of the ABA, NBA salaries increased four-fold.

WHA teams were granted admittance to the NBA and NHL, further expanding the markets of the existing leagues.

Ultimately, the lack of lucrative national television contracts probably led to the doom of the new rebel leagues. The ABA folded in 1977, the WHA in 1979 and the WFL in 1974. This emphasized to the existing league the importance of television broadcasting rights and may have influenced the newly emerging cable specialty channels in the early 1980's. What happened to Gary Davidson? Following the collapse of the WFL in 1974, Davidson liquidated all of his interests in the remaining leagues to become a poor man. He spent some time in Haiti in the agricultural industry, and then returned to Los Angeles where he is now a successful tax lawyer again. He has no interest in investing in professional sports again.

Source: The League Leader, Sports Illustrated, August 16, 1994, 49-57.

Chapter 7
The New Stadium Boom

The decades of the 1990's and 2000's saw a boom in new stadium construction that was unprecedented in the history of professional sports. Some of these new stadiums replaced outdated facilities and the rest were built to accommodate new franchises. Opulence and customer satisfaction are the key attributes of new stadiums to attract customers. The wealth of spending calls attention to several important issues that will be discussed in this chapter.

- A brief overview of the magnitude and cost of new stadium construction.

- The wide variety of sources of stadium revenues, with special emphasis on the economics of ticket pricing.

- Necessary team conditions for expansion of a stadium or construction of a new facility.

- The wide variety of licensing agreements and personal seat licenses used to subsidize constructions costs.

- How cities compete for new franchises by building new stadiums.

- The economics of new stadium construction and a discussion of the net benefits of new stadium construction to the public.

7.1 New Stadium Growth

A total of 64 new stadiums have been built since 1990 to service NFL, NBA, NHL and MLB clubs. The trend has been to build more luxurious facilities than in the past. Baseball stadiums have moved down in size but offer far more amenities than a bench to sit on. The movement towards high-tech stadiums is reflected in the Baltimore Ravens (NFL) $222 million stadium. It has 68,400 seats, all with excellent sight lines. Its 108 luxury suites are the most of any stadium in North America. State of the art 100-foot video screens are situated in each end zone, which are computer linked to a 1,900 speaker sound system. The stadium has 7,900 club seats with access to special food and drink services ($107 to $297 per game). Just over 54,200 personal seat licenses were sold at $100 to $5,000 each to help finance construction costs. The average season ticket holder to Ravens games earns an average of $75,000 per year. Tables 7.1 through 7.4 provide a partial list of new facilities with their estimated construction costs.

Baseball teams have been busy with 15 teams moving into new stadiums since the year 2000. The trend in MLB has been to build somewhat smaller stadiums than the cookie-cutter multi-purpose stadiums that were built in the 1970's to house MLB and NFL teams. The average capacity of the new facilities is just over 43,000, yet construction costs have increased dramatically since $175 million spent to build Jacobs Field in Cleveland to the $525 million to build Marlins Park in Miami. Excluding the $1.3 billion to build the new Yankee Stadium in New York (a significant portion being the cost to acquire the land), the average annual rate of increase in constructions costs is 11.1%.[80] Of course, MLB requires

---

[80] $\dfrac{((525-175)/175)}{18} = 0.111$

larger stadiums due to the size of the playing field and this makes larger seating possible.

Year completed	Stadium	Team	Cost	Capacity
2012	Marlins Park	Miami Marlins	$525 m	37,000
2010	Kaufmann Stadium	Kansas City Royals	$250 m	39,000
2010	Target Field	Minnesota Twins	$544 m	40,000
2009	Citi Field	New York Mets	$600 m	45,000
2009	Yankee Stadium	New York Yankees	$1.3 b	51,800
2008	Nationals Park	Washington Nationals	$611 m	41,888
2006	Busch Stadium	St. Louis Cardinals	$365 m	46,861
2004	Citizens Bank Park	Philadelphia Phillies	$346 m	43,000
2004	Petco Park	San Diego Padres	$457 m	46,000
2003	Great American Ballpark	Cincinnati Reds	$325 m	42,059
2001	Miller Park	Milwaukee Brewers	$400 m	43,000
2001	PNC Park	Pittsburgh Pirates	$262 m	38,365
2000	AT&T Park	San Francisco Giants	$357 m	41,503
2000	Comerica Park	Detroit Tigers	$300 m	40,950
2000	Minute Maid Park	Houston Astros	$250 m	42,000
1999	Safeco Field	Seattle Mariners	$518 m	47,476
1998	Bank One Ballpark	Arizona Diamondbacks	$354 m	48,500
1996	Turner Field	Atlanta Braves	$242 m	49,714
1995	Coors Field	Colorado Rockies	$215 m	50,381
1994	Jacobs Field	Cleveland Indians	$175 m	42,865
1994	The Ballpark at Arlington	Texas Rangers	$191 m	49,166

Table 7.1
New Stadium Construction in MLB
Source: www.ballparks.com

The new Yankee Stadium features the latest in amenities for both players and fans and demonstrates the new way of thinking in stadium design. It incorporates wider concourses and more space than any other baseball stadium so that sightlines are kept as unobstructed as possible. The stadium houses three restaurants, 25 concession areas, a team store and a Yankees museum full of valuable memorabilia. The fan experience is enhanced by 1,100 HD television screens so that the action is not missed anywhere in the stadium. The stadium also features the fourth largest HD scoreboard in MLB with 550 m^2 of viewing area.

Year completed	Stadium	Team	Cost	Capacity
2010	Arrowhead Stadium	Kansas City Chiefs	$375 m	79,451
2010	Met Life Stadium	NY Giants, NY Jets	$1.6 b	82,500
2009	AT&T Stadium	Dallas Cowboys	$1.15 b	80,000
2008	Lucas Oil Stadium	Indianapolis Colts	$720 m	63,000
2003	Lincoln Financial Field	Philadelphia Eagles	$512 m	68,532
2003	Soldier Field	Chicago Bears	$365 m	61,500
2002	CenturyLink Field	Seattle Seahawks	$360 m	67,000
2002	Ford Field	Detroit Lions	$300 m	65,000
2002	Gillette Stadium	New England Patriots	$325 m	68,000
2002	Reliant Stadium	Houston Texans	$325 m	69,500
2001	Sports Authority Field	Denver Broncos	$364 m	76,125
2001	Heinz Field	Pittsburgh Steelers	$281 m	64,450
2000	Paul Brown Stadium	Cincinnati Bengals	$380 m	66,846
1999	LP Stadium	Tennessee Titans	$292 m	67,700
1999	Browns Stadium	Cleveland Browns	$290 m	73,200
1998	M&T Bank Stadium	Baltimore Ravens	$220m	69,300
1998	Raymond James Stadium	Tampa Bay Buccaneers	$168 m	65,000
1997	FedEx Field	Washington Redskins	$251 m	78,600
1996	Ericcson Stadium	Carolina Panthers	$187 m	72,685
1995	Edward Jones Dome	St. Louis Rams	$300 m	70,000

Table 7.2
New Stadium Construction in NFL
Source: www.ballparks.com

The NFL has been even busier than MLB in building new stadiums with 21 teams moving into new digs since 1995. Football stadiums are larger than baseball stadiums largely due to fan demand for seats to NFL games. The average capacity of these new stadiums is just over 70,000 with ample room for luxury suites. Suite revenue is not shared under the NFL and MLB revenue sharing agreements so the trend is to substitute more luxury suites for fewer general seats. Construction costs range from the paltry $168 million to build Raymond James Stadium in Tampa Bay in 1998 to the record-setting $1.6 billion to build the Met Life Stadium in New York in 2010. Again, any stadium built in New York is not reflective of construction costs in general (nor the AT&T Stadium built for the Dallas Cowboys in 2009), which probably averaged an annual increase of 32.9% using the Lucas Oil Stadium construction cost (Arrowhead Stadium was an extensive renovation, not a completely new build).

The largest NFL stadium is the new Met Life Stadium in New York that houses the Giants and the Jets at 82,500 seats. It is also the most expensive stadium ever made in North America at $1.6 billion, all privately financed. The old Meadowlands Stadium can fit comfortably inside the new stadium. In order to house two NFL teams, Met Life Stadium is covered on its exterior with aluminum louvers that can pivot revealing the team colors of either the Giants or the Jets. Lighting inside the stadium can also change color schemes for the same purpose. The stadium includes 10,000 club seats and 218 luxury suites. Viewing is enhanced by 20 giant HD LED screens located at strategic points outside the stadium, while four larger HD screens are positioned inside. Delightful food options include five restaurants and a bevy of concession areas.

Table 7.3 lists new arena constructions in NBA cities. The average capacity of these new arenas is 19,500 and all are multi-use that also house NHL or minor-league hockey teams. The average annual increase in construction costs since the United Center in 1994 is only 7.3% using the Amway Center cost in 2010. This is despite the trend in the NBA to build new arenas in the downtown core where land can be expensive.

Unlike baseball and football stadiums, the majority of these new arenas involved significant public financing with the teams putting up little to no investment. The exception is Barclay's Center that houses the Brooklyn Nets (the NHL New York Islanders will become tenants for the 2015-16 season). The arena construction costs were entirely privately financed, however the city of Brooklyn invested $150 million to improve road and transit links to the new arena. The arena is the focal point of a new shopping plaza and subway station. Fans have their chose of food items from four restaurants and 14 different food vendors. A large number of luxury suites are available, including the Vault designed by Jay Z himself, which bills itself as the most exclusive luxury suite experience in the country.

Year completed	Arena	Team	Cost	Capacity
2010	Amway Center	Orlando Magic	$380 m	18,500
2010	Barclay's Center	Brooklyn Nets	$637 m	18,000
2008	Chesapeake Energy Arena	Oklahoma City Thunder	$201 m	19,599
2004	FedEx Forum	Memphis Grizzlies	$250 m	21,165
2002	AT&T Center	San Antonio Spurs	$186 m	18,797
1999	Bankers Life Fieldhouse	Indiana Pacers	$183 m	18,345
1999	New Orleans Arena	New Orleans Pelicans	$114 m	18,000
1999	Staples Center	LA Lakers, LA Clippers	$400 m	18,997
1997	MCI Center	Washington Wizards	$200 m	20,000
1995	Rose Garden	Portland Trailblazers	$262 m	21,538
1994	United Center	Chicago Bulls	$175 m	21,711

Table 7.3
New Stadium Construction in NBA
Source: www.ballparks.com

Many new arenas were constructed in the 1990's to house NHL teams, but no new arenas have been constructed since 2004. The average

266

new arena capacity is similar to the NBA at 18,774, slightly smaller due to the larger ice surface. New arena financing has been approved for the cities of Detroit (Red Wings) and Edmonton (Oilers), but these arenas will not be finished for some time yet. Construction costs have increased at about the same average annual rate as new NBA arenas.

The city of Edmonton will contribute $150 million towards the estimated $480 million construction cost of the new Rogers Place, due to be completed for the 2016-17 season. Oiler's owner Howard Katz will contribute $115 million with the remainder financed by the provincial and federal government. The arena will seat 18,500 spectators with room for approximately 2,000 more in luxury suites. From the exterior, the arena is designed as an oil drop reflecting the team name, but more importantly the staple resource output of the Alberta economy. A new community skating rink attached to the arena will seat 1,000 spectators for public skating and for watching practices by the home and visiting teams.

Year completed	Arena	Team	Cost	Capacity
2004	MTS Center	Winnipeg Jets	$134 m	15,015
2001	American Airlines Center	Dallas Stars	$420 m	18,532
2000	Excel Energy Center	Minnesota Wild	$130 m	18,064
2000	Nationwide Arena	Columbus Blue Jackets	$175 m	18,138
1999	PNC Arena	Carolina Hurricanes	$158 m	18,730
1999	Staples Center	Los Angeles Kings	$400 m	18,997
1998	National Car Rental Center	Florida Panthers	$185 m	19,452
1996	Molson Center	Montreal Canadiens	$230 m	21,631
1996	First Union Center	Philadelphia Flyers	$210 m	18,168
1996	Nashville Arena	Nashville Predators	$154 m	20,000
1996	Marine Midland Arena	Buffalo Sabres	$122 m	18,500
1996	Corel Center	Ottawa Senators	$200 m	18,500
1996	Ice Palace	Tampa Bay Lightning	$160 m	19,758
1995	GM Place	Vancouver Canucks	$160 m	19,193
1995	FleetCenter	Boston Bruins	$160 m	17,565

| 1994 | Kiel Center | St. Louis Blues | $135 m | 19,267 |

Table 7.4
New Stadium Construction in NHL
Source: www.ballparks.com

Obviously the cost of building a new facility is higher than it was years ago. Table 7.5 summarizes the construction and renovation costs of facilities for all four major leagues over three different eras. Generally construction costs have increased at a faster rate than the Consumer Price Index, but this partly reflects the increase in stadium quality and amenities.

League	2000-present	1990-99	1960-89	Pre-1960
MLB	$474 m	$223 m	$160 m	$27 m
NFL	$452 m	$224 m	$101 m	$55 m
NBA	$229 m	$162 m	$103 m	$8 m
NHL	$236 m	$165 m	$73 m	$30 m

Table 7.5
Average Arena Construction Costs
Source: T. Farrey, Getting Your Money's Worth, Sept. 18, 1998, www.espn.com and www.ballparks.com

State and local governments finance the majority of new stadiums in the United States. Typically special sales taxes are introduced to provide the needed funds. One notable exception is Pacific Bell Park in San Francisco (estimated construction costs are $262 million), which was financed both privately and through the sale of personal seat licenses. In Canada, the trend is to finance new stadiums privately as government has shown little interest in using public funds to benefit private teams. Table 7.6 lists a sample newly constructed stadiums and the share of the cost picked up by governments.

An interesting comparison between the expansion conditions facing American and Canadian teams is the case of the Florida Panthers and the Montreal Canadiens[81] in the 1990's. The new Molson Center in Montreal overcame two serious problems plaguing the old Forum: seating capacity (21,273 seats in the Molson Center versus 17,959 in the Forum) and luxury boxes (134 luxury boxes and four restaurants in the Molson Center versus none in the old Forum). The Molson Center also sports 2,600 club seats with special amenities and two levels of indoor parking. The benefits for the Canadiens in their first season at the Molson Center were immediate: an average of 21,002 tickets sold per game, the largest in the NHL. The construction cost of the arena was $270 million (Canadian) with $117 million in external private financing and the remaining $153 million paid by Molson's Breweries. Provincial and municipal government did not contribute at all to the new arena. In order to obtain approval for the new arena, the Canadiens had to participate in two public hearings and had to finance the cost of upgrading a nearby subway station. The club pays the highest property tax bill in the NHL at $11 million (Canadian) annually.

With the awarding of the Florida Panthers franchise in December of 1992, the team had less than a year to start operating. The only available facility was the 14,372 seat Miami Arena where the Panthers were the secondary tenant to the NBA's Miami Heat (who have since moved to a new arena). The Panthers took a five-year lease with no parking or concessions revenue and terrible home dates. Despite sell-outs, the club lost $60 million in the first five years of operating. In 1999, the Panthers moved to the new 19,088 seat National Car Rental (NCR) Center, built at a cost of $185 million. The new arena was financed entirely by public money: a new 2% hotel tax and an addition to the state sales tax will be

---

[81] This material is taken from M. Grange, U.S. unlike Canada, eager to pay price for sports facilities, Toronto Globe and Mail, Oct. 30, 1998.

used to pay off a public bond issue. The Panthers receive the first $18 million of arena profit and 80% of the remaining profit. The Panthers pay no property tax, no rent (a saving of $1 million annually) and receive free police and paramedic services for home games.

City	Facility	Opens	Cost	Public	Private
Seattle	Safeco Field	1999	$498	$372	$126
Cincinnati	Paul Brown Stadium	2000	$404	$404	$0
Seattle	Seattle Stadium	2002	$400	$300	$100
Milwaukee	Miller Park	1999	$367	$277	$90
Los Angeles	Staples Center	1999	$350	$45	$305
San Francisco	Pacific Bell Park	2000	$306	$0	$306
Detroit	Detroit Ballpark	2000	$295	$115	$180
Nashville	Tennessee Stadium	1999	$292	$292	$0
Houston	Ballpark at Union Station	2000	$266	$181	$85
Atlanta	Atlanta Arena	1999	$250	$210	$40
Dallas	Victory Arena	2000	$230	$125	$105
Detroit	Ford Stadium	2000	$230	$180	$50
Pittsburgh	Pittsburgh Stadium	2001	$223	$147	$76
Cleveland	Cleveland Stadium	1999	$220	$166	$54
Pittsburgh	PNC Park	2001	$209	$169	$40
Miami	American Airlines Arena	1999	$180	$0	$180
Denver	Pepsi Center	1999	$160	$7	$153
Raleigh	Sports Arena	1999	$158	$130	$28
Toronto	Air Canada Center	1999	$260 (Can.)	$0	$260

Table 7.6
Selected facilities with sources of financing ($ millions)
Source: M. Grange, U.S. unlike Canada, eager to pay price for sports facilities, Toronto Globe and Mail, Oct. 30, 1998.

The wide disparity in the fortunes of major league teams is reflected more generally in ticket prices. Figure 7.1 provides a scatter plot of the average ticket price in MLB parks versus the year the team moved into the stadium. Fenway Park (Boston Red Sox), Wrigley Field (Chicago

Cubs) and Dodger Stadium (L.A. Dodgers) are excluded due to their advanced ages. There is a weak positive association between average ticket price and year of construction with a correlation coefficient of 0.413, suggesting that newer stadiums tend to have higher ticket prices. However if the new Yankee Stadium is also excluded, the correlation coefficient falls to just 0.33. Economics does not predict that higher construction costs raise ticket prices, rather that higher demand raises ticket prices. It is more likely that the comfort, novelty and amenities of new arenas raise the demand for tickets, and prices. But for some teams with relatively new stadiums, such as the San Diego Padres, ticket prices are driven by the team performance and the local market size, not the attractiveness of the stadium

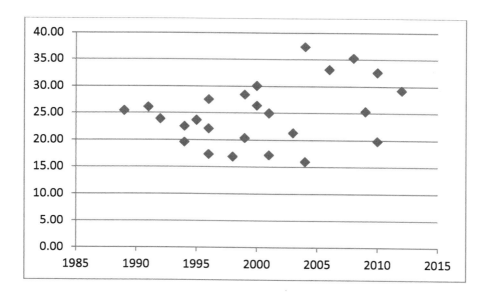

Figure 7.1
Average ticket prices versus year of stadium construction, MLB.

7.2 Stadium Financing

Sources of stadium revenue, other than ticket sales, are commercial licensing agreements, personal seat licenses and naming rights. Each is analyzed below[82].

7.2.1 Commercial Licensing Agreements

Concession providers normally enter into a commercial licensing agreement with the stadium owner in order to provide concession services at the stadium. The stadium owner can charge a royalty based on sales or a fixed fee not related to sales. Usually the agreement calls for a combination of a fixed fee and a royalty payment. Often fixed fees are collected even before the stadium has been completely built. Why should it make a difference if a concessionaire pays a fixed fee with lower royalty payments, or no fixed fee with higher royalty payments? After all, the stadium owner could charge no fixed up-front fee, get a loan to build the stadium, and then pay off the loan with higher future royalty payments. Or the stadium could be partly financed by large initial fixed fees with low royalty payments in the future.

A royalty is a form of sales tax that creates a disincentive to expand sales and results in a deadweight loss to society. Figure 7.2 demonstrates the effect of royalty payments. The royalty payment must be paid by the concessionaire to the stadium owner and usually takes the form of a percentage of sales. If $5 is the average price of a hot dog at a concession, the royalty payment raises the minimum price the concessionaire must receive to supply the equilibrium quantity of 10,000

---

[82] Portions of this section are drawn from R. Noll and A. Zimbalist, "Build the Stadium – Create the Jobs!" in <u>Sports, Jobs and Taxes</u> edited by R. Noll and A. Zimbalist, Brookings Institution, 1997.

hot dogs. Let's suppose the concession contract calls for a royalty payment of 10% to the stadium owner. This shifts the supply curve of hot dogs vertically by the royalty percentage times the equilibrium price of a hot dog, or 0.10($5) = $0.50 per hot dog. The minimum price the hot dog vendor needs to supply 10,000 hot dogs has increased by $0.50 to still earn the original $5. This cuts into the profit for the hot dog vendor so he or she will try to pass the royalty payment onto the fan by increasing the price of a hot dog. The vendor cannot pass on all of the royalty cost to fans due to the slope of the demand curve. The new concession price will increase to $5.25 with 9,500 hot dogs sold, where the demand curve and the new higher supply curve intersect. The triangle ABC is a *deadweight loss* to society. This area represents sales that would occur profitably if the royalty payment were not required. Hot dogs that would have formally been sold and added to GDP are not produced and sold. In this way, taxes create distortions in what and how much is produced.

The top half of the deadweight loss area is the loss in consumer surplus while the bottom half is the loss in producer surplus. The slope of the demand curve determines the ability of the hot dog vendor to pass on the royalty fee to the fan. Imagine that the demand curve for hot dogs at a game is completely flat (elastic) as is the case when there are many substitutes available for a hot dog. Shifting the supply curve for hot dogs vertically by $0.50 will not affect the equilibrium price of $5 because fans will not pay any price above $5. The hot dog vendor must then bear the full cost of the royalty tax by selling fewer hot dogs at the same price. Imagine now that there are no substitutes for a hot dog at a game (not likely). The demand curve for hot dogs is then completely vertical (inelastic). The royalty tax shifts the supply curve of hot dogs vertically by $0.50 and the equilibrium price rises to $5.50, where demand and supply intersect. In this case, the fan is paying the full cost of the royalty tax and the vendor is no worse off than without the tax.

This hot dog example illustrates what economists refer to as the *incidence of a tax*. The more inelastic (steeper) the demand curve for a taxed good, the more the consumer will pay of the tax and the more tax revenue will be generated. Sales will fall only slightly and the vendor is actually better off in terms of revenue (remember the elasticity condition). So governments prefer to tax goods with very inelastic demand, such as gasoline, tobacco and alcohol since it will generate a lot of tax revenue and not discourage sales too much for firms. Goods with elastic demand curves, such as milk and bread, are not taxed.

Fixed up-front fees will impose no deadweight loss, however if the team becomes successful, the stadium owner will not benefit from higher royalties, while the concessionaire will benefit from higher sales. Without royalty revenues, the stadium owner may attempt to benefit from team success by raising rental payments to the team, which may be passed on in the form of higher ticket prices. If the happens, consumers end up paying the royalties anyway, albeit in the form of higher ticket prices. Most commercial licensing agreements are a blend of fixed fees and royalty payments.

274

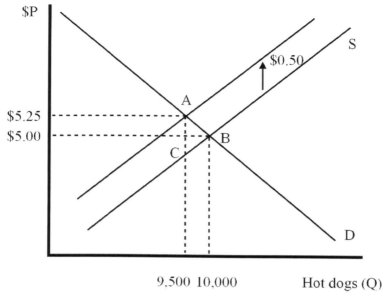

Figure 7.2
The royalty payment shifts the supply curve of hot dogs vertically by the royalty percentage of the price $5. The new equilibrium price will be $5.25 with 9,500 hot dogs sold. The shaded area is the deadweight loss to society.

7.2.2 Personal Seat Licenses

A personal seat license (PSL) is a fixed fee that gives the owner of the PSL the right to purchase a season ticket. The fee does not include the season ticket itself. PSL's are very common in the NFL, but not in the other four major leagues[83]. Its holder can sell a PSL to another consumer, however the team typically collects a commission on the sale price. Alternatively, the PSL can only be sold back to the team at a previously fixed price. The PSL was first used in 1968 to help finance the construction

---

[83] An exception is baseball's San Francisco Giants who sold PSL's to partly finance the construction of the recently opened Pacific Bell Park. These PSL's were perpetual, that is, they gave the owner of the PSL the right to purchase a season ticket forever, in theory.

Analytical example: Calculating the effect of a royalty.

Question: The demand curve for beer for the new Los Angeles Surfers NFL team is given by $P = 15 - 0.001Q$ where P is the price of a cup of beer and Q is the number of cups sold. The vendor's supply curve for cups of beer is given by $P = 2 + 0.001Q$. How many cups of beer will be sold and what will be the equilibrium price?

If the stadium owner imposes a 10% royalty tax on the beer vendor, what will be the new equilibrium price and quantity?

Answer: The equilibrium number of cups of beer is found by setting demand equal to supply.

$15 - 0.001Q = 2 + 0.001Q$

Now solve for Q.

$-0.002Q = -13$, $Q = -13/-0.002 = 6,500$ cups

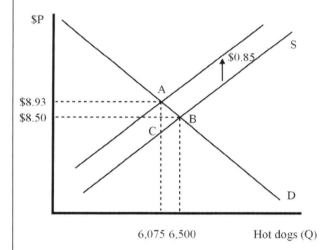

Substitute the quantity into the demand curve or the supply curve to find the equilibrium price.

$P = 2 + 0.001(6,500) = \$8.50$

The 10% tax shifts the supply curve vertically by $0.85. This increases the intercept of the supply curve by 0.85. Find the new quantities and price as before.

$15 - 0.001Q = 2.85 + 0.001Q$
$-0.002Q = -12.15$
$Q = -12.15/-0.002 = 6,075$ cups
$P = 2.85 + 0.001(6,075) = \$8.93$

of Texas Stadium for the Dallas Cowboys (NFL), but were not used again to finance new stadium construction until 1986 (Charlotte Hornets (NBA)). The sale of PSL's can raise significant revenues for teams: the Carolina Panthers (NFL) raised $150 million through the sale of PSL's, of which $100 million was directed towards construction of Ericcson Stadium. These PSL's ranged in price from $600 to $5,400.

Personal seat licenses have some advantages for helping finance the cost of new stadium construction. First, they reduce the exposure of the team, and the state and local governments, to risk. If the team and the stadium turn out to be a bust, the holders of the PSL's are left absorbing the loss. Since PSL's reduce the tax burden for new stadium construction, most voters prefer them. Second, PSL's tend to behave as a voluntary progressive tax on those who benefit from purchasing them. Those who have the greatest ability to pay taxes for new stadium construction should be the ones who pay. This idea runs counter to the approach taken for other large public construction projects where taxes are spread out evenly among a large number of people (like a state sales tax).

Economics predicts that PSL's should reduce season ticket prices. This is because consumers have limited incomes and will not pay high prices for both PSL's and season tickets. But lower season ticket prices may mean less team revenue and a lower quality team (less money for payrolls). If potential buyers of PSL's anticipate this, they may not be willing to pay as much for a PSL, since if they do not use it, the PSL will fall in value with a lower quality team.

If the sale of PSL's has the potential of lowering team quality, and thus the resale value of the PSL, why do consumers buy them? One argument is that the PSL gives the consumer priority access to season tickets and playoff tickets. This argument falls flat since season ticket holders, without PSL's, typically are given priority in purchasing playoff tickets and season tickets for the next season. In addition, consumers can sell their season tickets without holding a PSL, so it is not clear that owning a PSL grants the consumer any additional rights over a season ticket holder without a PSL. Another argument is that seats purchased by holders of PSL's typically have better sight lines and receive extra services that non-PSL holders do not receive. This may be true, but the value of the extra services is probably less than the cost of the PSL. A final argument for PSL's is that the cost is justified by the internalization of the value of a public good, that being the feeling of participating in the operations of the team.

Team owners prefer the sale of PSL's for two reasons. First, the sale of PSL's is a classic example of price discrimination where the owner attempts to capture any consumer surplus received by ticket holders. By charging different prices for PSL's, the team owner can extract the maximum amount wealthy consumers are willing to pay to attend home games. This translates into extra revenues for the team owner. A second, subtler economic argument for PSL's, involves revenue sharing. In the NFL, the current revenue sharing split is 60-40 in favor of the home team. The sale of PSL's may lower season ticket prices, lowering revenues for the home team. If the majority of visiting teams do not sell PSL's for their home games, the seller of the PSL's may benefit by receiving higher revenues from other clubs that the revenues paid out to them under revenue sharing. Essentially, visiting teams subsidize teams selling PSL's.

7.2.3 Stadium Naming Rights

A relatively recent method to obtain stadium revenue is to allow private companies to purchase the naming rights for the facility. For an annual fee, the company name and logo adorn the facility until the expiry date of the naming contract. For most facilities, this is not a large source of revenue but there are some notable exceptions. Table 7.7 contains a summary of these naming rights contracts. One would expect that the value of naming rights might be greater in newer facilities that are built in large urban centers. The value of naming rights increases further if the tenants of the facility are successful on the field and operate in a league with high television exposure.

Facility name	Company	Team	$ m	
Met Life Stadium	Met Life Financial	New York Giants and Jets	25.00	2027
Citi Field	Citi Financial	New York Mets	20.00	2026
Barclays Center	Barclays Bank	Brooklyn Nets	20.00	2028
Reliant Stadium	Reliant Energy	Houston Texans	10.00	2032
Phillips Arena	Royal Phillips Electronics	Atlanta Hawks	9.30	2019
CMGI Field	CMGI	New England Patriots	8.00	2017
FedEx Field	Federal Express	Washington Redskins	7.60	2025
Lincoln Financial Field	Lincoln Financial Group	Philadelphia Eagles	6.70	2022
American Airlines Center	American Airlines	Dallas Mavericks, Stars	6.50	2031
Invesco Field at Mile High	Invesco Funds	Denver Broncos	6.00	2021
Minute Maid Park	Coca Cola	Houston Astros	6.00	2030
Staples Center	Staples	Los Angeles Lakers, Kings, Clippers	5.80	2019
Gaylord Entertainment Center	Gaylord Entertainment	Nashville Predators	4.00	2018
Pepsi Center	PepsiCo	Denver Nuggets, Colorado Avalanche	3.40	2019
Compaq Center at San Jose	Compaq Computer	San Jose Sharks	3.10	2016
Raymond James Stadium	Raymond James Financial	Tampa Bay Buccaneers	3.10	2026

Xcel Energy	Xcel Energy	Minnesota Wild	3.00	2024
Heinz Field	H.J. Heinz	Pittsburgh Steelers	2.90	2021
Edward Jones Dome	Edward Jones	St. Louis Rams	2.65	2013
Edison International Field	Edison Intl.	Anaheim Angels	2.50	2018
Great American Ball Park	Great American Insur.	Cincinnati Reds	2.50	2033
Bank One Ballpark	Bank One	Arizona Diamondbacks	2.20	2028
Comerica Park	Comerica	Detroit Tigers	2.20	2030
MCI Center	MCI	Wash. Wizards, Caps, Mystics	2.20	2017
American Airlines Arena	American Airlines	Miami Heat	2.10	2019
Miller Park	Miller Brewing	Milwaukee Brewers	2.10	2020
SBC Center	SBC Communications	San Antonio Spurs	2.10	2022
Conseco Fieldhouse	Conseco	Indiana Pacers, Fever	2.00	2019
PNC Park	PNC Bank	Pittsburgh Pirates	2.00	2020
Safeco Field	Safeco Corp.	Seattle Mariners	2.00	2019
United Center	United Airlines	Chicago Blackhawks, Bulls	1.80	2014
Air Canada Centre	Air Canada	Toronto Maple Leafs, Raptors	1.50	2019
Tropicana Field	Tropicana	Tampa Bay Devil Rays	1.50	2026
First Union Center	First Union Bank	Philadelphia 76ers, Flyers	1.40	2023
Ford Field	Ford Motor Co.	Detroit Lions	1.00	2042

Table 7.7
Fees for Facility Naming Rights
Source: www.ballparks.com

Brief Review of Concepts

- A total of 33 new stadiums have been built in the 1990's to service NFL, NBA, NHL and MLB clubs. Constructions ranged from a low of $66 million (Delta Center) to a high of $1.6 billion (Met Life Stadium). Generally construction costs have increased at a faster rate than the Consumer Price Index, but this partly reflects the increase in stadium quality and amenities.
- New facilities built in the US typically require heavy public financing by local and state governments, while new facilities in

Canada are typically privately financed. Ticket prices tend to be higher in newer, more costly facilities. Individuals who attend professional sporting events tend to be more affluent than in the past.

- Sources of stadium revenue, other than ticket sales, are commercial licensing agreements and personal seat licenses. Commercial licensing agreements, such as concessions and parking, tend to raise ticket prices and create a deadweight loss for society. Fixed up-front fees create no deadweight loss but may not maximize profits for the concession owner.

- A personal seat license (PSL) is a fixed fee that gives the owner of the PSL the right to purchase a season ticket. The sale of PSL's can raise significant revenues for teams who are building a new facility. It is not clear why consumers purchase PSL's. Economics predicts PSL's may lower team quality in the future, lowering the value of the PSL.

7.3 Public Participation in Sports Facilities

New sports facilities often place a tremendous strain on local governments. New high-tech stadiums are expensive to build and often must uproot large neighborhoods. Consumers must endure additional sales taxes to pay for public bond issues to finance their construction. Those who benefit from new stadium construction and use are few in number compared to the number of taxpayers. Nevertheless, as indicated in Tables 7.1 through 7.4, new facility construction is experiencing a boom never before seen in the history of professional sports. State and local governments subsidize the construction and operation of sports facilities for a number of reasons[84].

---

[84] Portions of this section are drawn from R. Noll and A. Zimbalist, "The Economics Impact of Sports Teams and Facilities", in Sports, Jobs and Taxes edited by R. Noll and A. Zimbalist, Brookings Institution, 1997.

1. The social and psychological benefits of a local sports team may be large but cannot be measured and captured by local teams. A successful local sports team confers a positive externality on consumers. Fans can enjoy a sense of pride in their local team without actually paying to attend games. Local television and radio broadcasts can be freely enjoyed by all, merchandise can be purchased, etc.

2. Sports teams and facilities can generate significant economic benefits for the state and city. These benefits include stadium rental fees, employment in the stadium, temporary construction jobs, merchandising and tourism revenues.

3. Public ownership of sports facilities enables both teams and local governments to qualify for federal tax benefits for stadium construction. Essentially this transfers a portion of construction costs to taxpayers in other parts of the country.

4. The sports industry possesses great political power in influencing the decisions of local governments. Local governments can feel overwhelmed when facing the juggernaut of media and multinational corporations involved in the sports business.

In addition, professional sports leagues maintain a competitive market for new franchises by limiting the number of teams in the league. In order to acquire a new franchise, or even keep an existing one, cities must compete with another by offering new stadiums with generous lease agreements. Often the city that succeeds in acquiring a franchise suffers from the "winner's curse". The winning city will typically have to pay more for stadium construction and other amenities than the net benefit the team confers on the city. Net benefits are tricky to measure; their measurement is discussed in the next section.

Many professional sports teams simply cannot afford to build a new facility without public participation. In MLB, where the average construction cost of a new stadium is $474 million, only the New York Yankees and the Boston Red Sox could afford the usual 10% annual financing cost of $47.4 million based on their revenue estimates. If governments did not participate in financing stadium construction, it is quite likely that stadiums would be smaller and less elaborate. The then Ottawa Senators owner Rod Bryden financed the construction of the high-tech Corel Center almost entirely by borrowing. The $250 million project also required the private financing of a new highway overpass and road. With an annual financing cost of approximately $25 million, Bryden sold the team and the arena to Eugene Melnyk in 2003.

An alternative scheme to public financing of stadium construction is public financing of team losses. This might provide an incentive for team owners to build a better-quality team. Unfortunately a moral hazard problem would exist. Teams may decide to become perpetual losers knowing that all losses will be recovered. The real winners might be the players whose salaries will become inflated. Nobody wants local governments to transfer tax monies to professional sports players. The moral hazard effect might not be that large since most team owners would like to earn positive profits in the long run, implying no subsidy. Proper incentives could be put in place, such as salary caps and penalties, to ensure that team owners do not misuse the system.

Brief Review of Concepts

- In order for governments to participate in new stadium financing, the new stadium should confer significant social and psychological benefits and generate significant economic benefits.
- Local and state governments may able to qualify for federal tax benefits if local bond issues finance the new facility. Political lobbying may push a new stadium through even if the benefits are questionable.
- Winning bidders for new sports franchises usually suffer the "winner's curse".

7.4 Economic Impact Analysis of New Facilities

7.4.1 Concepts and Definitions

An economic impact analysis determines whether the construction of a new facility, using public funds, is justified. These public funds are raised through taxation in most cases, but in the case of sports facilities, governments will also use sales taxes and bond issues. The method can be applied to roads, bridges, or any other type of public infrastructure, as well as professional sports facilities. In order to pass the economic acid test, two broad criteria are required for any proposed use of public funds.

1. The project must provide total consumption benefits that are greater than the necessary expenditure to complete the project.
2. The project must make a net positive contribution to economic development in the community.

Direct consumption benefits do not include *public consumption benefits*, such as the psychic utility gained by consumers from the status of being a major-league sports city. The public need not attend a game or tune in to a broadcast to derive public consumption benefits. The positive externalities from a local major league team must be large, otherwise why would the media target this audience so heavily with broadcasting and advertising? In addition, consumers who never attend a game may be willing to pay to prevent the team from moving. Economists try to measure the size of these benefits using a technique called *contingent valuation*. A survey of consumers is contacted and each is presented with different scenarios that spend public funds on a set of investment projects.

Consumers are asked whether they are willing to pay an amount of tax to fund each project and are also asked to spend increasingly higher amounts. Projecting the sample results to the entire population of taxpayers allows for the estimation of a total amount consumers are willing to spend. This is then an estimate of the public consumption benefits.

Humphreys et al. (2011) used the contingent valuation method to estimate the public consumption benefits for Canadians from hosting the 2010 Winter Olympics in Vancouver.[85] Survey respondents were presented with different tax amounts to contribute towards the Own the Podium program used by the federal government to provide financial support to Canadian Olympic athletes. Projecting these results to the population of taxpayers resulted in an estimate of between $215 million and $3.4 billion. The contingent valuation method is not without its critics. The rather wide range of estimates of public consumption benefits, such as noted above, is a common problem and makes the results difficult to interpret.

Direct consumption benefits are measured by the increase in consumer surplus from stadium operations (games, broadcasts and concessions) over and above the consumer surplus for the goods and services the stadium operations will replace. When a new sports facility is constructed, particularly if it is built to house a new team in the city, other businesses may suffer or even disappear. Direct consumption benefits also include the incremental gain in consumer surplus from indirectly related consumption goods and services attributable to the new facility (motels, restaurants, etc.) over and above what existed before the new facility was built. Of course measuring consumer surplus requires a good idea what the demand curve looks like for stadium-related products and the products that will disappear. Positive direct consumption benefits are demonstrated in

[85]http://www.physedandrec.ualberta.ca/Faculty%20of%20Physical%20Education%20News/2011/12/Olympicsuccessintangiblebenefitsworthupto34billion.aspx

Figure 7.3. The consumer surplus arising from business directly or indirectly related to the new stadium is larger than the consumer surplus lost when other entertainment goods are replaced.

Analytical example: Calculating net direct consumption benefits.

Question: The demand curve for tickets for the new Los Angeles Surfers NFL team is given by $P = 100 - 0.001Q$. The team expects to sell 50,000 tickets per game and plays an 8-game home schedule.

The demand curve for other entertainment goods that will likely be replaced by the new football team (theater and so on) is given by $P = 200 - 0.0001Q$. Half a million consumers currently purchase tickets for these events.

Compute the net direct consumption benefits from the new stadium being built for the Surfers.

Answer: At 50,000 tickets per game, the Surfers can charge a ticket price of $100 - 0.001(50,000) = \$50$. The consumer surplus for a single game is

$0.5(100 - 50)50,000 = \$1.25$ million

Over 8 games, the consumer surplus is $12 million.

The ticket price for other entertainment goods is $200 - 0.0001(500,000) = \$150$. The consumer surplus is

$0.5(200 - 150)500,000 = \$12.5$ million

The net direct consumption benefit is $12 million - $12.5 million = -$500,000

Indirect consumption benefits are measured by any increase in incomes for city taxpayers and businesses over and above the incomes previously earned before the facility is constructed. These might include incomes from motels, restaurants, construction workers, stadium employees, merchandisers, etc. These increases in income are multiplied by a factor between 1 and 1.5 to account for multiplier effects on income. Income received by one person is partially spent, increasing someone else's income. Generally, direct consumption benefits are large and indirect consumption benefits are small, although stadium builders and governments argue the opposite since increases in income are more observable.

The *relevant costs* for an economic impact analysis include the annual team operating costs, annual stadium operating costs and any environmental and congestion costs. It is important to note that actual construction costs are not included as relevant costs since, in most cases, these are not true costs but instead transfers of income. For instance, wages paid to construction workers are not included as relevant costs or indirect consumption benefits. Governments collect taxes from consumers, and then transfer these taxes to other consumers when they pay construction wages, therefore there is no net gain income. This is true as long as the workers reside in the local area. If they are outside workers brought in from another city or state, their wages are included as a relevant cost since those wages will leave the local area when the workers are finished construction.

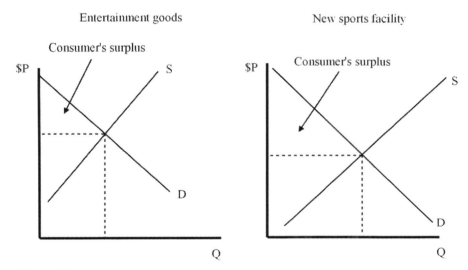

Figure 7.3

Direct consumption benefits are measured by the increase in consumer surplus from stadium operations over what goods were consumed before the stadium was built.

All of the relevant costs should be measured using opportunity costs, not accounting costs, since opportunity costs are relevant for economic decisions. The *opportunity cost* is the sacrifice in other activities required to undertake the investment, which is typically less than the accounting cost. If the city has fully employed resources, then the cost of the resources used is a good indicator of the opportunity cost. If the city has unemployed resources, the opportunity cost of using these resources is less than their accounting cost since their alternative uses are very limited. For instance, a skilled laborer who is unemployed has a much lower opportunity cost than a skilled laborer in a tight labor market earning a high wage.

If the new facility construction is ultimately financed by sales taxes on consumer goods, these taxes will reduce the supply of these goods and create a deadweight loss for each good, similar to the case of the royalty tax in Figure 7.2.If these taxes persist for a number of years, the deadweight losses in each year should be discounted to obtain their present value and included as a relevant cost when considering whether to build the facility. For instance, if the deadweight loss is expected to be $10 million every year for the ten years that a sales tax is in place, and the market rate of interest is 5%, then the present value of all of the deadweight losses is

$$PV = \frac{\$10\,m}{1.05} + \frac{\$10\,m}{1.05^2} + \cdots + \frac{\$10\,m}{1.05^{10}} \qquad (7.1)$$

That is a lot of calculations, but fortunately there is a short-cut formula that can be used when the discount rate and the deadweight loss are the same for every year.

$$PV = \frac{\$10\,m}{0.05}\left(1 - \frac{1}{(1+0.05)^{10}}\right) = \$77.22 \text{ million} \qquad (7.2)$$

Sales taxes have the same effect on consumers as royalties have on concessionaires. The deadweight loss of the sales tax is the extra consumer spending that would have taken place without the sales tax. These losses can be estimated statistically, and then discounted using an appropriate interest rate. The sales tax revenue is not included as a relevant cost since taxes are a transfer of income from consumers to owners of resources used to build the stadium.

Analytical example: Calculating indirect consumption benefits and relevant costs.

Question: An economic consulting team for the Los Angeles Surfers has estimated that the immediate increase in income for the city of Los Angeles if a new stadium is built will be $35 million per year for 10 years. Taxpayers in Los Angeles tend to spend about 25% of their incomes on consumer goods in the city. Construction costs for the new facility are $450 million, with $150 million in materials costs and with $100 million financed by the Surfers owner towards wages. It is hoped that all of the construction workers will be found within the city.

Congestion costs are anticipated to be small at $20 million per year for 10 years. The city will raise its share of the financing through a sales tax of 2.5% that will create an estimated deadweight loss of $35 million per year for 10

Answer: The increase in income over and above the existing level of income for the city is $35 per year. But the increase in the sales tax effectively reduces the increase in income to $35(1 − 0.025) = $34.125 million.

The relevant costs do not include the construction costs since the sales tax revenue will be used to pay the workers. This is just a transfer of income within the city. The net construction cost is the $150 million in materials costs. Since it is a one-time cost, it does not involve discounting.

The present value of the deadweight loss is and the congestions costs is

$$PV = \frac{\$55\,m}{0.05}\left(1 - \frac{1}{(1+0.05)^{10}}\right) = \$424.7$$
million

290

<table>
<tr>
<td>years. The market rate of interest is 5%. Calculate the indirect consumption benefits and the net costs of the project.</td>
<td>The total relevant cost is $574.7 million.</td>
</tr>
</table>

7.4.2 The Computation of Net Consumption Benefits

Generally any public investment project is economically beneficial in three situations.

1. There exist unemployed resources that are best used by subsidizing investment projects with public funds. In this case, the opportunity costs of these resources are low since they are not being used for anything else if the project does not move forward. Private financing may not be available or it may not be able to earn a sufficient profit. Private firms generally do not recognize the significant psychic and social benefits that can arise from new public infrastructure since they cannot profit from them.

2. If resources are fully employed, society may be consuming too much of its income and investing too little of its income. Investment spending is purchases of capital equipment to produce output using the economic definition. A lack of investment spending allows the capital stock to wear out so that future consumption may suffer due to reduced output. Normally a smaller capital stock will raise its marginal product and thus also its rate of return. This encourages investment and the stock of capital is replenished. To justify any public investment spending, it must be that capital markets are inefficient so that the rate of return on capital does not rise. Asymmetric information increases the

riskiness of private borrowers whereas public borrowers might not have this problem.[86]

3. The rate of return for the investment project (measured with current and future consumption benefits and relevant costs) exceeds the rate of return on all other public and private investment projects. If the public sector can internalize some of the public consumption benefits that the private sector cannot, the rate of return to public investment projects may be higher than the private sector.

Net consumption benefits are computed as

Direct consumption benefits + Indirect consumption benefits – Environmental and congestion costs – other relevant costs   (7.3)

Note that construction costs are not included if they merely transfer income within the local area. All benefits and costs are measured in present value terms. If net consumption benefits are positive, there is justification for the project to go forward. What is the statistical evidence on net consumption benefits for recent stadium construction? We present only a few examples here. The Target Center in Minneapolis, completed in 1991, faced an initial estimated construction cost of just $35 million, but quickly ballooned to $104 million during construction[87]. The majority of these construction costs were transfers of income and thus did not

---

[86] Asymmetric information of this type is called an *adverse selection* problem. Lenders cannot easily measure the riskiness of potential borrowers, so they lend at high rates of interest or do not lend at all. This means that low risk borrowers pay higher rates of interest than they should and may not borrow to undertake investment projects.

[87] J. Quirk, "Stadiums and Major League Sports", in Sports, Jobs and Taxes edited by R. Noll and A. Zimbalist, Brookings Institution, 1997.

influence the total net consumption benefits, estimated to be between $24 million and $26 million annually. These figures do not consider the fact that some of these expenditures might simply be diversions from other spending in the city, hence the net benefits may be greatly overestimated. The Target Center also attracted tenants away from two other arenas, the Met Center and the Civic Center Arena, so much so that the Civic Center Arena was demolished in 1994. This was also not taken into account in the initial estimate of the net consumption benefits. By 1995, the Target Center was losing so much money for its private owners that it was taken over by the local government.

Baseball's Cincinnati Reds and the NFL's Cincinnati Bengals have threatened to leave Cincinnati if a new stadium is not built to accommodate them. While it is not likely that MLB and the NFL would approve of the clubs relocating, the threat was taken seriously when the decision was made to conduct an economic impact analysis of a new facility[88]. The new stadium was estimated to cost $520 million to build and was to be financed entirely by government. The analysis concluded that total net consumption benefits would total only $6.11 million annually with a net employment gain of 461 jobs. That's a phenomenal $1.13 million in government construction subsidy per new job.

Cleveland's Jacobs Field and Gund Arena were constructed as part of a major downtown renewal project costing the public $467 million[89] for the two new stadiums. Besides the new stadiums, the project saw construction of new apartment buildings, restaurants, shopping and

---

[88] J. Blair and D. Swindell, "Sports, Politics and Economics", in Sports, Jobs and Taxes edited by R. Noll and A. Zimbalist, Brookings Institution, 1997.
[89] Z. Austrian and M. Rosentraub, "Cleveland's Gateway to the Future", in Sports, Jobs and Taxes edited by R. Noll and A. Zimbalist, Brookings Institution, 1997. Also see M. Rosentraub, Major League Losers: The Real Costs of Professional Sports and Who's Paying For It, Basic Books, 1997.

housing developments at a public cost of $289 million. Net employment and new business growth has been positive, although small. The subsidy cost per new job created was about $231,000, but future job growth may reduce that figure. Net consumption benefits were not estimated, rather the economic impact analysis focused on employment growth with the belief that the newly employed would spend their new incomes in Cleveland, resulting in a strong multiplier effect. Generally the overall results are negative.

San Francisco's new Pacific Bell Park (now AT&T Park) was financed entirely with private funds. Obviously the new owners must have believed that profits would be large enough to justify the cost of building the new stadium. An economic impact analysis was conducted in 1996 since the building of the new stadium required public approval from a city plebiscite. The city did have to absorb significant costs in the building of the private stadium: the loss of rental income from Candlestick Park, improvements to public transit to accommodate the new stadium and the alteration of existing road access to the new stadium. The annual net revenues generated for the city were estimated to be between a $2 million surplus and a $12 million loss. Net consumption benefits were not estimated.

Virtually every new sports facility that is built nowadays starts with an economic impact analysis. Generally the analyses overwhelmingly support construction even if the future net consumption benefits turn out to be negative. Economic impact analyses tend to suffer from the same sources of error.

- The usual assumption is that if the new facility is not built, the professional team will relocate in a different city. This may be true in a small number of cases, but league offices do not approve of teams relocating out of large media markets. This means the proper baseline to use for consumption benefits is the increase in benefits over the benefits if the team continued to play in the existing facility. For this reason, direct consumption benefits tend to be greatly overstated.

- The estimation of net direct consumption benefits usually does not subtract the direct consumption benefits from alternative forms of entertainment that already exist in the city. If the new stadium and team simply replace already existing benefits, the net direct consumption benefits are zero.

- The net indirect consumption benefits are usually grossly overstated for two reasons. First, the net increase in incomes in and around the new facility is overestimated since they do not subtract the loss of income in jobs that are eliminated. Second, the multiplier used to compute the final increase in local income is overly optimistic. Multipliers in the range of 1 to 1.5 are considered acceptable. Many studies assumed multipliers greater than 2.

Brief Review of Concepts

- *Direct consumption benefits* are measured by the increase in consumer surplus from stadium operations (games, broadcasts and concessions) over and above the consumer surplus for the goods and services the stadium operations replaced. Direct consumption benefits also include the incremental gain in consumer surplus from indirectly related consumption goods and services attributable to the new facility (motels, restaurants, etc.).
- *Indirect consumption benefits* are measured by any net increase in income over and above incomes previous to the stadium

construction. These might include incomes from motels, restaurants, construction workers, stadium employees, merchandisers, etc. These increases in income are multiplied by a factor between 1 and 1.5 to account for multiplier effects on income.

- The *relevant costs* for an economic impact analysis include the annual team operating costs, annual stadium operating costs and any environmental and congestion costs. It is important to note that actual construction costs are not included as relevant costs since, in most cases, these are not true costs but rather transfers of income.

- All relevant costs should be measured using opportunity costs, not accounting costs, since opportunity costs are relevant for economic decisions. Opportunity costs are typically less than accounting costs.

- Public investment projects are economically beneficial if unemployed resources are best used by subsidizing investment with public funds, private investment is too low due to distortions in capital markets, and the rate of return for the investment project (measured with current and future consumption benefits) exceeds the rate of return on all other public and private investment projects.

- *Net consumption benefits* are computed as direct consumption benefits + indirect consumption benefits − annual stadium operating costs − environmental and congestion costs − other relevant costs. All benefits and costs are stated in present value form.

Analytical example: Calculating net consumption benefits.

Question: We have already calculated the indirect consumption benefits and relevant costs for the Los Angeles Surfers new stadium project. So now compute the net consumption benefits and determine if the project should be financed with public funds.

Answer: The present value of the direct consumption benefits still needs to be calculated over the 10 year taxation period.

$$PV = \frac{-\$0.5\,m}{0.05}\left(1 - \frac{1}{(1+0.05)^{10}}\right) = -\$3.9 \text{ million}$$

The present value of the indirect consumption benefits is

296

$$PV = \frac{-\$34.1\,m}{0.05}\left(1 - \frac{1}{(1+0.05)^{10}}\right) = \$263.3$$
million

Using equation 7.3 gives the net consumption benefits.

-\$3.9+\$263-\$574.7 = -\$315.3 million

This project should not go forward.

Test Your Understanding

1. You have been hired as an economic consultant to assess the feasibility of building a new basketball arena in the city of Seattle. Your task is to estimate the net consumption benefits from the use of the new facility and to advise the committee overseeing the project. You have already estimated some of the relevant numbers needed to complete your assessment: the demand curve for attendance at the new arena is given by P = 580 − 0.02Q and average attendance per game (80 game season) is optimistically forecast to be 19,000; the demand curve for other entertainment goods which are thought to be substitutes for basketball games is given by P = 2000 − 0.0001Q and an estimated total of 100,000 tickets per year are sold for these events. Per capita income in Seattle is currently estimated to be \$25,000 per year, which is forecast to rise to \$25,100 after stadium construction is completed (local taxpaying population = 1.6 million).

Construction costs for the new arena are budgeted to total \$475 million with \$275 million in materials and land costs. The city will absorb the annual arena maintenance costs of \$3 million. The new team owner will contribute \$50 million of the construction costs. The rest will be financed by a sales tax of 1.5% for 10 years. You have estimated the annual deadweight loss from the sales tax to be \$45 million. The market rate of interest is 5%.

a) Compute an estimate of the net consumption benefits from the construction and operations of the new arena. What would you advise the board? What costs, if any, have not been taken into account?

b) If construction costs come in over budget at $525 million, does this change your assessment? What if average attendance is only 15,000 per game?

7.5 Competition for Franchises

Economics predicts that if professional sports teams operate in a competitive market, they will choose to locate where they can maximize profit. This profit will only be realized if the team chooses to locate where the local market demand for its product is the strongest. It also helps the bottom line if the local government can reduce costs for the team by providing a low cost or free facility to operate in. This government participation creates a distortion in where teams will find themselves operating that would not exist without government involvement. Teams would locate where consumers value their product the highest and are willing to pay the highest ticket prices. These would tend to be the largest cities, such as New York, Los Angeles and Toronto, to name a few. Teams would not locate in Columbus, Ohio (NHL Blue Jackets); Jacksonville, Florida (NFL Jaguars); or Sacramento, California (NBA Kings) without government subsidies to encourage them to locate there.

Competition for franchises by cities will lead to an inefficient allocation of teams (the invisible hand will not work) and an inefficient use of resources. Economic efficiency requires producing an output at the lowest average cost. If we include the cost to the taxpayer to the total costs of operating a professional sports team, efficiency is lost. Construction, marketing and so on will be spent in local markets that would not otherwise support a team. Unfortunately professional sports teams do not operate in a competitive market so the goal of efficiency must be thrown out. Teams agree to form a league that operates as a cartel to maximize league profits. The cartel restricts the number of new franchises so as not to reduce the profits of the existing teams. So by its very nature, a professional sports league is not economically efficient.

Cities compete with one another to attract new or existing franchises by offering subsidies to reduce the team owner's costs. These subsidies can take the form of financing the majority of the cost of building an opulent sports facility for the team to operate in. The franchise will choose to locate in the city that offers the highest "bid" in the form of a subsidy. The winning bid may not offer the highest facility subsidy since local broadcasting, advertising, concession and other royalties also supplement the package. Naturally larger market cities tend to attract franchises due to the value of these extras.

The city of Los Angeles wants the NFL to move back. The Los Angeles played in the 92,000 LA Coliseum and was the first NFL team to sign an African-American player, effectively ending racial segregation in the NFL. The stadium fell into disrepair and the team relocated to Anaheim in 1980, then left the state of California to move to St. Louis in 1994. The NFL Oakland Raiders moved into the vacated LA Coliseum in 1984, but experienced the same problems as the Rams with the facility and moved back to Oakland in 1994. Since 1994, the second largest television market in the United States has been without an NFL team.

The NFL has a keen interest in relocating one of its existing teams to Los Angeles but not if it means a long-term commitment to the ancient LA Coliseum. Three clubs have indicated interest in the move. The lease agreement the Oakland Raiders have with the Oakland-Alameda Coliseum expired at the end of the 2013 NFL season, so the team is free to move. The lease between the St. Louis Rams and the city of St. Louis for the Edward Jones Dome expires at the end of the 2014 season. The San Diego Chargers may execute a buy-out clause in their lease agreement for the aging Qualcomm Stadium in January of every year. Which team eventually moves to Los Angeles is anyone's guess, but a deal will not happen without a new stadium.

The city of Los Angeles has finished planning for a new stadium located beside the Staples Center in the downtown area. Tentatively named Farmers Field (after the Farmers Insurance company), total land and construction costs are estimated at $1.3 billion. The NFL has committed $200 million to the project regardless of what team moves in. San Diego Chargers owner Dean Spanos has offered $100 million, leaving the remaining $1 billion to be raised from public sources.[90] Such is the marketing power of the NFL that the city of Los Angeles will likely need to cough up significant funds that could be used to finance other vital public projects in order to attract an NFL team.

The NFL and MLB use a pooled revenue sharing system already detailed in Chapter 5. Revenue sharing reduces the profitability from filling a large stadium with standard seating since these revenues since one-third of these revenues must be contributed to the central fund. Revenue sharing makes public subsidies (low or zero stadium rental, luxury suites, etc.) more important to potential franchises, particularly in the NFL and MLB, and may allow the new franchise to extract higher subsidies from the local and state governments.

Cities that tend to win the battle for new franchises have the following characteristics.

1. The winning cities tend to experience greater net consumption benefits than the losing cities. This is an efficient outcome.

---

[90] http://espn.go.com/los-angeles/nfl/story/_/id/9500649/arash-markazi-no-team-arrives-years-nfl-not-return-los-angeles-long

2. Winning cities can import consumption benefits from other cities easily. These benefits may take the form of tourism and attendance drawn from non-major league cities in close proximity.

3. The net consumption benefits from the stadium and franchise tend to be contained within the winning city, that is, they are not exported to other cities. This tends to be true in larger cities.

Unfortunately it is often the case that cities overbid for new franchises or to host major sporting events, such as the Olympics or the World Cup. This is called the *winner's curse*. Let's assume that five major soccer countries wish to host a World Cup tournament and each formulates a bid to FIFA, the world governing body for professional soccer. The countries and their respective bids are listed below in Table 7.8. These bids take the form of new stadium construction and shares of the revenue to go to FIFA.

In an *English auction*, the bidding is observable by all of the participating countries. Bidding starts at a low value and increases until there is only one bidding country left that is then declared the winning bidder. As the bidding increases, the maximum bid each country is willing to make is revealed as the country declines to make a higher bid. The winning bidder will be Germany since it has the highest valuation of hosting the World Cup at $4.5 billion and it will be willing to bid up to this amount. However it need not bid this high, in fact, Germany only needs to bid slightly higher than the maximum bid of the next highest bidder which is England. So in theory, Germany can win the bidding with a bid of $4 billion + $1. This creates a surplus for Germany that is just less than $0.5 billion.

Country	Bid (US $)
Germany	$4.5 billion
England	$4 billion
Japan	$3.5 billion
Argentina	$3.25 billion
Italy	$3 billion

Table 7.8
Hypothetical bidding countries for the World Cup soccer tournament

Bidding for new franchises and major sporting events do not typically take place in an English auction, instead, they take place in a *sealed bid auction*. Each country formulates a maximum amount to bid and submits their bid in a sealed envelope. Each bidding country does not know what the bids are that are submitted by the other countries. To insure winning the auction each country will bid its maximum bid plus a little more. This is called *shading* one's bid. The uncertainty of the other bids encourages each bidder to bid more than their maximum valuation of hosting the event. The winning bidder will then bid more than the total net consumption benefits of hosting the World Cup, so winning the auction is really losing the auction in an economic sense. A cutting example of the winner's curse is the estimated $15 billion Greece spent to hose the 2004 Olympic Games. Most of the facilities lie in ruins partly due to poor Greek economy, but also by a lack of planning for their post-Olympics use.[91]

---

[91] "Why Athens has lived to regret hosting the Olympic games", http://www.thestar.com/news/world/2012/07/22/why_athens_has_lived_to_regret_ hosting_the_olympic_games.html. Video footage of the Olympic sites can be found at http://www.youtube.com/watch?v=UTY9ZzXTyW4

Chapter 8
The Market for Players

Most athletes playing in professional sports leagues earn a lot of money. The average annual salary in the NBA in 2016-17 was $6.2 million[92], $4.4 million in MLB, $2.9 million in the NHL and $2.1 million in the NFL.[93] The highest paid athlete in the four professional leagues for 2016-17 was MLB's Clayton Kershaw (L.A. Dodgers) who earned $32 million. Up to the 1960's, the average professional athlete did not earn much more than any other skilled professional. The average salary of a major-league baseball player in 1964 was only $14,800 and in 1966 only four players earned over $100,000. Today, professional athletes earn over twenty times what a skilled professional earns outside of sports. The trend is for the gap to continue to widen. Salaries in baseball increased by about 636% from 1990 to 2016, an annual average increase of 24.5%. The numbers are similar for the other professional sports leagues. Surely a hockey player cannot be worth that much more to society than a skilled doctor or a world leader. At the core of this chapter is the answer to the question of why professional athletes are paid so much. The important concepts covered in this chapter are listed below.

---

[92] Averages can be deceptively high if the distribution of player salaries is skewed. This means that a few very high salaries can pull up the average. The median is the midpoint of the salary distribution and is not influenced by very high or low salaries. The median salary in the NBA is $3.75 million, $1.5 million in MLB, $2.1 million in the NHL and $973,000 in the NFL.

[93] http://www.businessinsider.com/nfl-mlb-nba-nhl-average-sports-salaries-2016-11

- A brief history of the historical period up to free agency, with special emphasis on challenges to the reserve clause.
- A description of the different classes of free agents in each league and how they restrict player mobility.
- The economics of how player salaries are determined.
- Statistical evidence of human capital theory.

8.1 A Brief History of the Reserve Clause

The reserve system of contracting first appeared in baseball in 1879. A reserve clause states that if a player and an owner cannot reach an agreement on the player's salary for the coming season, the player can be "reserved" by the owner to play for the same salary as the previous season. This effectively binds the player to the owner for the length of the player's career, unless the owner chooses not to reserve the player. In that case, the player is a free agent and can sign a new contract with any team he or she chooses. Actually the reserve system in the National League initially gave the owner the right to reserve five players at the end of each season that could not be signed by other clubs. During the 1880's the reserve clause was extended to all player contracts. Owners further strengthened the clause in player contracts in 1889 due to legal challenges on the grounds that the reserve clause was vague. The first organized legal challenge to the reserve clause was by the Player's League in 1890. The Player's League did not adopt the reserve clause in its player contracts, rather players were signed to standard three-year contracts. These contract terms attracted 55% of National League players to defect to the new league. The rebel league was successful in court at proving the unfairness of the reserve clause, but the league folded after only one season due to financial difficulties[94]. From 1892 to 1903, the National League was the sole professional baseball league and the reserve clause became firmly entrenched.

The rival American League lured over 100 players from the National League by offering lucrative contracts with no reserve clause after it began operations in 1901. The huge success of the American League led to the National Agreement in 1903 that recognized both leagues operating as equal partners. It also saw the American League agree to institute a reserve clause and for owners from both leagues to honor each other's reserve clause contracts. Again players were bound to their teams for life, until the emergence of the rival Federal League in 1914. The Federal League operated eight teams for the 1914-15 season, but failed badly at the box office. The league challenged the reserve clause system of the National and American Leagues under the Sherman Act, but seven of the eight clubs dropped out of the lawsuit after they went out of business in 1915. The owner of the Baltimore Terrapins eventually won the case in 1922, but then lost on appeal, then lost again when the matter was appealed to the Supreme Court. The decision in *Federal League vs. Baseball* stated that the existing National and American leagues did not operate interstate commerce and thus were not subtract to the antitrust statutes of the Sherman Act. This meant that baseball teams did not operate as businesses when visiting other cities, even despite revenue sharing.

Curt Flood was an all-star outfielder for the St. Louis Cardinals in the 1960's. Towards the end of his career, Flood was traded to the Philadelphia Phillies in 1969. He refused to report to his new team and launched a legal challenge to the reserve clause in 1970 that was taken to

---

[94] The National League paid a total of $800,000 to the owners of Player's League clubs in compensation for folding. Players from the defunct league were allowed to return to their former National League clubs.

the Supreme Court. Flood lost his challenge in 1971, largely due to a lack of support from the player's union. The presiding judge noted that the reserve clause was clearly a violation of constitutional rights, but that the matter should be settled through collective bargaining and not the courts. Flood retired shortly after the decision, but his determination prompted a more vigilant attitude within the player's union. To avoid a player strike in 1973, owners agreed that in the future an arbitration panel would settle contract disputes for players with at least two years of major league service. This was a mistake by the owners and spelled the end of the reserve clause system.

Figure 8.1
Weeghman Park (now better known as Wrigley Field where the Chicago Cubs play) was home to the Chicago Whales of the Federal League. An upper terrace was added to the park in 1927.

Under advisement from Marvin Miller, the new head of the player's association, pitchers Dave McNally of the Montreal Expos and

Andy Messersmith of the Los Angeles Dodgers played the 1975 season without signing their contracts. At the end of the season, both declared themselves free agents since the reserve clause did not apply to a player without a contract for the previous season. The matter went to an independent arbitration committee headed by Peter Seitz. The three-person committee ruled in favor of the players, but the ruling was appealed and the owners fired Seitz. The owners lost the case in federal court. The court also ruled that any player playing out his one-year option at the end of the 1977 season was deemed a free agent and was free to sign with any team. The decision would have affect hundreds of players. In order to prevent a flood of free agents, and falling salaries, Miller negotiated a clause in the new collective agreement that free agents must have a minimum of six years of major league service. The owners happily agreed to Miller's shrewd tactic. In the 1994 collective agreement, players could become free agents after only four years of major league service.

The standard reserve clause in the NFL was more vague than in baseball, but was just as effective at limiting player movement. Adopted in 1922, the reserve system went unchallenged until 1957 when George Radovich, a star player, launched a legal challenge. Radovich played out his option, then wished to sign with a west coast team, but was prevented from doing so. He lost the case and was subsequently banned from playing in the NFL. In 1964, the NFL adopted the infamous Rozelle Rule, named after new NFL commissioner Pete Rozelle. The rule required any owner signing a player from another team to provide compensation to the former team. The compensation usually included quality players who were determined by Rozelle. The compensation was usually so onerous that player movement was rare. Of 176 players playing out their one-year options between 1963 and 1974, only 34 signed with other clubs. There were only four cases in which the Rozelle Rule was actually applied.

In 1972, 32 players sued the NFL for damages inflicted by the Rozelle Rule. The players won the case and received almost $16 million in damages. Despite this victory, the Rozelle Rule became even more restrictive over time. Between 1977 and 1988, between 125 and 150 players became free agents each year, but only three players moved to new teams. The NFL agreed with the players on a two-tiered free agent system in 1989. Roughly 65% of the available free agents still required compensation under the Rozelle Rule, but so-called Plan B free agents could be signed with no compensation. Currently the system is being adjusted to allow more player movement, albeit at the expense of the hard salary cap for each team. Teams are allowed to designate one "franchise player" each year who will require compensation if signed by another team. Teams must declare their franchise player at the start of each season. All other players can be restricted or unrestricted free agents (see next section).

The working of the reserve clause in basketball was basically the same as in football in the early years. Players were signed to one-year contracts with an option for a second year. The reserve clause insured that player movement was very restricted. In 1970, the NBA Players Association launched a lawsuit to prevent the proposed merger of the NBA and the new American Basketball Association (ABA). The players felt that a merger of the two leagues would prevent competitive bidding for players and hold down salaries. The lawsuit dragged on, preventing the merger. In 1974, the ABA Players Association (ABAPA) also launched a lawsuit against the NBA challenging the reserve clause. The NBA lost both cases that year, nixing the merger and allowing for more player movement across the two leagues. The ABA also had a standard reserve clause, so the ABAPA successfully launched an anti-trust lawsuit against the ABA in 1975. In addition, private lawsuits were launched by star players Wilt Chamberlain, Julius Irving and George McGinnis against the NBA. An out of court settlement was reached in these matters in 1976.

With the newly merged NBA reeling under player dissention, the collective agreement was changed to allow unrestricted free agents after the 1980 season. Following the 1983 season, the collective agreement was further adjusted to allow for team salary caps equal to each team's share of 53% of total NBA revenues. Player movement was not restricted by a reserve clause, but instead was restricted by the salary cap. The latest NBA collective agreement maintains the system of unrestricted free agency and raises the team salary cap to 55% of anticipated league revenues. Hard caps were instituted to limit the maximum salary of each player, depending on the number of years of NBA service. Under the "Larry Bird" clause, a team attempting to re-sign a player eligible for free agency may exceed the hard cap. In 2011, the NBA hard cap was reduced to 50% of anticipated league revenues.

The NHL had the same one-year plus an option contract that the NFL and NBA had up to the 1970's. Player movement was almost non-existent and salaries were low, particularly in the lengthy period of the "original six" teams. Rapid expansion in the 1960's put pressure on the league to allow more player movement to satisfy talent starved new teams. The NHL resisted and the rebel World Hockey Association (WHA) emerged as a haven for disgruntled players. In 1972, the WHA launched an anti-trust lawsuit against the NHL, citing that WHA teams were not allowed to play in NHL arenas. The reserve clause was also contested in several player suits, the most visible being the case of star player Bobby

Hull. Hull signed with the WHA Winnipeg Jets since the NHL's reserve clause severely limited his salary. The NHL responded by successfully lobbying for a ruling against Hull: he could not play professional hockey for any team, other than the NHL Chicago Blackhawks, anywhere in the state of Illinois. Whenever the WHA Jets traveled to play in Illinois, Hull could not play. The NHL eventually settled the suit out of court for a settlement of $2 million.

In 1974, the NHL and WHA agreed to respect each other's reserve clauses and WHA teams were allowed to play in NHL arenas. In the 1975 NHL collective agreements, players were allowed to become free agents after playing out their contracts, but the losing team required compensation to be determined by an independent arbitrator. The compensation was usually so large that player movement was severely restricted. In 1992, the collective agreement was changed to allow for unrestricted free agents after seven years of NHL service. Other free agents were restricted. The NHL adopted a salary cap in the 2005 CBA and today the salary cap stands at 50% of anticipated league revenue.

Focus Box: Charlie Finley

Charlie Finley purchased the Kansas City Athletics after the team had moved from Philadelphia in 1955. The club had always been a perennial loser and Finley did nothing to change its luck until he tried to move the team to Atlanta in the early 1960's. The Milwaukee Braves moved to Atlanta first, which angered Finley and began a tenuous relationship with the other baseball owners. Finley began negotiating with Oakland which was building a new stadium to house the AFL Raiders and offering a generous deal to entice the A's to move west. The AL owners refused to allow the move so Finley sued the other owners for the right to take his team wherever he wished. By this time, fans in Kansas City had all but abandoned the A's due to Finley's antics, so a move was inevitable. The AL finally granted permission to move the club and the A's began playing in Oakland in 1968[95].

Finley was a master salesman who tried many garish promotions to sell tickets. He dressed his players in polyester double-knit uniforms instead of the standard flannels. Team colors were white, yellow and green with white shoes worn in different color combinations for each game. Finley encouraged his players to grow mustaches, long hair and sideburns by paying them a $300 bonus. He lobbied baseball to adopt an orange ball. His lasting legacy is the designated hitter rule, which he lobbied baseball to adopt in response to a lack of hitting[96]. His teams were characterized by skilled players who hated each other as well as the manager and the owner. Yet his teams won World Series titles in 1972, 1973 and 1974. His final promotion before the sale of the team in 1978 was the hiring of a twelve-year old boy to call the radio play.

Finley is also notable for his ruthless dealings with players when it came to salary negotiations. In 1974, Jim "Catfish" Hunter went 25-12 for the World Series winners. He claimed that Finley failed to make certain performance payments under his contract, which Finley denied. An independent arbitration panel ruled in favor of Hunter, making him baseball's first free agent under the 1972 collective agreement. Hunter signed a multi-year contract with the New York Yankees for significantly more money. Following the Seitz ruling in 1976, Finley lost star

---

[95] Fearing an anti-trust lawsuit from Kansas City and Milwaukee over the moves, baseball promised that expansion teams would be granted to the two cities. These became the Royals and the Brewers (moved from Seattle).

[96] Only the AL adopted the designated hitter. Finley may have been right – the NL and AL batted a combined .250 in 1960 and offense dropped steadily through the decade. By 1967, hitting had dropped to a combined .236. Baseball responded by lowering the height of the pitching mound in 1968.

outfielders Reggie Jackson, Joe Rudi, catcher Sal Bando and pitcher Rollie Fingers to free agency. Finley was the last owner to try selling players to the highest bidder, a practice now informally disallowed in most professional sports. In 1976, Finley tried to sell pitcher Vida Blue, Reggie Jackson and Joe Rudi to other teams for a total of approximately $3 million. Commissioner Bowie Kuhn vetoed the sale stating the cash sales of players were not in the interests of baseball.

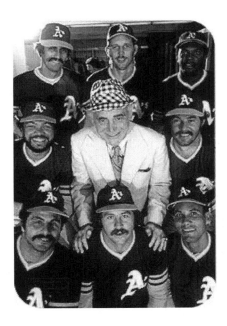

Charlie Finley pictured with his stable of star players. All of them would bolt from the A's within a few years for free agency.

8.2 Contract Terminology

Being a free agent is simple in baseball and basketball, but confusing in football and hockey. The points below list the most current contract and free agent categories in the existing collective bargaining agreements.

MLB

- All players can be unrestricted free agents (requiring no compensation from the new team to the former team) if the current players contract has expired and a new contract cannot be agreed upon. A minimum of six years of major league service is required for unrestricted free agency unless a renewing contract offer is not made.

- A drafted player is bound to the team that drafted him for three years of minor league service. At the end of this three-year period, the team must either sign the player to a contract that places him on the 40-man major league roster or release the player. If the player is kept, he must be placed on the major-league roster for three seasons, however the team has the ability to "option" the player to a minor-league team for one season in this period. Each player has a total of three options in their major league playing career.

- If the player is released after three years of minor league service, the player is eligible to participate in the Rule 5 draft. If drafted by another major-league team for $50,000, the player must be on the major league roster for the entire season, or be offered back to the original team for $25,000. Players need not participate in the Rule 5 draft and will remain as minor league free agents.

NBA

- All players can be unrestricted free agents (requiring no compensation) if the current player contract has expired and a new contract cannot be agreed upon. The salaries of new free agent players must fit under the annual league imposed team salary cap ($94.1 million for the 2016-17 season). A team may exceed its salary cap to resign a potential free agent player. A minimum of three years of NBA service is required for unrestricted free agency unless a renewing contract offer is not made.

- A team may choose to make a player a restricted free agent by making an offer (called a tender offer) of at least 125% of the previous year's salary plus $175,000 if the player is out of contract with the team. If the player does not sign with another team, the player is signed to a one-year contract with the offering team and then is an unrestricted free agent at the end of the contract.

- If another team wishes to sign a restricted free agent, it must extend an offer sheet to the player. If he signs it, the original team has seven days to match the offer. If they do not, there is no compensation.

NFL

- Unrestricted free agents (UFA): Players become unrestricted free agents when their current contract expires and they have at least four years of NFL service. The salaries of new free agent players must fit under the annual league imposed team salary cap ($155.3 million for the 2016 season). The signing period is February 12 to July 15. If still unsigned after the signing period, the player's rights revert back to his old club as long as a contract is offered by June 1.

- Restricted free agents: Players become restricted free agents when their current contract expires and they have three years of NFL service. The signing period is February 12 to April 12. The team must make a tender offer to the player based on the level of compensation required if the player is lost ($3.91 million for a first-round draft pick in 2017, $2.75 million for a second-round draft pick). If still unsigned after the signing period, the player's rights revert back to his old club. If the player accepts an offer from a new club, his old club can match the offer and retain his services (the "right of first refusal"). If the offer is not matched, the old club receives draft choice compensation depending upon the level of its last salary offer.

- Franchise players: Each club may designate one UFA player as its franchise player. The player must receive a minimum salary of the average salary of the top five paid players in his position, or 120% of his previous year's salary, whichever is greater. Failing this, the franchise player can declare free agency with the old club retaining the right of first refusal. Compensation is two first round draft choices.

- Transition players: Each club may designate one UFA player as its transition player. The player must receive a minimum salary of the average salary of the top ten paid players in his position, or 120% of his previous year's salary, whichever is greater. Failing this, the franchise player can declare free agency with the old club retaining the right of first refusal for seven days after a new offer is received. No compensation is awarded.

- Newly drafted players must sign a four contract with the team that drafted them. There is a maximum threshold contract value that is a complicated mix of salary and signing bonuses.

NHL

- Unrestricted free agents: Any player who is not re-signed upon expiration of his contract. Alternatively, a player who is at least 27 years old and has 7 years of NHL service. The salaries of new free agent players must fit under the annual league imposed team salary cap ($73 million for the 2016-17 season). No compensation is awarded.

- Restricted free agents: Any player whose contract expires and does not qualify as an UFA. The team may make a qualifying offer to retain the player for one season at the same salary as the previous season. If no qualifying offer is made, the team receives compensation if the player signs with another team. The player may also reject the qualifying offer. The team also retains the right to match the offer made by another team to keep the player.

- Newly drafted players must sign an entry level contract with the team that drafted them. The length of the contract is three years for players aged 18-21 and two years for players aged 22-23. Entry level contracts are two-way contracts meaning the salary will fall if the player is assigned to a minor-league team. The maximum NHL salary in the contract is $925,000 per season for 2013, but the minor-league salary is negotiated. After the entry level contract has expired, the player may sign a one-way with the NHL team that pays the same salary in the NHL and the minor leagues.

318

8.3 The Determination of Salaries

We have already seen in Chapter 3 that the salary paid to a player is determined by the marginal product of the team stock of talent and the stock of talent of the individual player. The marginal product is of talent the change in total output of the club (measured as ticket sales) when one more unit of talent is added to the team. Figure 2.11 demonstrated that the marginal product schedule is downward sloping due to the assumption of the law of diminishing returns. A club owner will hire talent up to the point where the marginal product is just equal to the going market wage per unit of talent. This is the case if the talent market is competitive and all teams settle down to the same market wage per unit of talent. If talent is scarce, such as it is in professional sports, the wage rate per unit of talent will be determined by how much talent the team owner hires. Figure 2.12 demonstrated that at this point, the owner receives the maximum surplus from the hiring of talent. This chapter extends the brief analysis of salary determination in Chapter 2 to account for market structure, talent supply and other real world issues.

In Chapter 6 we saw that it is realistic to think of a professional sports league as a number of teams operating as a cartel. Each team is a monopolist within its geographically protected area, which then colludes with other teams to form a market wide monopoly, or cartel. To ensure that the cartel does not fall apart, the league rations the available league market by controlling the growth of new expansion teams and the entry of players into the league (a draft system). Let's assume we are working in the short-run where talent is the only variable input. All other factors of production, such as coaching, equipment, training facilities, etc. are assumed to be constant. This is the economic distinction between the short run and the long run. In the short run, only labor can be changed, but in the long run, all factors of production can be changed.

8.3.1 Demand for Talent in the Short Run

In a competitive product market, we saw in Chapter 2 that a firm will hire talent up to the point where the value of the marginal product (VMP_T) just equals the going market wage per unit of talent (W_T). This maximizes the surplus to the owner from hiring talent. The VMP_T multiplies the marginal product of talent by the price of the firm's output, in this case, an average ticket price, and thus represents the change in the firm's revenue from hiring one more unit of talent. In a competitive product market, all teams would charge the same ticket price P.

$$VMP_T = P x MP_T = W_T$$ in a competitive talent and product market

In Figure 8.1, we have reproduced Figure 2.15. The VMP_T schedule is drawn as downward sloping to reflect the law of diminishing marginal product: when one more unit of talent is added to the production process, output increases at a diminishing rate holding constant all the other factors of production. This also can be considered the demand curve for talent since it gives the optimal level of talent to hire at each going wage rate per unit of talent. If the going market wage is $100 per unit of talent, the team owner will hire 200 units of talent in Figure 8.1.

Professional sports league cartels are not very competitive when it comes to ticket pricing. Each is a local monopolist and can charge the ticket price where $MR = MC$ for tickets, hence the factor-pricing rule above does not apply. Let's continue to assume that talent is available in

320

large supply. For a monopolist team owner, talent is hired up to the point where the marginal revenue product of talent (MRP_T) just equals the going market wage per unit of talent (W_T) that each team owner faces. Since the product price falls as the monopolist increases output (ticket sales), the MRP_T falls faster than the VMP_T as more talent is hired. This is because the ticket price must fall for all tickets in order to sell one more ticket, whereas in a competitive product market, the ticket price is constant and the same for all teams. The increase in revenue when one more ticket is sold is less than the price of the ticket.

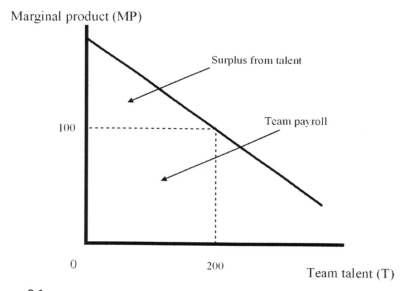

Figure 8.1
The player's salary is determined by his or her *VMP*. The difference between the value of the player's output (the area under the *VMP* schedule up to 200 talent units) and the team payroll ($25(100)(200) = $500,000) is the surplus value that the team owner receives.

Figure 8.2 demonstrates that the monopolist team owner will hire less talent than the competitive owner, at the wage rate per unit of talent of $100. The demand curve for talent for the monopolist is to the left of the demand curve for talent of the owner operating in a competitive market, since the marginal revenue earned from an additional ticket sold is less than the ticket price. The monopolist owner will wish to restrict the sale of tickets in order to achieve a higher profit-maximizing price. This in turn implies hiring less talent.

$$MRP_T = MRxMP_T = W_T$$ in a competitive talent market with a monopolist owner

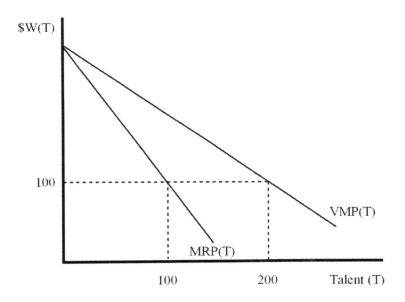

Figure 8.2
The monopolist hires only 100 units of talent which is less than the competitive owner who hires 200. The demand curve for talent for the team owner operating in a local monopoly is the MRP_T line.

8.3.2 Demand for talent in the long run: Competitive product market

In the long run, the firm can vary all of its factors of production, which complicates the determination of salaries. Let's assume that there are only two variable factors[97] of production, capital (K) and talent (T), and that the team owner operates in a competitive product market. This means that the ticket price is the same for all teams and that no owner can charge a higher ticket price without going out of business. The firm will hire increasing amounts of capital and talent up to the point where the value of the marginal product of capital (VMP_K) just equals the rental rate per unit of capital (r_K) and the VMP_T just equals the going market wage per unit of talent (W_T). This amount of hiring maximizes the surplus returned to the owner from hiring both talent and capital. So far this is just a generalization of the short run case where only talent is variable. The complication in the long run is that marginal product of talent MP_T, and therefore the VMP_T, may depend not only on the amount of talent that is hired, but also upon the amount of capital that is hired, and vice-versa.

To proceed further, we need to discuss how capital and talent can interact to determine the team's output (ticket sales). Capital and talent are said to be *complementary* factors if increasing the amount of one factor increases the marginal product of the other. Complementarity implies a synergy or positive interaction between the factors which raises output beyond just that attributable to hiring more of one factor. Examples are executives and secretaries, land and fertilizer, wood and carpenters, etc. If the hiring of more of one factor has no effect on the marginal product of the other factor, the two factors are said to be *independent*. Finally if hiring more of one factor reduces the marginal product of the other factor, the two

---

[97] In a strict sense, there must be a least one fixed factor, even in the long run. If all factors are variable, then the law of diminishing returns does not make sense and we cannot show that marginal product schedules are downward sloping.

factors are said to be *substitutes*. Examples here might be assembly line workers and machinery or different brands of the same good.

A complementary relationship between capital and talent is demonstrated in Figure 8.3. Assume again that the ticket price is the same for all teams (a competitive product market) and that capital and talent are both available in large supply (a competitive factor market). As the amount of capital hired rises from 100 to 150 units, the VMP_K decreases as we move down the VMP_K schedule. In a competitive factor market with lots of capital, a firm could use more capital if there is a decrease in the price of capital (P_K) beyond the control of any one of the firms. An example would be an increase in competition in the market for capital goods that reduces the price of capital. As a result, the VMP_T schedule shifts upwards in the right-side panel of Figure 8.3. With more units of capital per unit of talent used in production, talent becomes more productive (we can produce more output with the same amount of talent). Similarly if the amount of talent hired increases due to a fall in the market wage rate per unit of talent, the VMP_T will fall as more talent is hired and the VMP_K shifts vertically as capital is now more productive (not shown in Figure 8.2). If capital and talent were substitute factors instead, the shifts in the VMP schedules would be downward instead of upward.

324

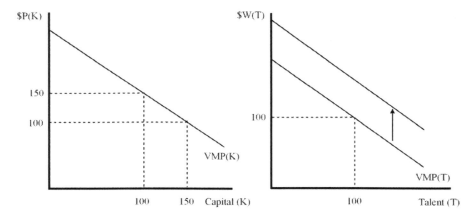

Figure 8.2
If capital and talent are complementary factors, an increase in the amount hired of one factor vertically shifts upward the *VMP* schedule of the other factor.

The marginal product story predicts that teams with greater stocks of capital and other factors of production will have more productive talent stocks, given the same stock of talent. Their VMP_T schedules will be positioned higher than other teams. Teams with greater access to good training facilities, better playing surfaces and equipment, and better coaching (human capital) will have more productive talent and will perform better on the field.

In the long run, the owners demand curves for talent and capital will be flatter, or more elastic, than is the case in the short run. This implies that the hiring of talent and capital will be more responsive to changes in factor prices in the long run. This is due to the interaction between the value of the marginal product schedules of capital and talent. In Figure 8.4, suppose the initial wage rate per unit of talent is $100 with 100 units of talent hired. The short run demand curve for talent is the VMP_T schedule for a given amount of capital equal to 100 units. Now suppose that W_T falls for whatever reason (perhaps the pool of available talent increases dramatically due to the failure of a rival league) to $65, so the owner hires more talent up to 150 units. This movement down along the VMP_T schedule shifts the VMP_K schedule upwards if the two factors are complementary. With the price of capital still equal to $150 per unit, more capital will be hired up to 150 units. But this is not the end of the long run story.

With the stock of capital increased to 150 units, the existing stock of 100 units of talent will be more productive. This shifts the VMP_T schedule upward, so that at $W_T = \$65$, more talent will be hired to 250 units. Connecting the two short run positions gives the long run talent demand curve that is flatter than either of the short run talent demand curves. In the long run, the owner will be better able to react to changes in factor prices by adjusting the optimal mix of factors. For the team owner facing higher player costs, the optimal mix of factors can be changed to reduce the stock of talent and hire a better manager.

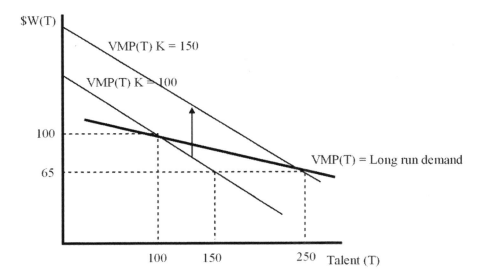

Figure 8.4
A short run increase in the amount of talent hired, from 100 to 150 units, shifts the value of the marginal product of capital schedule upwards (not pictured), resulting in more capital being hired. This shifts the VMP_T schedule to VMP_T K = 150 and

results in more talent being hired to 250 units. The long run demand curve for talent is more elastic than its short run demand curve.

8.3.3 Demand for Talent in the Long Run: Monopolist

In the case of a professional sports league that is a cartel, the industry demand curve for talent locally is the same as the team's demand curve for talent since the team is the industry (at least locally). The short run and long run demand curves for talent then look the same as in Figure 8.4, except that the demand curves are the MRP_T curves instead of the VMP_T curves. The result will be the same as for the competitive team owner: the long run demand for talent is more elastic than the short run demand for talent.

Analytical example: Hiring talent. Competition and Monopoly

Question: The table below gives the ticket price, talent stock and output (tickets per game) for the new NFL Los Angeles Surfers in the short run. Compute the MRP and the amount of talent that will be hired if the wage rate per unit of talent is $87.50.

Price $	T	Q
125	10,000	40,000
115	12,000	45,000
105	15,000	50,000
95	19,000	55,000
85	24,000	60,000

Answer: You need to compute the MRP from the table first. Use the formulae $MRP = MR \cdot MP$.

T	Q	$TR = PxQ$	$MR	MP
10,000	40,000	5,000,000		
12,000	45,000	5,175,000	35	2.5
15,000	50,000	5,250,000	15	1.67
19,000	55,000	5,225,000	-5	1.25
24,000	60,000	5,100,000	-25	1
30,000	65,000	4,875,000	-45	0.83

MRP is then

T	$MR	MP	$MRP

75 28,000 65,000	10,000			
	12,000	**35**	**2.5**	**87.50**
How much talent will the team	15,000	15	1.67	25.05
hire if the ticket price is fixed at	19,000	-5	1.25	-6.25
$55?	24,000	-25	1	-25
	30,000	-45	0.83	-37.35

The monopolist team owner will hire 12,000 units of talent. If the ticket price is constant at $55, then $MR = \$55$. In this case, the team owner will hire just under 15,000 units of talent since $VMP = \$55(1.67) = \$91.85$ at this point.

The responsiveness of the demand for talent to changes in W_T is determined by the elasticity of the team's talent demand curve (VMP_T curve for a competitive firm, MRP_T curve for a local monopolist). The more elastic (flatter) the demand curve, the more responsive owners will be to changes in W_T. Generally, this demand curve for talent will be more elastic:

1. the more elastic the demand curve for the team's product (tickets)
2. the more substitutes are available for current talent
3. the greater the share of team payroll in total team expenses, the more elastic is the supply of complimentary factors to talent.

An alternative approach to determining player salaries is to think of players like pieces of art that are auctioned only very infrequently. Teams bid for unrestricted free agents by bidding no more than their own private valuations of the players MRP. Ideally the winner of the auction bids slightly more than the private valuation of the second highest bidder. The decision for the player is when to move into the free agent market and when to accept a contract extension (or option year) from their current team. Rockerbie[98] developed an auction model of player salaries that predicts that the presence of one more free agent player (at a given playing position on the field) lowers the bids that all free agents will receive – not just the last free agent that enters the market. Players then must think strategically when deciding when to enter the free agent market.

8.3.4 Monopsony in the Talent Market

So far we have assumed that the supply of talent is essentially infinite at the going market wage W_T. This means one unit of talent is as good as another and if any player asks for more than the salary determined by $W_T \cdot t_i$, he or she will not find a job. This is clearly unrealistic for two reasons: professional athletes demonstrate differences in quality (inherent stocks of talent) which differentiate them, justifying different salaries, and; player's unions, free agent rules and draft systems restrict the supply of talent so that it is not infinite. With different qualities of talent in each player, salaries are now determined by the interaction of talent demand *and* supply, a point often ignored in empirical work in sports economics.

A *monopsonist* is the term used for a single buyer of a factor input. In this case, talent is in short supply and it has little use in any other industry. In the league cartel, each team hires a significant proportion of the total stock of talent in the league, hence the one team's hiring decisions affect the average market salary faced by all of the teams. Average salaries will increase if teams must bid away talented players from other teams due to a shortage of skilled players. The talent supply curve slopes upward in Figure 8.5 to reflect the increasing value of W_T as more talent is hired.

---

[98] D. Rockerbie, "Strategic Free Agency in Baseball", *Journal of Sports Economics*, 10(4), 2009, 278-291.

Essentially teams might have to bid away talent from other teams, which can raise W_T quickly if bidding is fierce. The *marginal resource cost of talent* (MRC_T) is the change in total talent cost when one more unit of talent is hired.

$$MRC_T = \frac{\Delta C}{\Delta T} \qquad\qquad (8.1)$$

This will be greater than the wage rate per unit of talent indicated by the talent supply curve since the talent supply curve gives the average W_T for all employed talent units, not the wage rate of the last unit of talent hired. The total talent resource cost rises quickly since to hire one more unit of talent, the wage rate per unit of talent must increase for all units of talent. It is as if the owners face an all or nothing choice when deciding how much talent to acquire, not an incremental choice. Hire 10,000 units of talent at a wage rate of $100 per unit or hire 11,000 units at a wage rate of $105. You can see that the total cost of talent rises quickly.

The owner will hire players up to the point where the marginal revenue product of talent (MRP_T) is just equal to the marginal resource cost of talent (MRC_T). The average W_T is still given by the talent supply curve at $100. The difference of ($150 - $100)10,000 = $500,000 is an extra surplus for the team owner in addition to the usual surplus that is the triangle above $150. This is because the team owner is the only buyer of talent and thus has strong bargaining power.

$MRP_T = MRC_T$ for a monopsonist buyer of talent with scarce talent supply

330

The wage rate per unit of talent is determined where the talent supply curve is intersected.

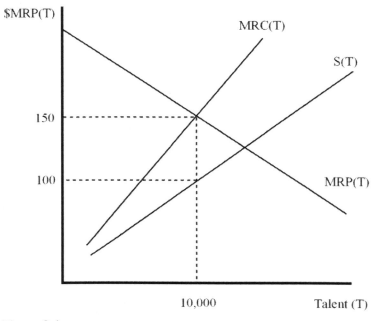

Figure 8.4
In a monopsonistic labor market, the owner will hire talent up to the point where the MRP_T just equals the MRC_T. The average W_T for talent is determined by the talent supply curve at 10,000 units.

Algebraically, we have a profit-maximizing monopolist who is also a monopsonist, $\pi = P(Q)Q - W(T)T$ where $Q = Q(T)$. We will assume that there are no other costs other than wage costs. Maximizing profit gives the first-order condition

$$P(Q) + \frac{\partial P}{\partial Q}\frac{\partial Q}{\partial w}\frac{\partial w}{\partial T} - \left(W(T) + \frac{dW}{dT}T\right) = 0$$

Since $\partial P/\partial Q < 0$, the first two terms compose the MRP_T represented by the downward-sloping demand for talent in Figure 8.4. The derivative

$\partial Q/\partial w$ is the shift in the ticket demand curve from an increase in the team winning percentage when more talent is acquired. The derivative $\partial w/\partial T$ could be substituted for from the logistic contest success function covered earlier, but we will not bother here. The derivative in the bracketed term is the positive slope of the talent supply curve in Figure 8.4. We can multiply and divide the bracketed term by W and simplify.

$$P(Q)\left[1 + \varepsilon_D^{-1}\frac{\partial Q}{\partial w}\frac{\partial w}{\partial T}\right] = W(T)[1 + \varepsilon_S]$$

The term ε_S is the wage elasticity of talent supply. Since $\varepsilon_S > 0$, $MRC_T > W_T$.

In a competitive labor market, the owner would hire more talent up to the point where the VMP_T just equals the wage rate per unit of talent given by the talent supply curve. This is not drawn in Figure 8.4 but it would be much larger than 10,000 units of talent. Hence the monopsonist owner hires less talent and pays a lower wage when facing a monopsonistic talent supply. This is because the monopolist owner maximizes profit at a smaller level of ticket sales and thus hires less talent.

Analytical example: Hiring talent. Monopsony

Question: Using the previous analytical example, suppose the market wage per unit of talent increases as more talent is hired.

T	W(T)
10,000	70

Answer: Calculate the total cost and the marginal resource cost.

T	W(T)	$C	$MRC	$MRP
10,000	70	700,000		
12,000	73	876,000	88	87.50
15,000	77	1,155,000	93	25.05
19,000	82	1,558,000	100.75	-6.25

12,000	73	24,000	88	2,112,000	110.80	-25
15,000	77	30,000	97	2,910,000	133	-37.35
19,000	82					
24,000	88	The team owner will reduce the team stock of				
30,000	97	talent slightly below 12,000 units. The wage rate				
		per unit of talent will fall to slightly below $73				
		from $87.50 in the previous example.				

Brief Review of Concepts

- In a competitive talent market and product market, the firm hires talent up to the point where the value of the marginal product (VMP_T) just equals the going market wage (W_T). This maximizes the amount of surplus the owner receives from the services of talent.

- In a competitive talent market and monopoly product market, the firm hires talent up to the point where the marginal revenue product (MRP_T) just equals the going market wage (W_T). Since $MRP_T < VMP_T$, the monopoly owner hires less talent.

- Capital and talent are said to be *complementary* if increased hiring of one raises the marginal product of the other. If hiring more of one factor reduces the marginal product of the other factor, the two factors are said to be *substitutes*.

- In the long run, the owners demand curves for talent and capital will be flatter, or more elastic, than is the case in the short run, if capital and talent are complimentary goods.

- The demand curve for talent will be more elastic: (1) the more elastic the demand curve for the team's product (tickets); (2) the more substitutes are available for current talent; (3) the greater the share of team payroll in total team expenses, and; (4) the more elastic is the supply of complimentary factors to talent.

- A monopsony occurs when there is only one buyer of talent. A league monopsony reduces the amount of talent employed and lowers the market wage.

8.4 Measuring a Player's Marginal Product

If we can measure the marginal product of a professional athlete, we are better able to determine if the athlete is being paid a fair salary. Human capital theory predicts that a player will be paid exactly his or her stock of talent multiplied by the marginal revenue product of talent for the team, but aberrations from this rule can occur. In the reserve clause era, player movement was restricted so owners could pay less than according to the marginal revenue product rule, with the owner capturing huge surpluses. In the free agency era, players can earn more than the marginal revenue product rule since they are free to sell their services to the highest bidder, thus transferring surplus from the owner to the player. The supply of professional players also complicates the theory. In a tight talent market, with few skilled players available, salaries may be bid up beyond the marginal revenue product rule.

Estimating the marginal revenue product of a player usually involves collecting historical performance data for the player in question: batting average, home runs, RBI's, ERA, goals, assists, shooting percentage, etc. These performance variables are thought to correlate strongly with the player's productivity and thus help form a picture of what the demand curve for talent looks like. In algebraic terms, we assume a relationship like the following:

MP_T = f(batting average, home runs, RBI, ERA, goals, assists, shooting %, etc.....)

The *independent variables* are chosen carefully to reflect the sport and position of the player(s). A variable is an independent variable when causation is assumed to run from it to the marginal product. The marginal product is called the *dependent* variable since it is assumed that the value is takes is dependent upon the values of the independent variables, but not vice-versa. Of course the marginal product is not observable and neither is the more relevant marginal revenue product. In this case, the number of team wins is used as the dependent variable.

Wins = f(batting average, home runs, RBI, ERA, goals, assists, shooting %, etc.....)

Multiple regression is a statistical technique used to estimate the marginal effect of each independent variable on the dependent variable. By marginal, we mean the effect that a 1-point increase in batting average has on the number of team wins, holding all the other independent variables constant. The lease squares method is used to compute a slope for each of the independent variables that estimates the marginal effects. Having estimated the slopes for a sample of teams, they can then be used to predict the number of wins the team would achieve without the services of the player of interest. The difference in the number of wins with and without the player is an estimate of the player's marginal product. Multiplying the difference in wins by the difference in gate receipts and broadcasting revenue per win gives the marginal revenue product, or predicted salary[99]. These predicted salaries are then compared to the actual salaries of the chosen players to determine if the marginal revenue product rule works.

Scully[100] used data from major league baseball for the 1968 and 1969 seasons to test the marginal revenue product rule. He estimated the marginal revenue product of a sample of pitchers and hitters, based on the

---

[99] A useful discussion of the approach is contained in Zech, C., "An Empirical Estimation of a Production Function: The Case of Major League Baseball", *American Economist*, 25, Fall 1981, 19-23.
[100] Scully, G., "Pay and Performance in Major League Baseball", *American Economic Review*, 64, Dec. 1974, 915-930.

player's effect on gate receipts and broadcast revenues. After deducting for associated expenses, such as player development costs, Scully determined a net MRP for each player in the sample. He then compared these figures to the salary paid to each player. The monopsony model predicts that players should be paid below their MRP, particularly with the reserve clause still in place during the sample period. The table below displays some of the results.

Actual salaries fell well below the estimated net *MRP* for each skill level, suggesting significant monopsony power. Apparently owners take a loss on mediocre players, but pay average and star players well below what they are worth to subsidize the loss.

One might suspect that monopsony power may have decreased significantly after the fall of the reserve clause in 1976. In the free agency period, players should make their MRP or even more. To test this hypothesis, Fort[101] improved upon the original work of Scully by utilizing additional independent variables to measure player performance and by using more detailed skill categories. To consider the effects of the move from the reserve clause to free agency, Fort used three sample periods: 1968, 1977 and 1990. Predicted salaries were computed based on the

	Skill level	Net mrp	Annual salary
Hitters	Mediocre	-$30,000	$17,200
	Average	$128,300	$29,100
	Star	$319,000	$52,100
Pitchers	Mediocre	-$10,600	$15,700
	Average	$159,600	$33,000
	Star	$405,300	$66,800

[101] Fort, R., "Pay and Performance: Is the Field of Dreams Barren?", in Diamonds Are Forever edited by P. Sommers, Brookings Institution, 1992.

Table 8.1
Estimates of MRP from Scully (1974).

player's estimated mrp, then compared to the actual salaries. For the 1968 season, almost all players included in the sample were paid well below their estimated MRP, reflecting the reserve clause and the monopsony labor market. By 1976, player salaries were still below their estimated MRP, but the gap narrowed somewhat from 1968. This was a transition year where the full impact of free agency had not yet become evident. For the 1990 season, all players in the sample earned salaries well above their estimated MRP, reflecting the ability of players to capture surpluses from the owners.

So why do professional athletes earn so much money? Economics suggests that it is because their services are valued so highly by owners. In most cases, the demand for skilled players drives up salaries, and owners only have themselves to blame. There are many examples of players who are paid very high salaries that are justified by their marginal revenue product. When Randy Johnson pitched for the Seattle Mariners in the mid-1990's, attendance would typically jump by over 20,000 fans per game that he pitched. Multiply that figure by an average of 20 home games he pitched, and an average ticket price of $15, Randy's MRP becomes a lofty $6 million per season. This is based only on his drawing power to the stadium, ignoring his stellar contributions to the team's performance overall. The Mariners paid Johnson $5 million for his last season as a Mariner (1998), which would seem a bargain. Michael Jordan had the same effect when playing road games - they almost always would sell out. That translates into a lot of windfall revenue for the owners, justifying his lofty salary of over $15 million for his final season in the NBA. Wayne Gretzky almost single-handedly saved the Los Angeles Kings from folding in the NHL, drawing in large numbers of fans that had never heard of ice hockey before his coming. His last season with the Kings, he was paid $5 million, all of it justified. Ultimately, players get paid what they do because profit-maximizing owners find it profit-maximizing to pay them, based on the marginal product rule.

Focus Box: Marginal product or rank-order finish?

Labor economists have long suspected that wages for workers might not be related to marginal product at all, rather, a worker's wage might depend on the worker's productivity ranking within an organization or industry[102]. If a player is viewed as one of the best in the league, he or she will receive compensation that is high relative to all other players, even though the marginal product of all players might be average or low. If a worker's output is difficult to measure, a salary as the outcome of a *rank-order tournament* might be optimal.

In some sports, players are definitely paid according to their finish in a rank-order tournament. Golf and tennis are good examples. Prize monies increase by order of finish and are determined before the start of the tournament. Players may perform well or poorly as a group (high or low marginal product), but their earnings depend only on their rank finish. Ehrenberg and Bognanno[103] studied the U.S. PGA (Professional Golfers Association) and European PGA golf tournaments and found that

---

[102] For instance, Lazear, E. and S. Rosen, "Rank-Order Tournaments as Optimum Labor Contracts", *Journal of Political Economy*, 89, Oct. 1981, 841-864 or Nalebuff, B. and J. Stiglitz, "Prizes and Incentives: An Economic Approach to Influence Activities in Organizations", *Bell Journal of Economics*, 14, Spring 1983, 21-43 to name a few.

[103] Ehrenberg, R. and M. Bognanno, "Do Tournaments Have Incentive Effects?", *Journal of Political Economy*, 98, Dec. 1990, 1307-1324.

tournaments that offer higher prize monies typically had lower golf scores. This suggests evidence for the rank-order tournament argument for player earnings. It could be true that, in other sports, larger playoff prize money improves team quality for those teams that make the playoffs. In the NBA, the winning team in the finals receives about $2.7 million. This prize money can be distributed as full or partial shares as the players and coaches see fit. The runner-up team receives about $1.8 million. Teams receive $224,000 each in the first round of the playoffs, $266,000 in the second round, and $440,000 in the third round. It could also be true that rank positions explain individual salaries better than performance statistics. These hypotheses have not yet been tested in the sports economics literature.

8.5 The Distribution of Player Salaries

The distribution of player salaries within a professional sports league is affected by a number of factors. Free agency allows players to earn what they are worth and thus has the effect of widening the salary distribution as compared to the reserve clause period. We have already seen that a luxury tax is born by the highest paid players in the league, reducing their salaries, and narrowing the salary distribution. Other efforts to promote league parity, such as salary caps and revenue sharing, should also narrow the salary distribution for players. Economics cannot say whether a narrow or wide salary distribution is preferred by society. Ideally players should earn their marginal revenue products. The distribution of salaries is what it is at the optimum. For this reason, any discussion of salary distributions is only descriptive.

A salary distribution is depicted graphically by assigning salary intervals from small to large, then plotting a bar for the number of times a player falls into each salary interval. The salary distribution for the NHL 2010-11 season is plotted in Figure 8.6

The salary distribution for all 706 NHL players is heavily skewed to the right, meaning that the majority of players earn salaries below the mean. This is typical of income distributions in other professions and in the macroeconomy, so NHL players are no different than other professions in terms of the shape of their income distribution, although their mean is much higher.

Salary inequality could be measured by computing the variance of NHL salaries in Figure 8.5, and then comparing the variance to the variance of salaries in some other year. Instead, the typical practice to measure salary inequality is to compute a Gini coefficient from a Lorenz curve. A Lorenz curve plots the percentage of total income earned against the percentage of income earners. This is demonstrated in Figure 8.6. With 706 players in the 2010-11 NHL season, the curve labeled "salary" is a running total of the player salaries after they are sorted from lowest to highest salary. Hence the left side of the graph contains the lowest salaried players – moving to the right increases the running total until the highest salaried player is reached. The line labeled "parity" assumes that each player is paid an equal share of the total league payroll. Taking a running total of this just gives a straight line.

The Lorenz curve would look like the straight line in Figure 8.6 if each player earned an equal share of the total league payroll. The more the Lorenz curve bows below the straight line, the less equal are player salaries since a large percentage of income earners (mediocre and average players) earn less than $(1/706)\%$ of the total league payroll, while a small number (star players) earn a much larger percentage. The Gini coefficient is computed by taking the area between the straight line and the Lorenz curve as a percentage of the total area below the straight line. The larger the Gini coefficient, the less equally distributed are salaries. The Gini coefficient for the 2010-11 NHL season was 0.56. For the 1999-2000 NHL season, the Gini coefficient was 0.471. Quirk and Fort (1997, p. 238) report a Gini coefficient for the 1989-1990 NHL season of only 0.284.

The large increase in the Gini coefficient suggests that salaries have become more inequitable in the NHL in the last 20 years, probably due to the relaxation in free agent rules in the NHL collective bargaining agreement and the compression of team payrolls by the salary cap. Quirk and Fort also report Gini coefficients of 0.529 and 0.427 for the 1989 baseball and NBA seasons respectively. More recent figures are not given, but the results suggest that the NHL has surpassed the other professional sports leagues in salary inequality.

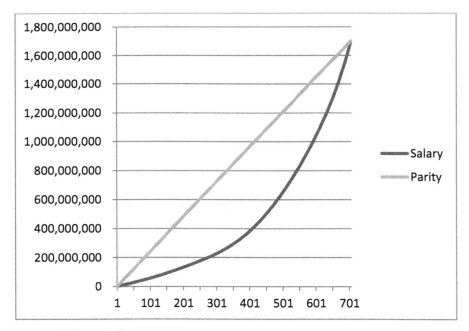

Figure 8.5
Salary Distribution for NHL Players, 2010-11.

Source: http://content.usatoday.com/sportsdata/hockey/nhl/salaries/team/

The Gini coefficient can be calculated using different formulae, each having different statistical properties. A popular formula is

$$G = \frac{2 \sum_{i=1}^{n} i y_i}{n \sum_{i=1}^{n} y_i} - \frac{n+1}{n}$$

First sort all of the observations (the y values) from smallest to largest. The number of observations is given by n. Each observation has a rank given by i where $i = 1$ is given to the smallest observation.

Economics cannot comment on whether more salary inequality is undesirable, even in the macroeconomy. The marginal product rule dictates that individuals are paid what their skills are worth in the labor market. The wider the dispersion of desired skills in workers, the wider will be the distribution of income. As the next focus box discusses, wider salary distributions may affect team performance.

Focus Box: Team salary distributions and team performance

The distribution of salaries within a team can have significant effects on the performance of the team. Bloom[104] identifies two contributing factors. First, a wider spread between different pay levels increases the rewards for better performance, creating a positive pay-performance link and an incentive for better future performance. Bloom calls this the *hierarchical* pay effect. Greater pay dispersion may motivate lower skilled players to improve and receive a larger future salary. Players

---

[104] M. Bloom, "The Performance Effects of Pay Dispersion on Individuals and Organizations", forthcoming *Academy of Management Journal*, 2000.

who are already star performers will prefer to play for a team with a hierarchical pay system since their high performance is rewarded with a large salary. On the other hand, hierarchical pay systems can create disincentives for cooperation among team players, instill feelings of inequity, and promote team dissention, reducing the quality of performance of the team. Players will tend to concentrate on their own performance to the exclusion of team goals, since they care most about moving up the pay distribution. A more compressed salary system (lower dispersion of salaries) may avoid this negative effect. Bloom calls this the *compressed pay effect*. The benefits of higher salaries, under the hierarchical pay system, accrue mainly to star players, not to the majority of players who are just average or mediocre. Hence the hierarchical system is a reward system whereas the compressed system protects average and mediocre players at the expense of the star players.

Bloom tested to see which pay system contributes most to team and organization performance using data for major league baseball teams from 1985 to 1993. Using several measures of team and organization performance as dependent variables, Bloom computed a series of multiple regression models. The independent variables included measures of team salary dispersion (Gini coefficient, coefficient of variation), a measure of the individual player's ranking within the team salary distribution, and control variables for external labor market conditions and team talent. The statistical results suggest the following.

- On the average, a greater dispersion in the team's salaries, the lower the performance of the player. This was true for both pitchers and fielders.

- A greater dispersion in the team's salaries, improved the performance of star players but lowered the performance of all other players.
- Teams with greater dispersions in salaries had poorer team performances, although the statistical evidence is not strong.

Overall the results favor the compressed pay system hypothesis, although as the author points out, the model fails to take into account the effect of one player's performance on that of another player. Players are factors in a team production function where the output of the team can be greater or less than the sum of the individual player performances. This team production aspect has not been explored greatly in the sports economics literature.

Test Your Understanding

1. Calculating a Lorenz curve and a Gini coefficient that includes all of the players in a league is a lot of work. It is easier to compute for one team and just as meaningful considering the discussion in the last focus box. The Tampa Bay Hooligans are a new expansion soccer team in MLS. The owner wants to create a buzz, so she has acquired two star players to play alongside lesser skilled players in the hopes of attracting fans. The salary for each of the 10 players is given below.

Jose Sanchez	$5 million
Nigel Forster	$4.5 million
James Easton	$550,000
John Humphries	$500,000
Steve Davis	$450,000

Skip Thomas	$150,000
Dave Engels	$125,000
Terry Mulligan	$115,000
Brad Jones	$105,000
Jeff Davidson	$90,000

Calculate the Gini coefficient for the Hooligans salary distribution. How does it compare to the Gini coefficients mentioned in the chapter for other leagues? What problems do you anticipate on the club given the discussion in the last focus box?

2. The posting system is an arrangement between MLB and the Nippon Professional Baseball League that allows a player on a Japanese club to be transferred to a MLB club if the player is not yet eligible for free agency. Between November 1 and February 1, a Japanese player can be "posted" by his Japanese club at his request. The MLB Commissioner notifies each MLB club and collects sealed bids for the negotiating rights to the player. The highest bid wins the auction, although the maximum bid was restricted to $20 million in the modified 2013 posting agreement. The Japanese player has until the end of January to negotiate a new contract with the winning bidder – if no contract is reached, the player's rights revert back to the Japanese club which then does not receive any of the winning bid. The highest bid came in 2012 when the Texas Rangers paid $51.7 million for the posting rights for pitcher Yu Darvish. Darvish settled for a six-year contract paying $60 million.

Use the monopsony model in Figure 8.4 to consider whether Darvish got a good deal. What is the maximum amount in the diagram that the Rangers would have bid to acquire the posting rights to Darvish? Finally, can you think of a situation where all three parties in the agreement came out with more profit?

Index

Made in the USA
Lexington, KY
10 January 2019